REFLECTIONS IN A MIRROR

REFLECTIONS
IN A
MIRROR

Of Love, Loss, Death, and Divorce

RAOUL FELDER

BARRICADE BOOKS
FORT LEE, NEW JERSEY

Published by Barricade Books Inc.
2037 Lemoine Ave.
Suite 362
Fort Lee, NJ 07024

www.barricadebooks.com

All unattributed quotations are by the author.

Library of Congress Cataloging-in-Publication Data

Felder, Raoul Lionel, 1934-
Reflections in a mirror: of love, loss, death, and divorce / by Raoul Felder.
    p. cm.
  Includes index
  ISBN 978-1-56980-470-4
1. Felder, Raoul Lionel, 1934-. 2. Lawyers--New York (State)--New York--Biography.
3. Public prosecutors--New York (State)--New York--Biography. I. Title.
KF373.F38A35 2012
345.7471'01262092--dc23
[B]
                                                                    2012015099

10 9 8 7 6 5 4 3 2 1

Manufactured in the United States of America

So we beat on, boats against the current,
borne back ceaselessly into the past.

F. Scott Fitzgerald, *The Great Gatsby*

I was young in that country:
These words are my life: these letters written
Cold on the page with the split ink and the shunt of the
Stubborn thumb: these marks at my fingers:
These are the shape of my own life ...

Archibald MacLeish, *Conquistador*

CONTENTS

CONTENTS

To my dead yesterdays, none of which I regret,
and for my granddaughter, Millie,
and her unborn tomorrows:

"... such stuff
As dreams are made ..."

The Tempest

1

PASSING OPEN WINDOWS

"... Man will not merely endure. He will prevail ..."
William Faulkner, Stockholm
December 10, 1950

Back, past the rivers of time, my—or "our"—story began. For my brother, it is a tale of a worse life best lived. For me, a better life mostly wasted. If Einstein was correct and past events continue to exist—fixed in a bundle of time, hurtling themselves through space—and could we but move fast enough, we would catch up with them. If that were so, somewhere, beyond my reach, it would all still be there: Williamsburg, Brooklyn, the Broadway el and the large orange-brick apartment building at the corner of McKibben Street and Manhattan Avenue. Upstairs, on the second floor of the corner apartment, the two beds were placed at opposite corners, and my brother's braces like two skeleton aluminum legs, each wrapped round with worn leather bands, lay beside his bed. While the phonograph's ten-cent needle scratched out Joe Turner shouting blues, our parents argued in the other room.

Measured by a lifetime, it all happened long ago, some of it seventy years or more. Over the years, I have buried much of it so deeply that it has become almost irretrievable. Memory, or lack of memory, caused me to invent some of it or forced me to lie about the rest, so that what happened no longer exists for me as one story with a beginning, an end and a fluid journey between the two. Rather, it is like traveling past open windows, and looking in, seeing in each a tableau of an event, and at the end of the trip, the sum of all the windows telling pretty much the whole story—or at least that much which is bearable. My mother, father and brother are gone, which leaves only me to tell our story.

* * *

In New York City, an address is a portentous thing. A proper address enables the owner of the building to demand more rent and affords the tenant an enhanced social status. In New York City, it is not unusual to find buildings with Fifth and Madison Avenue addresses when, in reality, only a small portion of the building is on the well-known thoroughfares, while the majority of the structure, including the entrance, is on a side street.

The official address of our house, grandly and presumptuously called "The Manhattan Arms" (or at least that was what was painted on the canvas canopy until my brother burned down the awning by tossing a lighted cigarette from the living-room window), was 75 Manhattan Avenue. In reality, the entrance was on the less-prestigious McKibben Street.

Manhattan Avenue ran the length of Williamsburg. It was not as spectacular as Broadway, with its elevated trains and trolley cars, considered to be the main street in Williamsburg, but certainly a street that was more desirable than the tenement-lined, pushcart-filled areas that intersected it, like Varet, Moore or Seigel streets.

If Christ stopped at Eboli, he would most certainly have stepped off the trolley at Delancey Street, the last stop before crossing the bridge into Williamsburg.

The economy began to recover from the Great Depression, national income rose 25 percent from 1933 to 1934; employment increased by more than 2,500,000. Fred Astaire teamed with Ginger Rogers. The Dionne quintuplets were born. Nylon was invented, and Flash Gordon, Li'l Abner and Donald Duck made their first appearances. On Broadway, Ethel Merman sang the Cole Porter song:

You're an Arrow collar.
You're the top!
You're a Coolidge dollar . . .
But if baby, I'm the bottom,
You're the top.

Nineteen thirty-four was the year the arguments began. It was a year when people thought they were going from bad to better. The truth was they were headed from bad to worse. Despite some improvement in the economy and rising spirits, there were still 18 million people on relief. In the Midwest, 150,000 square miles of farming land had turned to dust, blown wild by prairie storms that choked people and blotted out the sun, turning days into unending nights. Abroad, by contrivance and miscalculation, a nightmare began, one that would haunt the world for the next decade and whose effects would change it forever. Adolf Hitler was elected president of Germany by a 90-percent electoral plurality. The Nuremberg Laws, the first stage of Hitler's "final solution" to "the question of the Jews," were being drafted, and the first concentration camps were up and running. A year earlier, Hitler had unilaterally declared that Germany would not pay its obligation for reparations incurred as a result of the First World War. Following that sweeping pronouncement, he proceeded to sign a ten-year nonaggression pact with Poland, which he had no intention of honoring. The pact, however, lulled the Poles into complacency, believing that they did not have to react or fear the snarling German beast now poised to pounce along its borders.

Hitler's favorite saying was:

Mundus Vult Decipi
Ergo decipiatur

The world wants to be deceived,
Therefore let it be deceived.

* * *

In the 1940s in Williamsburg, snow did not float down in sleepy silent circles to languish on the thatched roofs of cottages nor spread itself lasciviously on the bowing branches of ancient trees. In Williamsburg, it was nasty. Once fallen, the white powder became flecked with city dirt, and depending on the weather, soon turned to dark, opaque ice or greasy slush.

Back then, weather forecasting was not advanced. Old bones, sensitive enough to give reasonable warnings of major snowstorms, were the barometer of bad weather. Waiting for the snow, there was quietness in empty streets draped in unnatural gathering darkness. Looking out of our windows, we shared an unhappy feeling—dreaded anticipation.

My brother, Jerome, could not go outdoors if there was snow on the ground. Polio had ravaged his limbs and made his system of locomotion primitive. He would move the crutch under his right arm forward and using that crutch as a lever, his right foot would follow, encased in a shoe that had a hole drilled through the heel. Two calipers were inserted in the bottom of the shoe, attaching it to two aluminum posts on either side of his leg running from ankle to hip. Leather wrappings sheathed his leg, joining the parallel aluminum posts, which swung forward with each step. Walking meant he would repeat the painful process with the left crutch under his left arm. Progress forward was slow, exhausting and caused boils to develop under his arms and where the leather cut into the tops of his legs. Crutch tips had to be frequently replaced and whether new or old, were unable to grip slippery ground.

Fortunately, our apartment was the only residential building in Williamsburg with an elevator. When the elevator broke down—which was frequently—my brother had to climb the two landings to get to our apartment. He accomplished this by sitting on a step and using one crutch to hoist himself to the next. He would say to me, "Hold the crutch," and I would stand *next*—he insisted I stand *next* to him, not on the step above or beneath him—to him and hold the crutch he was not using to hoist himself one step higher. If I stood on the step above him, I would impede his upward progress. If I stood on the step beneath him, I would not be able to hold the crutch in the necessary vertical position.

When he was in his late teens and early twenties, my brother became Doc Pomus, songwriter and singer. He would perform in local clubs in Bedford-Stuyvesant, a black ghetto that had a half-dozen "clubs" in the area. In those days, he would come home in the early morning hours and have to get up the stairs alone. Despite the misery of his physical condition, my brother was lucky. It is an inexorable law of economics that when times are bad, industries associated with entertainment, which offered escape from the misery of daily life at a reasonable price, flourish. To the people of Bed-Stuy, times were always bad. Their "bad" was always worse than other people's worst, and their "good" was always worse than other people's bad.

The clubs were unique institutions offering music, liquor, a bazaar for the sale and exchange of illegal drugs, a large performance space with stale cigarette smoke that hovered over the customers like a preternatural storm cloud. These were places where the musicians played with their hats on—perhaps because they had no other place to put them where they would not be stolen, or maybe they left their hats on to show a kind of insolence toward the audience. (This was different from the poseur club musicians of today who put their hats on *only* when they play.) They were piano, bass and guitar players with cigarettes dangling from their mouths: musicians who during breaks went into alleys behind the clubs to share reefers and Sneaky Pete. Honed in these musical boot camps, twenty years later, many gained national and international reputations.

Crime, in those days, in Bed-Stuy was treated differently than crime in other parts of the city. As long as it was contained in the community, it was met with official indifference, if not toleration—the acceptable price of containment.

"Shines. Another shine killing. That's what I rate after eighteen years in this man's police department. No pix, no space, not even four lines in the want-ad section." Farewell My Lovely, Raymond Chandler, 1940.

* * *

Since 1967, New York City's largest sewage plant has been in Greenpoint, next door to Williamsburg, receiving all of Manhattan's waste including that of Brooklyn. In much the same way, Williamsburg received successive waves of human refuse since the bridge from Manhattan opened in 1903, the last major horse-and-carriage bridge to be built in New York. Swarms of Italians and Jewish refugees from the overcrowded tenements of the Lower East Side extended the ghetto into Williamsburg. By 1920, Williamsburg was the most densely populated area in Brooklyn. Later in time, there were further waves of immigrants fleeing Europe before the Nazi onslaught—at least to the extent that the Roosevelt administration could not prevent them from entering the country while maintaining some semblance of morality. Stirred into this Williamsburg mix were pockets of blacks and Latinos enticed here by the prospect of a better life. However, in spite of hope and hard work, it was a place of losers. Some remained there forever, while others were lucky, and it became a way station to a better life.

That was Williamsburg in the mid-1930s, my boyhood home, far from the once-ubiquitous Ailanthus tree immortalized in *A Tree Grows in Brooklyn*, which had been replaced by soulless cement tenements. If my sense of time is often a jumble of people and events, there was one moment fixed in my mind as it was in history— December 7, 1941.

* * *

My father had a weekend routine that was as regular and predictable as a train schedule. Saturday mornings, he would go to his office at 66 Court Street in downtown Brooklyn where he would work for half a day. Around lunchtime, he would come home, eat and then stretch out on my bed in time to listen to the opera when it was in season. Each Saturday afternoon, the performance was broadcast as it was performed live from the stage of the Metropolitan Opera House. The announcer and commentator was Milton Cross, whose major distinction, aside from having an encyclopedic knowledge of opera, was the fact that he had a Brooklyn accent. Cross, in the verbal music of Brooklyn, would offer an extended dissertation on the opera and featured singers.

Sunday was another ritual. Every Sunday, unless there was a sporting event on the radio, my father would take me to visit his parents in Brighton Beach. My maternal grandfather, who lived with us and slept in the living room, was never included in any grandparent ritual. Every Sunday, he put on a clean white Sunday starched shirt, a newly pressed suit, carefully arranged his breast-pocket handkerchief and left the apartment on some mysterious errand, primarily to avoid my father. They rarely spoke.

Brighton is a resort area south of London. It has a boardwalk that runs parallel to the ocean. Between the boardwalk and the ocean is a narrow strip of rock-filled sand. Brighton's fame was not in its beach or boardwalk proximity to the ocean, but rather in the row of white gingerbread hotels standing beside the boardwalk, facing the ocean. They looked like a cross between the scenery from a second-rate production of Hansel and Gretel and a wedding-cake designer's nightmare. In one of these hotels, The Grand, on October 12, 1984, IRA member Patrick Magee set off a thirty-pound bomb, hoping to blow up the entire Conservative Party, including Prime Minister Margaret Thatcher, who was among those attending a conference at the hotel.

Three thousand and forty-six miles westward, on the banks of the same Atlantic Ocean, was Brighton Beach in Brooklyn. The Brooklyn Brighton was named in 1878 by Henry C. Murphy when he and a group of business associates built the then-elegant Hotel Brighton on a large tract of land in the southwestern part of Brooklyn between Manhattan Beach on its east, and Coney Island on its west. Coney Island was an area fabled in song and movies, but it has had a unremitting pitiless downward trajectory from playground of the rich to seedy, dilapidated, cobbled-together slums. On the other hand, Manhattan Beach was the final geographic dwelling place of immigrants who, over the course of a lifetime, were able to trudge up the economic ladder from tenements in Brownsville, Williamsburg and the Lower East Side, to elevated apartment houses in Flatbush, before moving on to two-family homes and finally, if they were lucky, finishing their lives in Manhattan Beach, in single-family houses of varying degrees of grandiosity and poor taste. It was a neighborhood of fulfilled dreams, of Jewish merchant princes and professional men.

Beginning in the 1920s until the 1960s, in Brighton Beach, older Jewish immigrants lived in neighborhoods of six-story, orange-brick buildings. These people had managed to save modest sums for retirement or they had successful children who supported them. In either case, there was not quite enough money for them to live in Manhattan Beach, but certainly enough to spare them the tawdriness of Coney Island. A usual sight would be a group of older residents sitting outside their apartment buildings on sunny days, the salt air drifting in from the ocean several blocks away, taking them back to other times and journeys across an ocean that delivered them to an alien land and unknown futures.

In the early years, our Sunday trip to Brighton involved an interminable ride on the BMT subway. Our journey to visit my paternal grandparents began at the Broadway el station where the D train ran on elevated tracks two stories above street level. Looking out from the train, the dark and dirty windows of battered tenements stared back at me like sightless eyes in ruined faces—tenements as bleak as blackened trees after a forest fire. When the train finally approached the Brighton Beach station, we could see the Atlantic Ocean behind and between the track-side buildings.

After the war ended, we owned a secondhand 1939 Dodge. My father would stack up several cushions so he could see out the windshield and drove us to visit his parents. In order to get to Brighton, we had to travel the length of Bedford Avenue. About halfway there, Bedford Avenue rises up in a long steep sloping hill, and in those days, near the top of the hill and on the right side of the avenue was Ebbets Field. On the left was a veterinary hospital owned by Doctor Spivack, a man who was my father's colleague when my father, during one professional incarnation, was a veterinarian. Unsuccessful as an animal doctor as he began his practice during the Great Depression when horses were phased out for commercial use and people had little money to feed themselves let alone household pets, he left Spivack's practice.

My father had great difficulty driving up the hill on Bedford Avenue. If he had to stop for a red light midway, as it was before the common use of automatic transmissions, the engine would have to be placed in neutral while waiting for the light to change. My father's problem was that when he stopped on the hill and put the car into neutral, the forces of gravity would take control, and we would then begin to slide down until he put his foot on the brake pedal. When the light changed, he would have to take his foot off the brake pedal so that he could step on the clutch pedal and place the car into first gear. Unfortunately, as soon as he removed his foot from the brake pedal, and before he could shift the car into a forward gear, we would again start our downhill slide, requiring him to attempt to stop the car again before he began a series of desperate maneuvers—his feet hopping between the brake and the clutch pedals, accompanied by the loud grinding of gears in order to get the car moving uphill.

Gradually, the hill began to obsess my father. By midweek, he had worked out different ways to attack his white whale of a hill on Bedford Avenue, the most successful of which was to stop at the foot of the hill, even if the light were green, and wait until the moment the light turned red. This would give him the maximum amount of time to go forward on green signals. When the traffic light became red, he waited, gunning the car's engine, like a crouching panther gathering its energy to pounce upon a prey. As soon as the light turned green, he would hurl the car up the hill, going past any traffic lights along the way that had changed to red. I would cheer him on—"Go, go"— until we got to the top. Often, when he arrived at the top, my father would pull the car over, climb out, walk a bit and take a much used, wrinkled handkerchief from his back pocket and wipe the sweat from his forehead.

My father's mother, Helen, was small and very old even in my first memory of her when she was no more than, perhaps, in her early sixties. She would shuffle around in what was then called a "housedress," a shapeless piece of flowered cotton, pulled around her body and fastened by a cord of the same material. Blinking behind her eyeglasses, it was obvious that Helen's world was always vaguely out of focus. My grandfather, Gustav, had a shiny bald head circled by a few wisps of white hair and a white walrus mustache. His belly was round, and he always wore a white shirt with a collar buttoned tightly around his neck. His pants were held up by suspenders, and I never remember him wearing either a tie or jacket. Our visits on Sundays were an obligation that my grandparents imposed on all their children. Always present were my father's six siblings and their children, taking turns sitting with the grandparents in their small living room, the children reading the comics.

My mother seldom came with us, for though she liked my grandfather, she never spoke of my grandmother without the word "mean," or "miserable," in the same sentence.

My brother never came with us. Travel with him entailed practical difficulties with his crutches, which, in turn, provided my father with a reasonable explanation and justification for his absence. The truth was that my father was uncomfortable when he was in public with my brother. At the same time, this provided my mother with a reason for not going. She could never leave my brother home alone.

On that infamous Sunday, a kind of tranquility had settled in our apartment. Each of us had retreated to our own invisible cocoon of space. My father, as was his Sunday afternoon custom, was stretched out on my bed. Since he was only a little more than five feet tall, there was considerable space above his head and below his feet causing him to appear even smaller. He chose our bedroom because it was furthest from the kitchen where my mother was omnipresent. Laying on the bed, half-asleep, the Sunday papers across his chest, he listened to the football game broadcast from the Polo Grounds.

On that day, there was a record crowd—55,051 cheering fans— who watched the Brooklyn Dodgers play their traditional rival, the New York Giants. The game was scheduled to begin at 2 P.M. Five minutes before the kickoff, at 1:55 P.M. New York time, 7:55 A.M. Hawaiian time, the Japanese attacked Pearl Harbor.

My brother, Jerome, not yet Doc Pomus, was on his bed, playing a game he created using a throw of dice to determine how far a player made a run in an imaginary football game. He would shake the dice and throw them on an open notebook, look at the number rolled and make a hoarse "hahhh" sound, signifying the roar of the crowd. He would then draw a vertical line in the notebook representing a player running or passing the football. Eventually, over the years, hundreds of notebooks with faux-marble, black-and-white cardboard covers were filled with pencil lines recounting thousands of games, all played to a stadium of one person. There were interruptions in the pregame broadcast giving vague details of the attack on Pearl Harbor. As the reports came in, my father became more awake, sitting up, newspapers falling to the floor. He said nothing, though a kind of unreleased tension, a sense of expectation like an unfinished sentence spread across the room to my brother's bed, who also listened to the news bulletins. Lying on the floor, drawing, I kept quiet and took refuge in the mindless drawings. When my father finally sat up and stared in disbelief at the radio—no one speaking—each of us suspending reality in our own way, and looking back, my brother and I both sensed that somehow things would never be the same.

During the game, more concrete and detailed announcements of the attack continued until the definitive reports were heard by us all. "There are unsubstantiated reports that Pearl Harbor, an American naval base located in the Hawaiian Islands, is under attack." "The Associated Press reports that Pearl Harbor has been bombed." "The War Department has issued a statement that Pearl Harbor has been bombed by Japanese planes." "Reuters reports that the Hawaiian Islands are preparing for an invasion by Japanese land forces." "The War Department has issued a statement that although there have been American casualties, our forces have fought back and succeeded in shooting down many of the attackers as well as sinking a Japanese submarine." "The White House has announced that the president will address a joint session of Congress tomorrow."

The ball game was played to its conclusion. The Brooklyn Dodgers beat the New York Giants 21 to 7.

We knew war raged in Europe. We understood that Asian and

American warships were unofficially at war on the high seas against German U-boats. For us, far away in Williamsburg, the fighting took place in the Movietone newsreels, *Life* magazine and on the radio. It was a world away. But the bombing of Pearl Harbor was somehow more dangerous, especially given the radio announcer's voice, which became increasingly excited.

My father finally found his voice. "Go inside, and call your mother. Something's happening."

I went into the kitchen. My mother was on her knees removing the pan from underneath the refrigerator. She carried the water-filled pan carefully to the sink to empty it.

"Come into the bedroom. Daddy says something's happening," I announced.

"The only thing that could be happening is your father waking up to help me. I'll come when I'm finished."

From the other room, my brother shouted, "Ma, come in."

Years later, it was falsely written, or at least I heard it said, probably twisted from something my brother said, that he developed his singing voice by having to call for my mother, who was in another room. If it was shouting that developed the power in his singing voice, it was the terrible shouting and screaming arguments that could be heard in the street one floor below our apartment that caused my mother to say that she was "ashamed to show my face in the neighborhood."

My brother called. My mother came running into the bedroom, a wet dishtowel in her hand. Actually, I never remember my mother with a dry dishtowel in her hand. She stood there, looking at my father, who by now was sitting on the edge of my bed, still staring intently at the radio.

"You don't have to just lie there [although, in fact, my father was sitting upright]. You could get up and do something."

My father stood, walked out of the room into his room. When he returned, he had put on a tie. In his code of conduct, events of such magnitude could not be faced without a tie. My mother now understood that the reason she was summoned had to do with events beyond our bedroom.

It was my brother who explained. "The Japs have bombed Pearl Harbor."

My mother, Millie, wore that special armor that certain mothers wear to protect their children from life's assaults, and this was especially so as it concerned my brother.

Mother, after a pause, replied, speaking only to my brother. "Don't worry, we'll be all right."

My brother was silent. This was unusual for him. He was never silent when something of importance happened. He cursed or laughed, belittled or praised, but almost never, as he was then, was he silent.

The radio was now broadcasting news interruptions, one after another—comments of various senators; travel-book descriptions of Pearl Harbor; news about Japanese submarines being washed ashore; warnings about saboteurs; castigations of Japanese Ambassador Nomura and special envoy Karushu who were in Secretary of State Cordell Hull's waiting room when the attack began; estimates of American casualties; foreign reactions to the attacks. The announcements gave way to analyses by various experts suggesting a quick victory by the United States, pointing out that the Japanese lived in paper and wood houses and that one good air raid would burn their cities to the ground; that the Japanese were all nearsighted and could therefore never produce pilots equal to ours; that the average Japanese was too short to handle a full-sized infantry rifle. All of these predictions, slurs and false reports were interspersed throughout the day with strains of "The Star-Spangled Banner" and Kate Smith singing "God Bless America."

At one point, my father went to consult the set of encyclopedias that was in a bookcase in the hall. The books were purchased by way of a monthly payment plan. Although our sixty-five dollar a month rent, on some months, could not be met without borrowing from Mister Milch, who owned the appetizing store on Moore Street, there always seemed to be enough money for books, even for a large embossed, leather-covered volume of Shakespeare, which my mother also bought "on time." Bringing one volume back into my bedroom, he informed us that Pearl Harbor was "far away" before he left the room to continue listening to the radio in the living room.

My mother stayed in my room, put her arms around my brother and me, while listening to the radio and repeating that the war would all be over quickly. The words of the radio announcer did nothing to comfort us, as he kept announcing that hostilities seemed to be spreading to other places and that everyone should listen to President Roosevelt's address to the Congress and to the nation the following day.

Over the last half-century, when I sometimes thought of my mother, the lyrics of an old English folk song come to mind. The song is about a mother who sent her boy away to the wars, and as she waited for his return at shipside, they carried him down the gang-plank. Confused at first as she saw that his legs were missing, the song explained "That a little cannonball on the first of May took them two fine legs from him away." She declared with the eternal fearsome indifference that mothers have, to even the might of empires, when it involved harm to their children,

> *". . . Of foreign wars, I know not of,*
> *Between Napoleon and the King of Spain,*
> *But by heaven I'll make them rue the day,*
> *When they took the legs from a boy of mine."*

On that day, December 7, 1941, even my mother couldn't console us. We were all frightened.

2

ALL OF US

We called it "the hall" though it was not that at all. It was a corridor that ran from the entrance to the apartment directly into a space we called the "foyer." That too was not quite accurate as the space was little more than a broadening of the corridor. A small table sat there on which was a Bakelite phone whose cord could stretch into the kitchen. With the kitchen door closed, some privacy was possible for someone on the phone unless there happened to be a family member in the kitchen, which was usually the case. Going in the opposite direction from the kitchen, off the hall, was my parent's bedroom; next to it was my brother's and my room. The door was always open. The bathroom was at the end of the hall on the left. The configuration of the apartment afforded all of us little privacy though we considered ourselves fortunate to have more space than most other people back then.

If a novel is autobiography to the degree that its author infuses each character with himself or at least his own sensibilities, then an autobiography becomes a novel and therefore fiction, at least to the degree that it is born in the author's imagination and musings. In my story, the villain is memory itself, albeit an honest criminal or at least one without motives other than to protect the seeker from his own past.

* * *

My father was a bit more than five feet tall. He suffered from a curvature of the spine. In less than polite circles, he would be called a hunchback, a term we never used. Rarely, my father would refer to himself as "having a problem with my back." The curvature of the spine caused him difficulty buying suits. Levy, a tailor whose shop was on the other side of Manhattan Avenue, dealt with the deformity by padding the right side of my father's jackets to make the left side even with the right. The thing about Levy that made him different from most tailors was that he was never a walking advertisement for his work. He worked in a wrinkled shirt, no tie and had wrinkled trousers held up by wide suspenders. Another thing about Levy was when he began working on a suit, he would circle the customer much like a buzzard closing in on helpless prey. Following him around the customer was his grandson, matching him step by step as he analyzed every nuance of anatomy or deformity relevant to his sartorial solution. Muttering to himself in a foreign tongue as he walked and calculated, he would pause occasionally to make a note on a pad until he seemed satisfied with his appraisal. My father required many circles by Levy and his grandson. He was a difficult case.

Everybody said Levy was a lucky man. He came to America in the late thirties with his wife, son, daughter-in-law and infant grandson a step ahead of the Wehrmacht as it goose-stepped its way across Europe. The family was able to enter the country just before America turned off the immigration spigot. When that happened, it became a simple dynamic. Those who were not allowed sanctuary in America died in concentration camps. Those who were admitted, lived. Immigrants who were turned away were forced to return to their native lands to become slaves of Germany's New Order—unless they were too young or too old or too worked out, and then they were marched into gas chambers. One block down from Levy's shop, on McKibben Street, at P.S. 141, each day the school children mumbled the pledge of allegiance that ended with "…one nation, indivisible, with liberty and justice for all." Well, maybe it was not for everyone, but Levy was one of the lucky ones.

The room my brother and I shared had windows overlooking McKibben Street on one side and Manhattan Avenue on the other. I usually would look out the McKibben Street windows since the head of my brother's bed was on the Manhattan Avenue side. Because our apartment was on the second floor, I was close enough to the street to see expressions on faces, to hear voices, and yet I was safely far enough away to be protected and unseen. I saw fires and automobile accidents, games played, business conducted and violent confrontations. When that happened, I would press my body against the wall and peek out, afraid that if someone saw me, they would come upstairs and force me to be a witness. Rain fascinated me, and I would watch it endlessly as the streets turned black and shiny, and rainbows appeared in oil puddles in the gutters. When the window became misted from the condensation, I would draw pictures with my finger on the windowpanes.

One late spring afternoon, as I was watching the rain, I heard loud voices on Manhattan Avenue. Looking down, there was a small body lying in the middle of the street. It was Levy's grandson on the tar-black, rain-slicked road, his body like that of a broken doll; arms and legs unnaturally bent in only the way death makes possible. The car that killed him was stopped nearby, both its doors open. Levy ran out of the shop, hugged the boy's body, swaying forward and back, as in prayer, looking up to the sky, wailing in some unknown language as the rain came down. I can still hear that cry sixty years later.

Levy's luck ran out that day.

* * *

My father was the oldest of eight children that survived their birth. He was born Moritz Felder in Vienna in 1896 and came to America on the steamship *Rhynland*, arriving here on March 17, 1906. He traveled with his mother, listed on the ship's manifest as Helene, together with two of his sisters, Gitela and Berthold.

Parents are free to pick any names for newborn children as are owners for their pets. But if individuals want to *change* their first or second name, they can pick a name of choice, provided it is not both well-known and already taken, like Bill Gates, Barack Obama or Madonna. They then go through a judicial process, and after many forms are filled out and a lawyer paid, a judge ultimately signs an order allowing the use of the new name of choice, unless the new name includes a "von" or "Sir" since the United States Constitution abolished hereditary titles.

However, in those days, it was the custom for immigration officers to dispense new Anglicized names upon the immigrants, whether desired by them or not, without the interference of lawyers, courts or judges. Upon landing, Helene therefore became Helen, Gitela became Gisela, Berthold became Birdie, and my father became Morris.

My father never spoke of Vienna, although he was ten years old when he left and should have had some memories of the place. His only connection with his former home was that he would pronounce "w" in place of "v," vinegar always becoming "winegar." Aside from this connection with Austria was the wooden plaque that marked the place where his ashes, contained in an empty coffee tin, were buried—until they were moved to a proper cemetery with a tombstone engraved, "Morris Felder, born, Vienna, January 24, 1896—died, New York, February 12, 1983."

He was buried several rows down from my mother in a group plot purchased by the United Friends Mutual Aid Society. Although his ashes were contained in a coffee tin, he was placed in a full-sized grave.

When the great wave of immigrants came to America, one of their concerns was that when they died, they would have a place to be buried. Many Chinese immigrants who came here saved their money, enduring a miserable lifestyle so that they could be buried with their ancestors in China. Jews, being practical, had no such desire to have their families pay to have their bodies shipped back to the place from which they fled when they were alive.

The United Friends Mutual Aid Society owned a large plot of land in an orthodox Jewish cemetery. A man—women could not be members— joined the society to be assured of a burial place for himself and his family. When a member died, a call was immediately made to the organization's social secretary. The social secretary's job was to arrange with the undertaker and the cemetery for a grave to be made available in the society's plot.

After he died, I buried my father's ashes in the woods, next to my country home. Ten years later, when I was about to sell the place, I wanted to move my father to a proper cemetery. Since he had been a member of the organization, I assumed that he could be buried in the society's plot. I discovered, however, that I had a problem. All of the United Friends, including the social secretary, had long since died, so I had to deal directly with the cemetery itself. I explained that I only needed a small piece of land in the society's plot. Initially, the cemetery agreed to let me have the space at a proportionately lower price. Then they realized that there was still money to be made from the Mutual Aid Society and forced me to buy a full-sized grave site, which is how my father, whose ashes rested in a tin coffee can, came to occupy a full plot. There was, I thought, something altogether fitting and proper that now in death, he was able at last to enjoy superior accommodations or at least, more spacious ones than his neighbors.

*   *   *

To say that Brooklyn was a Democratic Party stronghold equated, in the real world, with saying that Asians live in China. Except for that brief time of madness and even greater than usual dishonesty when Vito Marcantonio imported boatloads of Puerto Ricans to vote and elect him congressman under the American Labor Party banner, virtually every voter in Brooklyn voted Democratic. The few votes received by the Republican Party were usually the result of elderly or visually impaired voters who pulled down the wrong lever when the Democratic "inspectors" neglected or were too drunk to go into their polling booths and pull the lever down for them.

In those difficult economic times, the twenty-five dollars paid for a day's work at the polling place was significant. In Williamsburg, there was no shortage of people looking for these jobs. On the Monday evening—during the year, Monday night was the usual meeting night—before the following Tuesday's Election Day, applicants who wanted to work on Election Day would line up at the local clubhouses. The people who were chosen would have their names placed on lists then sent to the Board of Elections. Since the board was controlled by the Democratic Party organization, and the lists of people applying for jobs as poll watchers and election inspectors had been forwarded to it by the local Democratic clubhouses, a Republican had as much chance of getting elected as Marcel Proust had of going twelve rounds with Lennox Lewis. Additionally, the Brooklyn judiciary was either elected or appointed by the Democratic mayor and was comprised entirely of clubhouse Democrats except traditionally, by the grace of the Democratic leadership, one token Republican. In order to ensure elections adhered to principals of constitutional fairness, there was one Brooklyn State Supreme Court judge on duty

Election Day and evening to hear and decide voting disputes. Decisions by that judge had to be made on the spot since the appeal process to higher courts lasting months was not completed until long after the election and even perhaps after the elected official had already assumed office and would be at best, meaningless and at worst, create ministerial chaos.

In Brooklyn, becoming a judge—a municipal or criminal court judge's salary: $12,000 a year—was the goal of every Jewish lawyer. This meant, for all practical purposes, give or take a small number of Italian-American lawyers living in the borough, it was the goal of *all* lawyers. The trajectory began with minor political appointments— counsel to this or that commission—then secretary to a judge or state assemblymen until finally, a judgeship.

Municipal court judges were elected and criminal court judges enjoyed ten-year terms and were appointed by the mayor. In both cases, the process began at the local clubhouse level until the name of the prospective judge arrived either at the desk of the mayor, for his signature on the certificate of appointment, or that of the Brooklyn borough president, a tyrant named John Cashmore, who had the final say over the names appearing on the ballot. Judgeships were freely bought and sold and then sometimes even on the installment plan, payments being spread out over a number of years.

Fifty years later, this system continued. Addressing itself to an upcoming election, a November 2, 2002, editorial in *The New York Times* commented:

> *"Defenders of this farcical system [the method of choosing judges] talk piously about voter choice and preserving democracy. But as this year's judicial elections underscore that the only thing really preserved is clubhouse control of lucrative courthouse patronage."*

If the past is prologue or as can reasonably be anticipated, the human condition, with all its frailties and instincts toward greed and power lust, remains constant, fifty years hence this editorial could be reprinted with the same cogency it had in our time or could have had a half-century ago.

* * *

Somewhere in the past, before my memory of it, my father held appointed office. He was associate counsel for the Transit Commission of the State of New York—the title I suspect more grandiose than the job itself—a position he enjoyed for ten years until the transit commission was abolished in one of the periodic restructurings of local government. My father never mentioned anything about the position he held or anything about the job to me, except once, when he told me it enabled him to go on the subway without paying the fare. I learned about this job because mention of it appeared in the campaign literature he distributed in his half-dozen unsuccessful attempts at public office. His various campaigns were in primary elections, by which he attempted to become the Democratic nominee for elective offices.

In Brooklyn, to have the Democratic nomination for an office was tantamount to being elected to it. The only people who could vote in the primary elections were registered Democrats who, for the most part, did exactly as requested by their local "captain." A captain was in charge of an election district. His job was to dispense minor favors—fixing a traffic ticket, obtaining a day's work handing out leaflets on Election Day, getting someone on the home-relief rolls—for voters in his district. In return for doing these things, he could expect his constituent's fealty in the form of a vote for the organization's candidate on Election Day. Since an election district was little more than two city blocks in size, the captain occupied the lowest place on the political totem pole. The district captain would receive his orders from the assembly district leader—the boss of the neighborhood clubhouse—who, in turn received his directions from God—the county leader.

My father never really believed he could garner enough votes in the Democratic primary election to actually win the nomination. His goal was to be enough of a pain in the neck to the regular organization for them to award him with a respectable job or eventually the brass ring—a judgeship—simply to get rid of him. After several campaigns, each with a successively poorer showing, my father abandoned his attempts at elective office and ended up a district captain, standing at the polling places distributing campaign literature. At this point in life, he was too old for appointment to any political office. His goal was to receive appointments as a special guardian from the surrogate.

The surrogate—one for each county in the city—except for New York County that had two—presided over the disposition of the estates of those persons that lived in the county at the time of their death. This presented the last opportunity for the politicians to get at a citizen's money. Anytime a person dies with a minor child in his or her immediate family or had an incompetent relative stashed away, living in some attic or in an old-age home or molding away in Miami Beach, the surrogate would appoint a special guardian to protect that person's interests. The special guardian was supposed to investigate matters and write a report, in return for which he would receive a fee awarded by the surrogate, the money for the fee to be taken from the decedent's estate. Back in the real world, the special guardian slipped a court clerk who was assigned to such matters anywhere from fifty dollars upward to write and arrange for the approval of the guardian's report.

When I had just graduated law school, having no prospects of gainful employment, or even any sense of my future, on Monday nights, my father would take me to the clubhouse to see "the Leader"—the boss of the assembly district. My mother would watch me leave with him, a look on her face akin to that of a mother watching her son going off to war. I could see in her eyes that she looked past me, down a road and saw the beginnings of my retracing my father's steps through life.

I hated to go to the clubhouse. The clubhouse was located in an ancient frame building up a flight of stairs over—what in those days was called—a bar and grill. The stairway smelled of stale beer and the wet, decaying wood of old wooden houses, and I climbed the stairs as I would a gallows. The clubhouse scene looked like a bad day at Lourdes. It was a large room with perhaps fifty poorly dressed men sitting on folding chairs and twenty or so other men standing around the room, waiting for an audience with the Leader—Dr. Josiah Greenberg—who sat behind a table at one end of the room alongside an American flag on a pole. Doctor Greenberg, a physician with no practice other than that of politics, was always referred to as, "The Doctor" or "The Leader." I never heard him called or addressed by his first name, nor as I learned later, did he have any friends or social life other than politics. The people who had major problems waited to speak to The Leader himself, and those requiring lesser miracles met with minor officeholders standing together along one of the walls. The walls were decorated with a few grimy photographs of men with handlebar mustaches.

My father stood on the side of the room waiting for The Leader to give him a glance, acknowledging his presence. I would sit in a vacant seat and bury my head in a book and was careful in my choice of books so that anyone seeing their titles would not think me too smart or threatening. My father always told me not "...to be showy" or as he would say, "It is always the nail that sticks up that gets hit with the hammer."

After a while, my father would tell me to stop reading and stand up so that The Leader could see me. Once there had been a nod of recognition from The Leader, my father would say, "He's seen us. Now we can go."

Years later, when I had developed something of a reputation in family law, Manny Shultz came to me for a consultation. Shultz, or "Shultzie" as he was called, owned the bar over which the clubhouse had been located. He succeeded Doctor Greenberg as leader and held that post during my father's final years in politics. At that point, we had moved out of Williamsburg, but my father preserved the fiction of living there in order to maintain a political base.

Shultzie came to my office, wearing mismatched jacket and trousers, no tie and a black shirt buttoned to the collar in a style worn by lounge lizards a decade earlier. He had long since retired and moved to Miami Beach. This was the first time that I remember his ever having spoken to me. He explained to me in the kind of English spoken by people to whom English is not their native language, but who are, in fact, literate in no language, about a predicament he had gotten himself into involving two widows and bogus condominium deeds.

"I had never told any of them two that they was getting the real deed. They should had knowed that I meant in the future when I would have gotten it myself. It was their own fault. They should have knowed it. Anybody would of."

I derived an uncommon pleasure in telling him I was too busy to get involved in his matter.

3

POLIO

*He is chastened also with pain upon his bed, and the
multitude of his bones with strong pain.*

Job 33:19

There was nothing infantile about infantile paralysis. The disease
struck adults and children, its most famous victim being Franklin
Roosevelt, the president of the United States.

Polio, as it was called, had no respect for class, gender or geography
as it reached epidemic proportions during the summer months of
1934.

Treatment was primitive, cruel, painful and most significantly,
ineffective. One treatment was surgery that immobilized a patient's
legs, feet and ankles. Another treatment was the amputation of a
patient's legs followed by their replacement with prosthetic limbs.
Sister Kenny and her followers believed in massage, application of
warm compresses and painful stretching of legs. None of these methods changed the paralysis and emotional devastation that the bacil-
lus left in the wake of its invasion. During the initial onslaught of
the virus, the victim was usually only able to survive with the aid

of an iron lung, a crude metal canister similar in appearance to a basement boiler. It encased the body from neck to ankles, leaving only the face exposed. A slanted mirror was affixed above the head to allow some view of the room, which delineated the contours of the patient's life.

The virus' host was human waste. Modern drainage systems allowed waste to be separated from drinking water. Before these drainage systems became universally available, infants were exposed to the virus through contaminated water. After a mild bout with the illness, they became immune. Children living in large cities with sophisticated sewerage systems did not enjoy this protection. Those unprotected children from metropolitan areas often swam in communal pools or played with large groups of other children, some of whom were carriers of the disease.

During the summer of 1934, mothers in populated American cities lived in fear that their children would contract the deadly disease. Beginning each fall, they began concocting schemes to get their children out of the city and into the country. For the poor, labor unions, social, religious and charitable organizations maintained summer camps that they made available to children of their members. People joined these organizations simply to obtain the right to send their children to camp. Others borrowed money from banks and other lending institutions to pay camp fees.

In 1934, my mother managed to enroll my cousin, Maxie, twelve, and my brother, Jerome, who was ten. They were sent away together for the summer.

Back then there was no television. Newspapers recounted the horrors of polio, sometimes in strictly factual stories on page three or four about a few cases reported in Staten Island or in the Forest Hills section of Queens or some other local neighborhood. Sometimes, when a dozen or more cases turned up in an area, the word "epidemic" shouted hysterically from the front pages. Even those who never purchased a newspaper were not immune from the terror of the word. Inescapable to people on their way to work in the mornings were the headlines of the daily papers spread out at the ubiquitous newsstands found at entrances to subways or elevated trains. In some places the Newsies, like town criers of another age, would cry, "Polio Epidemic. Read all about it."

My brother was not happy about being sent away. My brother did not read the newspapers, which made him ignorant of the reasons why my mother was so intent on sending him away for the summer. After much research, she decided upon a camp for predominantly Jewish children—Camp Mohican—though most came from more affluent neighborhoods than ours.

It was a summer that would never be spoken about by either my mother or my brother. Fifty years later, I managed to piece together bits and pieces of the story during hushed conversations with relatives, friends and neighbors and former employees of Camp Mohican.

"Ma, I don't want to go to camp," Jerome pleaded. "I want to rest this summer, and besides, I have plenty of things to do."

"Is this your father talking?" my mother argued. "You want to end up in the hospital? You *have* to get away from this place this summer. Maxie is going with you, and you'll both have uniforms. Now please stop arguing. The money has already been paid." Turning to my father, she added, "Morris, you tell him he has to go."

Typical of my father, his response was to remove two sheets of paper from his jacket pocket, read them and nod his head in agreement. "Here," he said to my brother, "look at this. These are the things you need to bring with you. Two uniforms, a pocketknife, a flashlight ... it's expensive. I'll take you to the office. Downstairs is Schwartzman, a Boy Scout supply house—the only one in Brooklyn. We'll get a good price on things because he's in the same building."

Arrangements were made to go to Schwartzman's the following day.

Summer camp was no longer in dispute.

From that day on, my brother's life changed forever.

On June 15, 1934, five years before I was born, my father, mother, brother and cousin Maxie, together with two duffle bags filled with the required camp necessities, boarded the GG train for Schermerhorn Street in downtown Brooklyn—the gathering place for the departing Mohican campers. While my brother was only reconciled to going, Maxie was looking forward to the experience. If the event had been recorded in a police report, the words used to describe their departure would be "without incident."

My parents watched the lumbering bus drive off into the distance, happy in the knowledge that they were able to protect my brother from the expected polio epidemic.

Upon arrival at camp, the counselors called out the names of their charges. Soon the orderly scene was transformed into chaos, a tableau of boys running to the bus, trying to sort out and claim their luggage before running back to assemble with their assigned counselors, some suitcases breaking open, spilling their contents, boys asking to have names repeated, other boys shouting that their names had not been called. The camp director, Uncle Bob, watched the commotion and offered words of encouragement on the order of "That's the way, Mohicans." As for the bus driver, he observed the scene without interest, having seen it replayed each year in the dozen or more summer camps in the area.

The counselors walked their charges down a path in the woods. Jerome would later describe it as about "two blocks," as his only frame of reference was calculated that way. The bunkhouses were a row of seven single-story, dormitory-style wooden structures, three steps above the ground and connected by common walls. Jerome's counselor, Stewie, led my brother and his thirteen bunkmates into their new summer home, one long large room. The walls were bare wooden planks with crossbeams on the ceiling. The smell of wet wood permeated the cabin. Decades of rainwater that had seeped through the wood had never quite dried. For the rest of his life, when the cool, nutlike scent of wet wood was in the air, Jerome had to stop himself from thinking about that summer when memories carried him back to dark places in his mind.

That first night, in the dining hall, Uncle Bob stood up before the entire camp. Next to him was a tall, elderly woman in a shapeless dark-flowered dress and men's walking shoes. Beside her was a short, bald man, his huge stomach falling over the waist of too-tight trousers, held up by bright red suspenders. He wore a white dress shirt that framed his round beet-red face, a white stubble on his cheeks matching the wisps of white hair around his ears.

"Campers," Uncle Bob began, "before we say grace, I want to introduce you to our medical staff. Mrs. Worth is our nurse who happens to be a registered nurse—if you care to write that to your parents to put their minds at ease. She will have regular hours at the infirmary, but since she lives in camp, she is available anytime for emergencies. Doctor Sternmeyer is a respected doctor from the town of Lake Mohican and is available to come to the camp if Nurse Worth feels it is necessary. Now let us bow our heads and have a moment of silent grace before dinner."

Jerome sat with his bunkmates at one table and at an adjacent table was Maxie. They exchanged glances and held out their hands, palms up, delivering the message, "Who knows what comes next?" to each other. At one end of the room sat the older teenaged campers who, as the time passed, became increasingly noisier, finally ending with the chant "food, food, food," accompanied by the metronomic clanking of forks against glasses. Following the inexorable law of human nature that makes revolution possible, Uncle Bob, who like a person in the midst of an unruly mob left with no choice other than to make an instant decision between resistance or participation invariably chooses the latter, was soon energetically swinging his fork against his water glass accompanied by his own jovial cries of "food, food, food."

Shortly thereafter, with the cheery energy of chorus girls bouncing on stage in response to the stamping of feet and whistles of an expectant audience, the waitresses came out—town girls in shorts and T-shirts—carrying large trays piled high with broiled rib steaks, which they set down—one on a plate. These were boys who back home had to be coaxed and pleaded with by their mothers to eat steak that was obtained by mothers at the sacrifice of some personal pleasure: a new housedress, a night at the movies, money that could have been sent overseas to relatives—sure in the belief that steak had mystical powers to make their young sons grow tall and healthy. At the appearance of the platters of steaks stacked high, carried like the trophies of heads of vanquished foe, the boys made such noises of delight as one would suspect to have heard if there were a simultaneous discovery of pearls at a dinner of oyster fanciers. Uncle Bob was moved (and troubled) enough to push back his chair, rise and announce to his campers, "Now, we don't want to get you spoiled and expect steak every night. Tonight, we just want to give you a proper welcome."

The teenage boys from the upper bunks looked the town girls over like soldiers with pockets full of chocolates occupying an enemy village. Not looking at the girls directly, they giggled boastful obscenities to each other.

After dinner, Jerome fell behind the other boys as they walked back to the bunk. He had never been in the country before, let alone the country at night. Sensations came that were new to him: the uneven ground beneath his steps, the endless vacuum of darkness surrounding him that surrendered only to the rays of the boys' flashlights—and then just for a moment and just for a sliver of space—the breezes from out of the darkness, cool against his face, carrying the cacophony of scents of trees and plants and fallen leaves and mosses and flowers in their arc of life and decay. He felt alone and helpless as never before in his life and helpless to even declare his helplessness.

After they arrived at the bunk, as the boys prepared for bed, they ran about, tossing things to each other. Jerome did not join in. He sat on the edge of his bed exhausted, waves of tiredness sweeping down from his neck to toes until, happily, Stewie told them it will be "Lights out" in ten minutes. In bed, Jerome felt as if he were floating downward into a soft blackness and in a moment was in a deep dreamless sleep.

That old whore, Our Lady of Pain, lavish and indiscreet in her embrace and soon to be his constant companion paid her first visit in the early hours of the next day when even the dying night sounds of the woods became muffled by the slowly settling dew—the hours when the night creatures had fled the coming dawn and the sounds of a wakening day were not yet heard.

It began as a dream, or at least he thought it was a dream—a weight upon his neck progressing down his back and legs. And then he awakened, his head and body hot and feverish—the cool night air unable to breach the carpet of heat that lay upon his body. He began to shake, his teeth chattered and his legs trembled, his neck became stiff, and then suddenly, as an army deserting a field of battle, it stopped. He lay exhausted. Fever damp, he drifted off to sleep.

It was 7 A.M. From some far-off place, a staccato bugle call announced the new day to the campers. He was awakened by a worm of pain deep inside his legs that pulsed outward ending up in his lower back. The waves of pain were unconnected to any motion of his body, and when he tried to move his legs, they would not respond. His face was burning; his mouth, hot and dry. He was barely able to swallow. He could not turn his head. His neck was as a rusted mechanical gear that with great effort was able to be turned one click at a time.

All around him movement: Bunkmates shouted to each other, pillows thrown about, boys running back and forth in the bunkhouse.

"I can't move. They don't move," he screamed, the scream fading into a rasp.

The boys crowded around him, at first joking, calling to each other, then all of them silent, like children at their first sight of a dead person. More than mere awareness, there was a sense of being in the presence of something implacable and baleful, beyond their world of games and arguments, disappointments and pleasures, one-upmanship, bullying and cowardice, something not comprehensible or at least not wanting to be comprehended, but yet something that resonated with the contagion of their parent's fears: the disease of paralysis. "Call Stewie."

Stewie, having heard the noise and seen the boys crowded around Jerome's bed, was already at the rear of the group and pushing the boys aside.

"All of you go back to your bunks."

He bent over Jerome. "What's the matter?" He looked back over his shoulder to the other campers still standing together some distance from Jerome's bunk.

"I said *now*," he shouted to them over his shoulder.

"My legs, I can't move them, my neck."

"I want one of you to run over to Miltie's office and tell him what's going on, and he should tell Uncle Bob that I think the nurse should come over."

He looked down at Jerome, whose face was flushed crimson and now, surrounding his head, was a halo of sweat upon the pillowcase.

"Just, just ..." he moved his now shaking hands toward Jerome, then stopped them midway: two helpless birds fluttering in midair. Stewie was paralyzed into inaction, indecisive, ignorant of what to do, angry at himself now being thrust into a role beyond his ability to play and angry to be afraid as he was in that special way when the source of the fear is beyond logic or understanding and therefore impossible to end or even hide.

Turning to the campers, now silently huddled together at the other side of the bunkhouse, he shouted, "All right, I've had enough of all of you. Get out of the bunkhouse. Immediately. I don't care where you go, but get out *now*."

The campers ran out of the bunk in fear and confusion leaving Stewie and Jerome alone in the bunkhouse. Outside, at the perimeter of the crowd that had accumulated, which now included other campers and counselors, was cousin Maxie.

Uncle Bob arrived at Jerome's bed accompanied by the nurse, Mrs. Worth. Over bright-red pajamas, Uncle Bob wore a flannel bathrobe decorated with Indian designs. It was held closed by a knotted twisted silk rope. The bedroom slippers on his feet were wet from plodding through the dewy grass. He seemed annoyed and walking through the door of the bunk, halfway to Jerome's bed, called out, "Now let's see what this is all about." Following him was the nurse, wearing a topcoat over a longer nightgown whose hem was wet and discolored from the walk across the grass. Her bare feet were in men's shoes that seemed several sizes too large for her, and on her head, she wore a hair net.

"Bob, why don't you wait here by the door and make sure nobody comes in while I'm examining him." Walking over to Jerome's bed, she loomed above him, tall and thin, dark against the light coming into the bunk from the windows at the opposite wall. Not bending over, she placed her hand on his head and paused. "Do you hurt anywhere? Your head feels hot."

"My neck is stiff," she had to bend over to hear him, "and my legs, can't move them."

She looked down, paused and then frowned, "Let's cover you. Probably the flu, but we'll have Doctor Sternmeyer come in to look at you. Meantime, just rest, and I'll stay until he gets here."

She walked across the bunk to Uncle Bob and whispered, "It doesn't look good. It could be meningitis or ... you know."

"How can you be sure? It may be nothing, and you know these kids ... maybe he's making it up to get out of activities."

"Don't be stupid. Get Doctor Sternmeyer."

"But, if word ever got out what you suspect, we will have a riot here. The parents will drag their kids out, they'll want their money back. The season will be ruined … if they ever even bring them back next year. No, let's wait."

"If you don't call him, I will, and if I call him, I'll announce the situation to the campers, who will call their parents, and then you *will* have a riot on your hands."

"You're trying to ruin me. I've had enough of you. Either way, you're finished here."

"Go to hell. I'm calling Sternmeyer."

"No, no, I'll make the call. God knows what you'll say, and you'll overdramatize it."

Uncle Bob left the bunk to walk to his office. He had forgotten about the campers who were gathered outside the bunkhouse, all still wearing their pajamas. Now, he realized he would have to tell them something.

"Campers, we are going to have first day take-it-easy party. Er … it's a new tradition we are starting at Camp Mohican. Everybody go to the mess hall as you are. Stewie, notify the other counselors about it."

"But, Uncle Bob …"

He grabbed Stewie by the collar of his bathrobe, pulling him close, and in a fury, whispered into his ear, "Just do it. Do it, and shut up."

Uncle Bob crossed the common lawn in front of the bunkhouses, turned right down a path that led to the mess hall, continued further down the path until it ended in front of a wooden structure. It stood, hardly larger than a good-sized room, resting on cement blocks, several feet above the ground. He walked up some crudely built wooden steps and opened a door that had nailed to it a sign with the word "Administration" on it. He walked into his office containing a desk and one chair in front of it and one behind. The desk was clear of papers, the room unadorned save for a long, horizontal photo of last year's smiling campers arranged in rows by height and standing alongside them, a group of people posing behind a sign that said "Staff."

He sat behind his desk, hesitated, rested his face in his hands, then stared at the telephone. After a few minutes, he sighed, then picked up the instrument and slowly dialed a number.

"Yeah, I know it's early, but we got a problem here ... Yeah, a sick kid, but we can't wait. This is big trouble. Mrs. Worth saw the kid and said it could be meningitis or ... worse. You know what that means. It means we're finished.... No, not just for the season. We would be finished for good ... have to give the parents back the money, and who would ever send their kid here again? Maybe even sue me ... No, I don't want a goddamn specialist called. I want *you* here ... Wake up! If I'm finished, so are you. Then you can go back to treating the yokels' pimples and getting paid in cornhusks.... No, an hour is *not* good enough. Be here in ten minutes, and act like a doctor. I have enough trouble with all these lousy kids wanting to know what's wrong and can only shut them up for so long, and then it's them wanting to call their parents. Just *get* here!"

He hung up the telephone receiver, took a soiled handkerchief from his bathrobe pocket and wiped the perspiration from his face and sweat-beaded bald head. He sat there, staring straight ahead locked in a paroxysm of indecision and despair. After a while, he arose, left the office and walked the long path leading back to Jerome's bunk. He carefully avoided the mess hall where now all the campers were gathered.

When he entered Jerome's bunkhouse, it was empty save for Jerome and the reed-thin stooped-over figure of Nurse Worth standing beside him. As he approached the bed, he heard Jerome's moans. He turned to the nurse, who continued to look down at her patient while Uncle Bob spoke to her. "How is he?"

"He is in pain. I can't tell if he is asleep or ... He just doesn't answer me. I wanted to get something for the pain ... aspirin, at least, but I was afraid to leave him."

"I called Doctor Sternmeyer. He will be right over."

"The boy needs a *real* doctor, not that quack."

"Doctor Sternmeyer has a great deal of experience. We've used him for the campers for years … and he understands the reality of the situation, the … er, problems this can create."

"You must mean that old fake can cover it up. Well, this can't be covered up. This boy might die if we don't get him to a hospital."

"Let's not get all excited. You're no doctor, between you and your bottle, you couldn't even be a *nurse* in a *real* hospital. Don't forget, it's your job too if this is … you know."

"Drop dead! I may have had my problems, but you're not even a human being."

Jerome stirred and mumbled a cascade of pain-propelled disjointed words. Nurse Worth hissed at Uncle Bob, "Shut up, he can hear you."

They waited in silence for the doctor.

4

DOCTOR STERNMEYER

No one living in the tenements of Williamsburg has ever seen a sunrise. At the end of night, the sun snakes its way over the horizon of rooftops, through the alleys and streets, through the spaces between buildings, spreads its dawn light on the streets and gutters, laps at the foundations of buildings, rises up their walls and through their windows.

On that July day in 1925, it flowed through the open windows of the second-floor McKibben Street apartment and touched the bed of Morris and Millie who slept backs toward each other on the furthest sides of the double bed, the space between them inviolable by unspoken agreement, unbreachable as if there were a wall of mortar and stone. They slept having gone to bed secure in the knowledge that whatever the detritus that remained of their union, there was at least one perfect son.

As the sun splayed itself across the foot of the bed, she suddenly sat bolt upright, her hand flung to her mouth stifling a scream more silent than spoken, drawn from her out of the depths of her sleep by some vision of unknown and impending terror.

* * *

Marcus Sternmeyer —Doctor Sternmeyer—was almost a doctor, and "almost" was good enough for the inhabitants of the town of Lake Mohican—particularly if they did not know that there was an "almost" involved. Sternmeyer did, in fact, at a late age, after his failure as a pharmacist and the bankruptcy of his apoteck, briefly attend the once-renowned medical school in Antwerp. But then in 1914 came the Great War, and Antwerp was occupied by the Hun. In the battles that accompanied their coming and then being driven out, most of the great buildings of the city were destroyed. All that remained of the university were standing fragments of walls that created vast landscapes of brick stalagmites.

When peace finally came in 1918, the city, like a patient recovering from a stupor, slowly came alive. People, hungry, clothing in tatters, carrying cardboard suitcases, pillowcases and baby carriages filled with their possessions, some pushing wagons and most by foot, began to return to the city. The Sternmeyer family came back from the farm where they, hidden from the invaders, spent the war.

When Marcus Sternmeyer finally returned to the medical school, he saw that amidst the mounds of rubble and the brick skeletons of building walls, wooden desks had been set up in spaces of cleared debris. Behind the desks, conducting the business of the university, were a handful of the surviving former senior administration officials, now mostly elderly, most in threadbare clothing.

Sternmeyer made inquiry at one desk and was then sent to another. Since the Sternmeyers had relatives in America, they hoped to immigrate there, and he sought to obtain a certificate memorializing his academic record. However, all the university records were destroyed, and he learned there were not even any municipal records that survived the war. Speaking to the administration officials, he discovered that, upon proof being given, these people were, indeed, providing certificates attesting to an individual's academic achievements at the university. But how could proof be given if there were no records in existence? The official was sympathetic, and drawing Marcus closer, explained how the necessary documentation could be obtained. And so it was that another trip to the farm was made, and by the delivery of a wagon containing a side of pork, sausages and several chickens to a certain address, his medical diploma was forthcoming. Thus did Marcus Sternmeyer become Doctor Sternmeyer.

* * *

After the call from Uncle Bob, he lay in bed for several minutes staring at the ceiling, adrift in the land between sleep and awakening, his mind slowly pulling together what had to be done in the next few hours, using the certainty of these things to tear himself away from sleep—his forgiving and smothering mistress.

He knew he had to make the house call at the camp just as he knew there was nothing he could do, and worse, the time taken up and wasted by his visit should have been better spent by calling for an ambulance from the big hospital in Peekskill, the Hudson Valley Hospital Center.

He drove away the thought that the time lost could have made a difference in the patient's recovery or even whether it could have made the difference between the patient's living or not.

These thoughts he filed away in the part of his brain where he kept a ledger awaiting payment for all the ugliness and horrors he had committed or had been spared while others were not. Over the years, these things accumulated until now, they were at an almost unbearable level.

He arose in segments. First he sat up, then swung his legs over the side of the bed so that his feet rested on the floor. He stood erect and steadied himself by putting the flat of his hand against the wall.

His clothes were already laid out across the back of a chair, wallet, money and keys all placed in their assigned pockets. He did this each night before going to sleep, he explained to people, so that if he were called in the middle of the night on a medical emergency, he would save time in dressing, often enabling him to arrive on the scene before the volunteer fire department ambulance. Actually, this was not completely true. It was a habit formed when he and his family hid at the farm. At the first sign of Germans coming down the farm's dirt road, the family could immediately toss on their clothes and run out through the back door into the woods. The Germans never did come, and the truth was that now, since there was a new young doctor in the town of Lake Mohican—a town that could barely support even one doctor—the nighttime emergency calls were less frequent, and those that did come in were mostly from elderly patients whose problems could have waited until morning. Most really just wanted to have someone they knew and trusted share some time with them during a lonely country night. Since his wife died and children had gone off, he understood—and shared—that need for *something*—often *anything*—to help get him through the night. He and the patients shared the same kind of mornings—mornings that stretched out before them like empty yawning chasms. So, when the night call came, it was, "I'll be right over." He would toss on his clothes, go out to the driveway, start up the car and drive off, his medical bag on the seat beside him.

Lately, he walked about the house, and to his benign amusement, as if he were a third party listening to someone tell a barely funny anecdote, he became aware that it was his own voice speaking aloud to himself. Sometimes, there were words or one word repeated over and over or bits and snatches of conversations. That morning after the call came from Uncle Bob, as he dressed, he kept repeating the word "empty" and thought, with a half-formed smile, "Now why did I say that?"

He peered at his face in the mirror as he shaved and realized that this was the only time during the day when he really looked at his face. Other times, he would glance in a mirror to look at his tie to make sure it was on straight or to see whether his jacket fit or matched his trousers or to comb his fringe of hair.

Every morning, looking in the mirror when shaving, guiding the razor, he studied the contours of his jaw, jowls, chin and neck, the landscape of his cheeks, not really seeing his face. Today though, he stood back and looked at his face, as a face, reflected in the medicine-chest mirror, behind whose swinging door he kept the hoarded bottle of Seconal purchased in the names of a dozen nonexistent people. The pills, he knew, gave him the power, when the time came, to soar beyond unhappiness, loneliness, pain and humiliation.

His face, he thought, was a good and kind face for an almost-doctor: round in a way that fit a body not particularly tall, in fact— in this moment of honesty between mirror and person—a body that was, or at least might appear to some, short and fat. A face that was creased and too red, teeth small and uneven, skin that sagged under his chin traveling directly to his collarbone, burying his neck beneath the plump flesh, a head smooth and hairless except for some few wisps of white hair that clung 'round his head above his ears.

He went out into the cool country air, started the car. He knew that this was not a case for him. He would do the customary things, ask the questions, use the stethoscope, cluck sympathetically, shake his head and say that this was a case that had to go to the big hospital in Peekskill, wait an appropriate period of time for the ambulance to arrive, and if it had not yet arrived, avoid Uncle Bob and say that he had to leave in order to make another house call.

5

THE DOCTOR, A NURSE, AND A LIMOUSINE

God never made his work for man to mend.

John Dryden

As the doctor got older he, with a certain sense of bemused detachment, observed, as one sitting at a sidewalk café might view the passing world, that when unpleasant thoughts took hold of him, he could not, as could a playwright, transmute them into happier ones by making piecemeal changes—substituting one element for another, swelling a scene, diminishing another—but rather, he was forced to accept these thoughts as having a life of their own, coming upon him as a complete, full-blown mise-en-scène.

Now, when this happened and memories of suffered loss, ruminations over past humiliations and failures or unpleasant anticipations gnawed their way into his psyche, taking up entrenched positions, it was not difficult to overwhelm these barricades with wholly new and different scenarios. He believed it was not a bad thing that his mind was no longer able to allow the unpleasant to ward off assaults from completely new thoughts that brought with them entirely new and unrelated visions. Here, the old thoughts, like he himself, had lost the power to resist assault. And so, for him, the thoughts, if not happy in their entirety, were at least, bearable. This accommodation to the memories of a life he believed to be filled with unhappiness, caused him to draw upon a meager inventory of grassy summers, fishing on a still and silent lake, walks in damp and dark fragrant woods or of a girl with long black hair he had met at a certain dance when he was young and without conscience. It was these mental pictures that unreeled themselves in his mind as he drove to the camp and allowed him not to contemplate the pain he would see and the humiliation at his helplessness to do anything about it and indeed, because he was an *almost* doctor, his complicity in the pain.

He drove the short distance along a dusty country road to the camp. Bouncing on the seat next to him was his worn leather doctor's bag containing the armamentarium of modern medicine, which in cases such as the one he would shortly see, he knew to be as useless as a shaman's bag of dried bones. It was, however, his protection and one that could be held up before his detractors, shielding him like a policeman's badge or a wooden cross.

He drove through the gates, parked in the almost-vacant lot and dreading the meeting, slowly walked the distance to the bunkhouse, feeling as though he walked on the stumps of his legs.

The sun had struggled over the horizon, its country fierceness making the morning, even at this early hour, already bright. But when he opened the door to the bunkhouse, the large room was in twilight darkness. As one might observe in a cathedral or church, solid bands of dusty light streamed through the window. On each side of the bunk, the beds were lined up in precise and impersonal rows like gravestones in a cemetery.

The shadow figure of the nurse, curved over like a dark sickle, arced above a bed midway down the left-hand row. Several feet away, Uncle Bob paced back and forth. The figure on the bed was a huddled mass of darkness.

Now having walked over to the bed, he was able to observe that the boy was covered with several blankets and yet was shivering, teeth chattering. Standing at the foot of the bed, he turned to the nurse, not acknowledging the boy, and questioned her as if they were discussing a third party who was not present or if present, was not capable of hearing or divining that he was the subject of their conversation.

"How long has he been like this?"

"Probably since sometime late at night or early after midnight."

"What have you given him?"

She shook her head from side to side, not looking at him.

"Why didn't you call somebody?"

She tossed her head in the direction of Uncle Bob and then averted her gaze away from the doctor and looked down at the boy. The doctor understood, aware of his own complicity by silence in similar situations involving Uncle Bob. He knew that as an almost-doctor, he was helpless to resist Uncle Bob or at least had made himself helpless by his submission over the years to Uncle Bob—who he never addressed, even in thought, as anything other than Uncle Bob—so that he was now like a car driven in deep ruts, unable to traverse the tire-muddy channels.

He turned to the nurse, "Well, what's done is done, and it probably would not have made any difference."

"What do we do now?"

"The only thing we can do. Call the hospital."

"Don't I have to get his OK?" motioning with a toss of her head toward Uncle Bob.

"I'll call myself."

"No, I can … will do it. You stay with the boy."

He, not trusting her to make the call, but also driven by the shamed knowledge from some half-hidden recess of himself that he simply wanted to flee the scene of his helplessness, whispered to her, "You may have a problem with Uncle Bob. Better I call."

He did not wait for her to answer nor did he look at Uncle Bob, who was now standing in the darkness at a corner of the room, leaning on a windowsill, staring out at the breeze-blown shifting summer foliage that grew in the shadow of the bunkhouse. The doctor quickly left the building. Once outside, he stopped, breathed deeply and then walked steadily across the field and up the road to the office.

The telephone calls in this rural area had to be placed through a central operator sitting before a console in an otherwise empty room over the town's hardware store. This morning, it was Ruth. Her considerable girth spilled over the small round stool upon which she sat, in front of the telephone switchboard, painting her nails Pagan Red, the same color that *Movie Life* magazine said was worn by Marlene Dietrich.

Ruth performed her beautification chores while plugging cords into small, winking red-lighted holes located in the apparatus in front of her. A red light—and its accompanying buzz—signaled that someone wished to place a call. Ruth, after inquiring who the caller wished to contact, then reached the desired recipient of the call by yanking out a cord from another row and plugging it into the board facing her, making the connection and at the same time, flipping a small lever causing the phone at the requested number to ring until the instrument was picked up thus completing the connection. Between doing all of this and painting her nails and listening in on the conversations, Ruth had her hands full this morning.

The doctor knew it would be without effect to ask her not to listen in on his conversation and indeed, would only guarantee it would happen if he made the request. He had to be careful in what he said to the hospital since, with Ruth's eavesdropping, it would be the equivalent of taking an advertisement or, at least an article, on the front page of the local Duchess County paper announcing a polio epidemic.

"Peekskill General."

"Give me Laura in Admissions, please." A short pause and then he was connected.

"Laura?"

"Doctor, what are you doing up so early?"

"I know it's early, but I wanted to catch you before you go off. I need an ambulance at the camp."

"Is it an emergency, or can it wait for Emma? I was just about to sign off."

"It's not an emergency, but I'd like to get back to sleep, and if I wait for Emma to gear up, I'll be stuck here for another hour. Please do me a favor."

"I'll walk over to the ambulance bay, and if there's one there, I'll send it out. If not, you'll just have to wait for Emma."

"I appreciate it."

* * *

The 1932 Packard began life as a limousine ordered in 1931 from the company by the owner of a Peekskill lumber mill. When it came time for delivery, the lumber mill was closed down, a victim of the Depression, and the mill owner was closed down due to an overabundance of gas or more exactly, in the vernacular of those unhappy time, "He took the gas pipe"—which in fact had nothing to do with taking any pipe, but described a desperate scene involving a person without hope or the internal strength to survive a fall from economic grace and was played out in a kitchen with its windows closed and the music of hissing gas jets sending the person, slumped over a kitchen chair, to a place of no pain and no monetary obligations. It happened so often in those days that the police usually spent little time searching for a note that even if found, was usually banal in its sameness to all other notes.

The car was delivered to the local Packard dealer, who was able to remain in business only because the expense of maintaining the store was underwritten by the motor-car company itself. The company's reasoning in keeping the local dealerships afloat being that times would eventually get better. When the customers returned, they had to have a place to purchase their cars. So it was decided that it would be a case of waiting out the Depression. And besides, there might be a local dowager or bootlegger in need of a fancy car.

Since, in those times, an unpurchased limousine would have few potential buyers, it remained at the end of the lot like an overdressed flapper sitting at the side of a dance floor with no takers.

After remaining there for a year, it became almost a part of the real estate, and people passing by accepted it as they would a lamp-post or discarded armchair left in a backyard. Then the manager of the agency had an idea. He visited one of the two undertakers in town and offered it for sale as a hearse. He discovered that in those times, funerals with hearses were an item of discretionary spending. People had simple graveside ceremonies with the main personage at the event usually delivered to his or her final destination in a pine box in the back of a pickup truck. He did not bother to visit the town's other undertaker.

His next thought was to try Peekskill General Hospital. He had seen the hospital's present ancient ambulance careen through the streets of town, wobbling on its skeletal wheels. It often broke down on the muddy roads outside of town, announcing the fact by its siren that continued to scream, reminding him of a trumpeting elephant sinking in mud.

He met with the hospital administrator, and between coffee cups, tooth-picking and negotiations that rose and fell like North Atlantic swells, a deal was made: Packard Motor Car Company would tear out the insides of the limousine, put two beds in the car, and the hospital would pay for it over ten years. The hospital now owned a first-class ambulance.

6

ALOIS

Strange to wander in the mist, each time is alone.
No tree knows his neighbour. Each is alone.

Hermann Hesse

Alois Wyckopf was a man with a pinched little mouth, dirt under his fingernails and small black eyes that darted around like minnows in a pond. In 1916, he drove a truck making deliveries from seven in the morning until seven in the evening on a circular route starting and ending at the company's garage in an unheated building that smelled of gasoline and rubber, its floors slick from oil that dripped from the bellies of the trucks left parked overnight.

He lived in a rented room on the top floor of a shingled boardinghouse. There were four other tenants, or "boarders" as the widow liked to call them, with whom he shared a bathroom but seldom saw. The widow who ran the house knocked on his door promptly at seven A.M. on the first of every month calling out "Rent's due." After he was there several months, he left ten dollars wrapped in half a sheet of newspaper propped against his door on the last day of each month. This avoided the need to deal with the landlady and suited them both just fine.

He had no friends at work even though, in hope of engendered camaraderie, he had introduced himself as "Al." He ate his meals at local diners taking the last seat at the counter so that no one, at least on one side, could sit next to him. As soon as the countermen recognized him as a returning customer and tried to make conversation, he changed diners.

He was slight of build, just over five-and-a-half feet tall and returned exhausted to the garage each day after maneuvering the large brown truck along its circular route dropping off packages and small furniture to local businesses. If the proprietor was waiting on a customer, the unspoken understanding in his employment was for the driver to wait to have his receipt slip signed even if it ultimately caused Alois to return to the garage late and not to be paid for his overtime. Sometimes he delivered packages to homes to be met by women who spoke to him through partly opened doors clutching tattered housecoats around themselves in the delusion of needed modesty and who frequently did not have the money due for the delivery telling him "to come back tomorrow."

"Al, you go back only once. If they still don't got the money, it gets returned to the sender. The hell with them. And don't let them dames sweet-talk you."

Several times he asked the foreman to supply him with a helper, only to be met with the reply, "Al, if you can't do the job, there's plenty out there that can." He felt his circumscribed life was as without promise of change as was the daily drive from and to the garage on Division Street.

He worked there a year and then, one evening, after returning to the garage, he parked his truck and was about to leave the building. The foreman, fiftyish, fat with a small round red chin resting on the pillow of his double chins, motioned him to come back into the building. Arms crossed, the foreman looked down at him, "Al, we lost two more men who joined up. There's just not enough guys to go around."

Al tried to remember the foreman's name and at the same time, tried to think of a response. As he was about to reply, the foreman continued. "I just got to ask you to work Saturdays."

"But that wasn't part of my job when I was hired, and as it is, I am bummed out from working my hours."

"Look, I just pass it on as it's given to me. There's a war starting, we're short, and that's the way it is."

Alois looked down at the floor, his hands in his pockets, balled into fists. "The last time, when I asked for a helper, you told me there were plenty of guys for my job. Now you tell me that you are short."

The foreman stepped closer to Al, raising his voice so that it echoed in the cavernous empty garage. "That's then, now's now. I don't got to explain anything to you. If it wasn't for you Krauts, *Alois*, we would not be having this conversation."

They remained, scarcely a foot apart, wordless, the foreman breathing hard, his beer and baloney sandwiched-laden breath passing down in waves over Al's face. Al's fists tightened, his fingernails cutting into his palms. He began to take his fists out of his pockets, stopped, turned and left the garage.

He walked through the dark streets to home oblivious of traffic and people, the roar of his angry blood in his ears. Entering the boardinghouse, he passed his landlady, ignored her greeting and entered his darkened room. He lay down on his bed fully clothed and fell asleep.

The next morning, he arose, washed his face and still wearing the clothes from the prior day, went downtown to the Post Office building.

In the recruiting office, the sergeant, smart and regular army, too old to actively serve and resembling a retired boxer, casually looked up from his paperwork, glanced at Al with all the interest of a bidder at a racehorse auction looking at a prospect for a glue factory, went back to his work and nodded at a pile of literature at the end of the counter. "Pamphlets are over there. Help yourself."

"I want to join up."

The sergeant put his pencil down and slowly looked up at Al again.

The sergeant slid into the standard phrases that recruiting sergeants across the country had been taught, smiled, reached for a form and said, "Sit down lad. Let's see all your country has to offer you and what it wants in return." Ten minutes and some paperwork later, the sergeant stood up, put his cap on his head, walked Al to the corner of the room where stood an American flag and with some solemnity, swore Al into the army of the United States of America.

Inductees hated the ninety days of basic training—Al found them comforting—being one gear in a hundred surrounding gears: human connective tissue. He was but a synapse between himself, the man before him and the next man—he could exist or not exist, the machine would continue to work with or without him—comforted by the warm embrace that comes from supplication to authority: orders given, orders taken—all with the predictability of a kabuki dance.

In order to determine their future assignments, shortly before the end of basic training, the inductees were given questionnaires to be filled in detailing their work histories and skills together with their preferences for their future career in the army. The artillery was Alois' choice. The thought that he could, by his pull on a lanyard, send fifty pounds of steel packed with high explosives hurling through the air at people a half-mile away—at people he never would meet, people over whom he had the power to take their life—enthralled, no, exhilarated, him.

On his last day of training, the forms that were filled out were returned to the recruits. His was stamped "Ambulance Corps."

He sat on the barrack's wooden steps reading the form as the sergeant was about to enter.

"Sergeant, could I have a word?"

"Quick, I have to check the lockers."

"It's my assignment request. I wanted artillery, and I got ambulance corps."

"Maybe you should have asked for ambulance, then you would of got artillery."

"But then what was the point of the forms?"

"I seen what you filled out. You were a driver, and so you're ambulance. Lots of guys want artillery because it's way behind the front and the ambulance guys keep getting killed. Take what you get, and shut up."

"What can I do to change things?"

"Write to your congressman or see the captain. But I don't think you should do neither."

At the end of training, Alois reported to the ambulance section, a one-room wooden hut located on the other side of the camp. The only piece of furniture in the room, other than a coat rack, was a desk. Behind the desk sat a corporal, his hair, flecked with gray, was uncombed, his face was unshaven, his little mouth twisted in a smile as if he had just told himself a dirty joke. He handed the corporal his assignment. The corporal tossed it on a pile of papers and turned to Alois. "They have a hold on ambulance drivers. The trucks can't get close enough to the trenches to do any good, so you're lucky you just stay here for now."

"What will I do?"

"You wait. But for now you relieve me at the desk. I do nine hours on, and then you take over. You get the night hours. Don't make any waves. We got a good thing going on, and we don't hardly never see an officer."

For the next two years, Alois sat in the chair behind the desk from five in the evening until two in the morning. He shuffled paper, formally changing the orders as he received written instruction posting drivers in France from one base to another and entering it in their service record. Drivers who were eligible to be sent home on rotation were instead given leaves in the large cities of France or Belgium, and ultimately, in Germany. A determination had been made that it did not make sense either economically or in terms of manpower to spend the time to ship them home only to have them return again, and besides, the war was always "Just about over".

For two years, during the course of which, through no effort of his own, Alois was promoted to the rank of sergeant, he spent every Saturday night at the local USO club, watching a movie. Then it was coffee and a doughnut sitting by himself and back to the noncommissioned officers barracks. Sunday was spent mostly in bed. Since each of the other occupants of his barrack had different work assignments as well as different schedules, other than a grunted greeting, he had little to do with them.

After two years and the war's end, he returned to Peekskill, a civilian, possessing a uniform with all insignia removed, three sets of army-issue underwear, a toothbrush and two hundred dollars in mustering-out pay. After several days of unsuccessful job hunting, in the local paper he saw an ad for an ambulance driver at Peekskill General Hospital. He explained at the interview that he had been an ambulance driver in France for the last two years. He was hired.

7

PEEKSKILL GENERAL

Because of summer polio outbreaks, the New York State Department of Health decreed that for every three counties, there had to be at least one designated institution set up for the emergency treatment of polio cases. This facility was required to have at least twenty-four iron lungs available during the summer epidemic period, together with adequate nurses, aides and doctors sufficiently trained to treat the patients and operate the machines. Peekskill General was such a hospital.

* * *

Trouble came barreling down the hall with sausage-shaped legs stuffed into mens' shoes, a white hospital gown draped around her like a tent. She hurried along the corridor, her gown flapping in her wake. The corridor was in semidarkness, on the one side was the emergency room, now empty and lit only by a single lamp. On the other side of the corridor, there were three darkened rooms. Rushing down the corridor, she paused before each room, looked in and called out, "Al, you there? Are you in there?" Muttering to herself, puffing and out of breath, she traveled the length of the corridor until it terminated at the ambulance well. There were no lights in the Packard ambulance parked in the dock.

"Al, you in there? It's Laura. You got to make a run." Still no reply.

She reached across the open space between the cement edge of the dock to the wide rear door of the ambulance and grasping it, opened the door. Balancing herself between the edge of the dock and the automobile by hanging onto the door's rear handle, she peered into the darkened vehicle.

"Al, you lazy sonuvabitch. I know you're in there. Come out, or I'll get Steven to come down and get a light and haul your ass outta there and outta the whole hospital. You got a run to make."

"Wait, wait. I was just fixing something in front of the wagon."

"Like hell you are." She sneered, "Fixing? In the dark? You know damn well that you were sleeping on our time."

Alois came to the rear end of the vehicle and shouted through the open door at Laura. "I weren't sleeping, and I would never lie on the beds back there. No telling what kind of diseases the people wot laid on these beds had."

"Doc Sternmeyer just telephoned, and you have to make a call at the camp. No hurry, not an emergency, but don't go back to sleep."

Alois climbed out of the back of the ambulance and jumped across the short distance to the cement loading dock.

"I need a route sheet and an order."

"You don't need nothing. Just go to Mohican, ask for the nurse, Worth, and pick up a kid. You can go alone since he don't sound too sick, and he can get himself into the ambulance. It is no emergency, and I'll give you the paperwork when you come back."

"This ain't the way it's supposed to be done."

"You ain't supposed to be sleeping in the truck, neither. Now just get going."

Alois descended the five steps to street level and walked slowly to the front of the vehicle, climbed into the driver's seat and started up the engine. He eased the ambulance out of its darkened well into the sunlight of a summer Peekskill morning. Traffic was building as he headed east toward the country road that led to the camps. He had made this trip many times before.

After driving for about fifteen minutes, he was at the outskirts of the city. On the other side of the road was a wooden hamburger shack. It was a small square building constructed of unpainted, weathered wooden planks with a large glassless window and on its sill, a serving counter opened to the street. A hand-lettered sign above the opening said "Fresh Hamburgers 30¢." Beneath that sign hung another, with the word "*open*" scribbled in large painted black letters.

Alois made a U-turn and parked in front of the shack. Behind the counter was a thin man in an undershirt, over this he wore a soiled white apron. His arms were embossed with faded nautical tattoos. Alois got out of the ambulance and said to the man, "Gimme one with all the fixings."

He received the hamburger wrapped in a napkin, paid the counterman-chef fifty cents and returned to the ambulance to eat his breakfast. Watching the traffic go by, he ate slowly, his mind still fogged from sleep and numbed by the hypnotic sameness of passing cars. When he finished breakfast, he left the ambulance, strolled over to the shack and asked the counterman if he could use the bathroom. The man said he could use the one in the house and jerked his thumb in the direction of a ramshackle house about twenty yards behind the hamburger stand. Alois walked slowly across the pathless, hard-packed dry earth to the house.

Fifteen minutes later, he returned to the car, started it up, headed toward the camp.

The roads led to progressively narrower roads and finally, ones that were little more than country paths made firmer and wider by a generation of automobiles passing over them on the way to and from the summer camps. He drove past several, all with Indian names hand-painted on wooden plaques. The hand lettering was a clumsy effort to achieve at least an ersatz rusticity. But, even in this modest intention, it failed. Finally, Alois arrived at Camp Mohican and turned into the driveway.

At the foot of the driveway stood Uncle Bob and Doctor Sternmeyer. Uncle Bob was still in his red pajamas and flannel bathrobe. The doctor began to give Alois some instructions, but Uncle Bob pushed him aside and led the driver a few feet away from the ambulance and the doctor. He put his arm around Alois' shoulders, and in the soft voice of one conspirator talking to another said to him, "You know these doctors. Everything is a big deal. The boy has a touch of the flu, and Sternmeyer and the nurse are in a tizzy over it. I'm sorry I called him in the first place."

"Look, mister, none of this is my business. I pick them up and take them to the hospital, and that's it."

"I know, but we wouldn't like to have you mention it to anybody else at the hospital. That's how rumors start, and pretty soon, everybody gets excited. You wouldn't want that to happen, would you?"

As he said this, Uncle Bob pressed a ten-dollar bill into Alois' palm. Alois glanced down at his open hand containing the moist crumpled bill.

"Sure boss, ain't no use getting people excited."

Leaving Doctor Sternmeyer to find his own way on foot, Uncle Bob climbed on the running board of the ambulance and directed Alois toward the bunkhouse. When they arrived at their destination, they entered the large room, now vacant but for the boy's bed and Nurse Worth, who stood beside the bed, hands clasped, still wearing her topcoat over her nightgown. The boy's eyes were closed; his face fever-red and perspiration damp. His moans trailed off into silence.

Uncle Bob looked down at him and shouted as one might to a

person hard of hearing or as an ignorant person might to someone who has difficulty with the language in the hope that volume would penetrate ignorance.

"Son, you're going to be all right. You just gotta take a trip to the hospital. This boy here's gonna take you, and you will be right as rain. Yes sir, right as rain! So, let's see that old Mohican spirit, and you'll soon be right back here. Right as rain!"

The boy did not respond.

Nurse Worth said she wanted to ride along with the boy to the hospital, adding they would have to wait while she went back to her cabin to get dressed.

Unconscious, the boy drifted on merciful clouds that silently smothered his pain. He was unaware of his moans that came from an unknown place within him that felt the pain that he was unable to feel.

Alois brought in a stretcher on wheels and rolled it beside the boy's bed.

"I need somebody to help me get him on the stretcher."

"Wait for the nurse. She's riding back with you anyway."

The two moved away from the bed to another part of the bunk-house where they would not hear the sounds from the boy.

After about fifteen minutes, Worth walked in carrying a small overnight bag. She wore a starched white dress that could reasonably pass for a nurse's uniform.

She and Alois walked over to the boy's bed.

"Ma'am, you take the bottom end of the sheet, and I'll take the top, and we'll just slide him onto the stretcher."

The boy felt himself being lifted and then the sleeping provinces of each motionless joint of his body screamed at him. He felt himself carried into the ambulance—each sway and bump of the stretcher, each footstep of the bearers, caused a new wave of searing pain. Then it suddenly stopped. He was now inside the ambulance.

The ambulance started forward. Nurse Worth sat beside him,

staring straight ahead, holding his hand. As the ambulance passed over rough patches in the road, pain—unspeakable and terrible—stabbed and tore at his child's muscles; pain beyond endurance; pain clubbing him into welcomed unconsciousness to be only awakened by the car when driven over ruts in the road—brief wakeful voyages between nightmare pain.

By the time they reached the hospital, the day had become overcast. The hospital loomed large and ominous against the clay-colored sky. The building itself, gothic and turreted, was dark gray and built of large rough-hewn stones. Behind and to the sides of the building, there were buildings of newer and lighter brick, designed with an indifference to the principal structure. The myth-rumor enjoyed by the hospital staff was that the original building had been the home of an upstate robber baron that he had built, copied from a European castle, as a gift to his bride. She became ill shortly after the wedding and died. He left it, never to return and, at his death, it was bequeathed to the city of Peekskill. Subsequently, when municipal administrations had sufficient funds, additional buildings were added to the original facility.

Alois glided the twelve-cylinder Packard up the long curving driveway and backed it into the emergency-room parking well. He climbed out, went to the rear of the ambulance and opened the door. He called for an orderly to help him remove the stretcher from the car. Together, they wheeled it down the corridor to the emergency room.

The boy was awake, unable to move, but as he was rushed toward the emergency room his eyes fixed at the ceiling, the bare electric light bulbs seemed like a moving necklace rapidly marching past him. And, again the pain returned, now constant, invading his powerless limbs, thrusting itself into their every sinew and fiber, filling his mind, his reason, driving out all thought and memory until there was only searing, scolding pain that encapsulated his existence, until his very being was but a vehicle for the pain that now owned him.

They turned on the lights in the emergency room. Nurse Worth whispered a few words to the intern on duty that were sufficient to cause the young doctor not to examine the boy, but rather call for the neurological resident.

Alois, the nurse and the intern, while waiting for the neurologist, stood next to the boy, serious and silent, looking off into nothing, like hearse drivers at a funeral in a cemetery.

After about fifteen minutes, he appeared, a middle-aged man, unshaven, harried, wearing a many-colored, open-collared sport shirt and dungarees under an unbuttoned white coat. Ignoring Alois, he nodded to the intern and Nurse Worth.

He took Nurse Worth aside and obtained a brief history from her. He then examined the boy, testing his reflexes with a small triangular rubber hammer. First he tapped his bent elbow. No reaction. Then he tapped his knee with the hammer. No reaction. "Try to touch your chest with your chin." The boy could not.

He again took the nurse aside and asked the intern to join them at the side of the room, once more ignoring Alois.

"The boy has polio. His arms and legs are paralyzed, and he is in enormous pain, but his breathing has not been compromised . . . yet. We can't give him anything for the pain because it will suppress his breathing ability, which is the only thing he has going for him at this point. But, he immediately has to be admitted to the third-floor isolation unit. Also make sure they have a lung available . . . just in case. Why on earth wasn't he brought in sooner?"

"We have a procedure I've had to follow, and . . ."

"No matter. It will not make any difference in the prognosis. In the end, I don't think anything we do will make a difference. If you give me the family's phone number, I'll call. They will have a lot of questions. Lord, I hope they don't start bringing in city specialists. In the meantime, get masks and gowns, get him upstairs and wash yourselves down . . . thoroughly."

8

THE IRON LUNG

Philip Drinker and Louis Shaw invented the modern iron lung in 1929. This was made possible by a seven-thousand-dollar grant from the Consolidated Gas Company of New York.

Four-hundred million years earlier, the human lung evolved when fishes climbed out of the primordial ooze and their oxygen-exchange mechanism— their gills— proved to be insufficient for the breathing requirements of a terrestrial life.

The inventors of the iron lung sued John Emerson, the developer of a later, more efficient apparatus. Emerson won the lawsuit by proving that virtually every element of the Drinker/Shaw lung had been appropriated from the earlier work of others.

The iron lung is rigid, ugly, noisy, uncomfortable and often painful to its user. It needs electricity in order to function and is primitive in its application, being dependent on basic physical laws: the human lung inflating and deflating in response to the fall and rise in external air pressure.

The human lung continued to evolve by virtue of necessity and adaptation. It is a superb and gentle instrument consisting of fifteen hundred miles of airways, soft and spongy in consistence, requiring but .23 seconds for the carbon dioxide/oxygen exchange to take place in red blood cells. It is responsible for supplying its host with oxygen, controlling the temperature and humidity of the air intake and the expelling of harmful substances breathed in, and it requires no external power source to perform these functions but . . . it can fail.

* * *

The third-floor isolation unit was designed to prevent the spread of disease from patient to visitors and from patient to patient. The unit was divided into a number of individual rooms, each only large enough for one hospital bed around which was mosquito netting draped from the ceiling, a chair and a small bedside table. Pasted on the large glass window that was set in the door was a sign that read:

Caution!
This is a quarantined area.
Contagion precautions are required.

Nurses and doctors who entered the room wore cotton masks, gowns and rubber surgical gloves. The nurse's aides bagged the waste and ultimately burned it in the hospital incinerator. Visitors to the unit were not allowed to enter the patient rooms and were confined to a waiting room directly across from the elevators. If permission to see a patient was granted, contact was limited to looking at the patient through the glass window in the door.

* * *

Things moved slowly in the summer in Williamsburg. The evening sky is light until late; the molten sinking sun dying blood-red far off behind the elevated train tracks running along Broadway. The cars are parked at curbside for the night; the laundry hung out to dry on clotheslines has been hauled indoors; kitchen tables cleared of dinner dishes; the water trays under iceboxes have been emptied; people leaned out of windows, resting their elbows on folded towels, hoping to catch a vagrant breeze; some brought mattresses out onto fire escapes for a night's cool sleep. That night across McKibben Street and down the block, a few Puerto Ricans sat on the steps of a tenement, one with a guitar, quietly strumming, while further up the steps, a card game was in progress. The six-story building at 75 Manhattan Avenue was in its last stage of construction, looming dark and silent, save for a few light bulbs in a construction shack. It was to be the first building with an elevator in Williamsburg. Next door, across from Goldie's bridal shop, three boys, one in an undershirt, all in short pants, sat on a stoop, watching a large water bug, its shiny black shell catching the last flickers of the setting sun, slowly drag its belly across the sidewalk. The boys furtively passed a cigarette, each taking turns at a puff.

The air was still and held the faintly acrid smell of cooling tar from gutters made soft from the heat of the day. From somewhere down the street, through an open window, a tinny radio broadcast a society band performing at the Rough Rider Room of the Hotel Roosevelt on Madison Avenue, across the bridge and two miles uptown—a universe away.

Around the corner, over Rudy's luncheonette, Morris and Millie shared the now-empty, two-bedroom, second-floor apartment. With no child at home the apartment had the unlived-in neatness of a spinster teacher's rented room. That evening, an evening that changed their world, an evening that was so painful to recollect that it was buried deep, without ceremony or discussion, never to be spoken of again, in that final place of internment where all past terrible things are entombed, never to be disinterred.

That evening, chores were done, dinner prepared and eaten, dishes washed and put in racks to drain, evening paper read and tossed away, windows opened for the night, with hardly a word exchanged between them. They went to bed, and after an hour, the night quiet was torn by the ringing of the phone in the foyer. She sat bolt upright, paused and got out of bed.

It *had* to be bad news; people only call if there is bad news. Somebody must have died, all else could have waited until morning. As she ran to the phone, her mind raced through the lists of relatives close enough to have shattered the night with a telephone call. Her sister, Yettie and her family … Morris' family, no … not likely. She did not dare to think the next thought for to think it would be to give it life. And then she picked up the phone and to herself, the unspoken thought, "Jerome … away from home … Jerome. Not Jerome. Oh God, please, not Jerome."

"Hello?"

"Hello. Mrs. Felder?"

"Yes?"

"This is Doctor Samson. I'm a neurologist at Peekskill General."

She put her hand against the wall of the foyer to steady herself, heart pounding, a roaring in her ears. She lowered her arm so that the telephone receiver was at her side. From out of the telephone, hurtling over the wires, the faint, distant-thin voice that she could barely hear from the phone she was unable to put against her ear, as if holding it away could keep the bad news away.

Her husband came out of the bedroom, with one hand clutching the bunched-up waistband of his pajamas, with the other putting on his eyeglasses.

"What is it? What's the matter?"

"The hospital …"

"Who is it?"

She did not answer.

"Answer me. What is it?"

"A doctor at the hospital."

"What happened?"

"Mrs. Felder, are you there? This is Doctor Samson..."

She turned away from her husband and put the telephone to her ear. "I'm here, Doctor. Tell me."

"I'm afraid the news is not good."

"It's polio, isn't it?"

"It looks like it."

She paused. Thoughts, bits and pieces, disconnected and fragmented raced through her mind, colliding and crisscrossing with one another. She pulled herself together as if forcing herself awake from a nightmare.

"How bad is it?"

"We really don't know. It has not affected his breathing... so far. And this is obviously a good thing."

"His legs?"

"As of now, he can't move his arms and legs. But we're still in the acute stage, and they very well may come back. We will, of course, do a spinal tap, but basically we will just have to wait and see."

"I'll come immediately."

"Why not wait? He's in the isolation unit and can't have visitors, so you won't even be able to be with him."

"I *will* come. I'll leave now... no, it's night... first thing in the morning."

"Well of course, it's up to you." Her hand trembled as she replaced the receiver on the telephone and turned to her husband.

"It's polio. I have to go in the morning."

Now wearing his eyeglasses as if they somehow allowed him to focus his thinking as well as vision: What did he say? How serious?

"He can't move his arms and legs. I don't know. But, he can still breathe." She heard her words as if coming from another person,

"Still breathe? Did I say that? My God how did this happen? Oh my God!"

They remained standing at the telephone—the now silent instrument of their destruction—without speaking, bound together, by these last several moments that would forever change their lives: collateral damage caused by some pulsating evil bit of unseeable matter that had attacked their son on a summer's evening many miles away.

* * *

She took a cab from the train station and had difficulty saying the words "Peekskill General" when she directed the cab driver. After a short ride, the taxi drove up the long circular driveway, the hospital, a massive gray presence hovering over them, a place, she thought, from which there was no return.

She entered a vast, cool, dimly lit room with a high vaulted ceiling. On the walls were faded murals, painted flat, without a perspective of depth, of knights on rearing horses with ladies wearing tall cone-shaped hats and veils, running either to or from the horsemen and all about them were dark and swirling plants and flowers.

In the center of the room was a woman with gray-white hair tinged with blue, who sat behind a round desk upon which were several address files and telephones. She told the woman she was there to see Doctor Samson. The lady paged the doctor with a lack of enthusiasm born of her boredom. Her voice over the paging system—monotoned and controlled—reverberated throughout the labyrinthine corridors.

"Doctor Samson, please come to reception. Doctor Samson to reception."

After several minutes, one of the phones on the desk rang. She answered it and informed the visitor that the doctor was just finishing rounds and would be down in a minute.

A half-hour later, Doctor Samson arrived. He was unshaven, wearing a wrinkled white coat, open-collared sport shirt, the uncoiled snake of a stethoscope protruding from his coat pocket. His eyes, tired and sad, were set deep in the gray and sagging flesh of his face. He greeted the visitor, "I'm sorry you had to wait." He led her to a marble bench on the side of the room.

"We are overloaded. Four new polio cases were just admitted, and this puts a strain on our resources. I'll tell you what we know so far about your son's condition ... and more importantly, what we don't know. As of this morning, the nurses tell me he is stabilized."

"The *nurses* told you?"

"I have not yet seen him today. We do the best we can. I had to deal with the incoming emergencies, but he is constantly monitored, and they page me if there is any change in his condition ... and I have not slept in two days. We are doing the *best* we can."

"I want to see him."

"You understand that since he is in quarantine, all you can do is to *look* at him through the door window, and to tell you the truth, from my experience, this is probably all the more upsetting for the children and the parents."

"We can discuss that later, but ..." her voice rising, "I want to see my son."

The woman at the desk looked up upon hearing the mother's raised voice and observing its source, quickly looked away, busying herself by examining the papers on her desk with a theatrical intensity.

"I can appreciate your feelings. God knows I've been through this with enough parents, but I still can't imagine how you feel or what you are going through." He paused, ran his fingers through his tousled hair, put his head down and in thought said, "Tell you what. You wait here. I have to deal with several emergencies. Then I'll come down and take you upstairs, and you can see the boy, and I'll introduce you to the nurses."

She waited for a half-hour until he reappeared. He led her down seemingly endless dark corridors through two other buildings that had been added on and then joined with the main hospital building. They came to an elevator that had a small sign above the call button reading, *This elevator for isolation floor only.* The elevator was small with scratched wooden walls. All the buttons designating floors had been taped over except the one for the third floor. On the third floor, the elevator opened into a small enclosed waiting room that contained three overstuffed and overaged easy chairs. Her housewifely eye told her that an administrator at the hospital must have had his home redecorated, and his demanding wife insisted that the old furniture be thrown out. With furniture as with people, she thought, the hospital is the alternative to the garbage pail. The chairs told her something else: the people who sat in them had to make themselves comfortable for a long wait.

The doctor said, "I'll go in to see him and make sure everything is OK. I'll be back for you in about ten minutes."

As the doctor turned to leave the room, a nurse came through the doors on her way to the elevator. Seeing the doctor, she turned to him, "Doctor Samson, we have been paging you. We have a ..."

She glanced at the woman sitting in the easy chair, stopped midsentence and whispered in his ear. After a moment, the nurse and doctor quickly left the room.

* * *

It began as heaviness on his chest: a gentle pressure, almost the caress of a resting hand. Then the pressure increased, slow, steady and increasingly heavier, confining his small chest, making it impossible to take an inward breath, leaving him feeling as if he had just run a great distance, unable to gulp air.

The monitoring devices set off warning signals at the nurse's station. The rules required that one nurse must always be present at the station to hear the electric call for help; a signaling of a failure of a body function: the desperate plea of a dying organ. They raced into his room. His eyelids were fluttering their last signals of his descent into nothingness.

The nurses had seen this many times before. The choreography had been well rehearsed; the actors well knew their roles. It was to be the iron lung, but he would never last the transfer without help breathing. His life now consisted of existing until the next breath, straining, gasping, never quite making the next full breath, his lungs arrested in their travails; air around him, people swimming in air, air surrounding and suffusing everything he could see, and yet this air, like a solid thing crashed into a fathomless and unseen wall, unable to penetrate into his body.

They immediately placed an emergency ventilator over his mouth and nose, a mask attached to a rubber bulb about the size of a grapefruit that a nurse running alongside his wheeled stretcher, rhythmically squeezed, forcing air into his bronchial passageways as he was taken to the iron lung.

His mother sat in the waiting room unaware of what was happening thirty feet away behind the hospital doors.

* * *

They brought him into the room through the swinging double doors. On his back, he saw only the ceiling and fly-specked bare light bulbs, but he heard the sound of the machine, as regular and impersonal as the beat of a metronome, hcump-huh, hcump-hah: the breathing of the iron monsters. It was the sound of the rhythm of the bellows taking the place of lungs for the twenty-two children and two adults encased in the devices. He was wheeled between two rows of twelve iron cylinders to what was to be his place of entombment, his home: the twenty-third iron lung, next to the last in the column on the right.

The lungs were cast iron with heavy protruding rivets and had all the charm of tugboat boilers. At one end, the head of the patient—looking more like that of a victim of a medieval torture device than of a patient—rested on a pillow outside the cylinder, a slanted mirror fixed above the person's head, providing the patient a partial view of the outside world . . . limited to about three feet. There were rubber portholes so that the nurses could insert their arms in order to perform chores on the patients. Above each porthole was a rectangular curved glass window so that the nurse could see what she was doing when she put her hands through the portholes.

When it came time to transfer the boy into the encasing iron prison, the nurse stopped squeezing the rubber bulb that forced air into his lungs. The moment that the nurse stopped breathing for him, his stilled lungs were helpless. The heavy dull weight came down upon his chest, and the suffocation began. He tried to scream, but the wisps of air remaining in his lungs were hopelessly spent on producing an unintelligible rasp.

Once in the lung, his existence was encapsulated by what he could see in the slanted mirror above his head and the walls of the iron prison and the rhythmic monotone sound of the beating of the machine's iron heart—hcump-huh, hcump-huh, hcump-huh—that enabled his own lungs to intake and expel air and that separated him from the world.

Because polio attacks the nerve fibers that send messages to the muscles of the arms and legs, these limbs become little more than useless; flaccid masses of protoplasm. However, the paralysis can affect more than just the muscles that control breathing and locomotion.

Each child and adult held prisoner in the lungs wore a diaper that the nurses changed once a day. If the patient's diapers had been soiled early in the day, it would have to stay that way for hours until the nurse came to attend to it. The nurses would say, "You've been a naughty boy [girl]" to both the children and adults.

Initially, the disease left most of its victims unable to move their hands or arms and even the ones who could were unable to take them out of the machine. Because of this, the nurses had to spoon-feed them.

A child might call for a nurse to change the position of his head or to change the towel around her neck, placed there to ease the chafing from the machine's collar or to do any one of the myriad of tiny things that, outside this room, outside of this disease, a person could, without thought, do for themselves—the accumulation of threads making the fabric of a day's life: brushing hair away from one's eyes, an itch to be scratched, clearing mucus from a throat now unable to cough, wiping away a tear. After finally arriving to attend to them, the nurses would treat them as misbehaving children.

Whether by design, ignorance or happenstance, it was not long until they all—children and adults—became infantilized.

Parents were allowed in the room for several brief periods during the day. This was done as much for the benefit of the nurses as for the children, since children who were occupied by a parent combing a child's hair or reading to them, were less likely to call for a nurse. But, the unspoken—and perhaps unconsciously thought-out idea— was the same as the template of armies and religions: sweet supplication to authority; the warm smothering embrace of authority that removes the necessity, then the desire and ultimately, the ability for independent thought or action.

There were times that the patient had to be removed from the machine in order for the staff to attend to some need: medical tests to be performed; a physical examination that had to be made; bedsores to debride; or limbs to be wrapped in scalding wool bandages in the vain hope of keeping muscles supple.

Usually, the patient was slid out of the machine for a few minutes, but the second he was removed from that machine, his breathing stopped, or mostly so—eyes bulging, lips becoming colored the faint purple prelude to death, chest heaving and straining, and soon the skin already pale, now turned to blue-tinged ivory. Often, the patient was already unconscious before being returned to the life-giving chamber. When he was back in the breathing chamber and awake, the nurses would say, "You acted like a big baby" or some variation of this remark.

* * *

After two months, the doctors determined that the disease had completed its raging swath, wreaking destruction—some temporary, some permanent—through the territories of his body. His legs, they believed, would never again function as legs, but thought that he would regain the ability to breathe on his own. So now came the process of teaching him to breathe again—a process begun nine years earlier with a simple slap on his bloody infant's back. But now, it was considerably more difficult.

A doctor and two nurses stood at the head of the machine, opened it and then slid him out until, heart pounding, tearing itself from his chest, gasping and opening and closing his mouth, trying to raise his head to catch the air that eluded him, straining without success to gulp the unseen medium of his existence until he began to sink into a bottomless and peaceful black void where air was irrelevant and pain existed not even in memory.

Afterward, they scolded him for not being able to remain out of the machine for a longer period. Their plan was simple: keep him out of the machine for progressively longer periods of time so that eventually he would be able to sustain his own breathing. Since, when they attempted this, it did not seem to work out, they decided on a different approach. They would slide him out of the machine gently while he slept, and when he awoke from lack of oxygen, they would return him into the machine. They would measure the time he was out of the lung each day, and they would, as his lungs got stronger, increase the intervals.

The first time they did this, almost immediately he was awakened by his inability to breathe, but added to this was the naked terror of being wrenched from the dark and quiet refuge of his world of sleep to one where the lack of air wove itself into a fleeting nightmare that seemed to go on and on until he was back in the world of doctors and nurses and was panting for air: a beached and dying fish, its gills helpless, clasping and opening on nothing.

They decided they were on the right track and continued the process the next night. Soon he came to dread the night and fought sleep. Eventually, he would fall asleep from exhaustion until the armies of terror would descend upon him, sliding him out of his iron cocoon until he was returned to the lung. It worked. After a month and a half, he was able to breathe on his own and ready to be transferred to the rehabilitation floor.

9

REHABILITATION

Most any definition of the word "rehabilitation" suggests restoring something damaged to a former condition or at least, to a good or better condition. However, sometimes the damage or degradation that had occurred was so great that restoration is not possible, or what happened was of such immensity that it had been obliterated from memory or at least those memories have but the gauzy substance of the mere wisps of old dreams. Then, "rehabilitation" becomes a meaningless term: a label now hung on a new and compromised state of being.

* * *

It was the sound that he did not hear—the thumping metronome from the mechanical hearts of the iron lungs—that caught his attention as he was wheeled through the swinging double doors.

There was also the noise from the children—not all, but some, those who were able to sit upright or could use their arms and legs in varying degrees.

Once again, there were two rows of beds lined up facing each other in as neat and exact precision as eggs in a carton. Between the rows of beds were two desks, one behind the other. Nurses sat behind the desks.

As they rolled him to a vacant bed midway in the row to the left of him, the children—those who could—sat up to look at him. Some gave a greeting, some waved welcome with a hand gesture or nod.

Once he was set up, in the bed to his right was Andy, twelve, red-headed and freckle-faced, whose legs were paralyzed and who immediately tried to engage him in conversation.

"It's pretty good here except the rehab stuff is tough, and they are really down on you if you don't get it. Yeah, oh yeah except for Old Steinpus when he comes around. Him, you gotta look out for. But he was just here two days ago—that's how you got the bed—so he won't be coming back for a week. I'll tell you what to do before he gets to you. It never fails. I'm here three months and never been picked."

On the bed to the left of him was a boy, perhaps eight years old. Only his pale round face resting on a mass of unkempt hair was outside the blankets, brown against the white pillows; his thin lips pursed and closed tight; his eyes open, wide and unblinking, pupils motionless, unfocused, staring at the ceiling.

He turned to look at the silent figure on the bed and said, "Hi." There was a long pause, louder now, he called out, "Hi. Can you hear me?" Andy said to him, "It won't do you no good to talk to him. He came in yesterday and hasn't said a word. I tried to talk to him, but he just lays there and don't answer. Even when they come to feed him, he don't talk. The nurses say he can, but just won't."

"Can he move?"

"Nurses say he can't, but he can talk."

"Can he hear?"

"Dunno."

When evening came and they announced that the lights were going to be lowered, he looked over to his left at the boy who remained, eyes open, still staring at the ceiling.

He was tired from the move and the having to absorb all the newness of the change and fell quickly asleep. He thought he awakened during the night and looked over at the boy in the bed on his left. In the morning, he remembered that the boy's eyes were open even in the night—or at least he thought that was what he saw—or maybe it was just a dream.

* * *

In the early morning hours, while still asleep, he dreamed that an animal with large teeth had locked its jaws on his ankles. The dream crossed a threshold into the place of nightmares and as he struggled to free himself from this terror of the night, the animal transformed itself into the disembodied teeth of a headless beast whose teeth bit deeper and deeper until screaming, he was thrust into consciousness.

Swimming into his focus, at the foot of his bed were two nurses bent over his feet, pulling at them, now twisting them, straining to attach his feet to a board affixed horizontally to the foot of the bed. One nurse, the older one, went about her task with the relentlessness of a Mack truck hurtling down a straight and endless highway. She had a square and wrinkled face now beet red. She pursed her lips tightly together as she pulled and grunted, twisting his legs and trying to attach his feet to the board. The other, younger nurse stood next to her, hands clasped, waiting for instructions from the other. "Hold down the leg while I get it into place." "Quick, put the strap on while I have it against the board." She did as she was told, not looking at the boy.

His leg muscles lacking power were unable to resist the twisting and turning of his feet. While one nurse turned his foot, holding it in a vertical position, the other strapped it to the board. Soon, both feet were affixed to the board. After a few moments, the pain radiated from his ankles to his knees then to his hips. He cried out for them to stop. They did for a moment, the older nurse turning to him, looked down at him, her hands on her hips and said,

"Now don't be such a baby. We want to make sure that your legs stay nice and straight, so we are doing what you can't do yourself. We will help you every morning until things are all right. Just be thankful we are here to do it and *no*, understand *no* complaining. It is just going to make things worse." Bending over him, her mouth close to his ear, she said, "I don't want to hear any whining, or you will have to stay this way double time."

She patted him on his shoulder, and the two nurses left to go to another sleeping child in the next row.

When they left, Andy said to him, "Yeah, I forgot to tell you about the leg handcuffs. Nothing you can do about it."

He tried to contort his hips to ease the pain, first, trying to lift one hip and then, unable to do so, the other and finally, by twisting his torso, lifting one side of his upper body and putting all of his weight on the other, for a moment—just a moment—he could relieve the pain from one leg. And then, he would fall back panting, exhausted.

Pain flowed up his back until finally it stabbed at the muscles of his neck. At first, he would cry out, but the nurses ignored him. After a while, his feet and legs became numb to the pain, but also to any other sensation. It felt as if his legs were tied off from the rest of his body and that his legs and feet existed, if at all, as a separate entity. The pain in his upper body spread round his torso and gripped his chest and stomach muscles, increasing in intensity until he felt as though his burning muscles would tear through the skin that imprisoned them.

The other children on the ward would fall into silence while he or another patient was strapped to the boards.

They came to tie his feet every day for two weeks. He tried to fight sleep; he thought that by doing this, somehow, they would not come. He could not stay awake, and of course, they came and would continue to come whether he was awake or sleeping.

After two weeks, they released his feet from the board. The older nurse said to him, "Well, that's all we can do. I don't think you really appreciated everything we did."

* * *

Early mornings, they came into the ward, the younger nurse wheeling a cart piled high with very hot, wet wool blankets fresh from the large stainless-steel vats that were used to sterilize hospital equipment. The steam from the blankets rose to the high ceiling of the room in a shimmering tower that in its upward climb changed and distorted the forms of what was viewed from its other side. The children, denied the natural phenomenon of life—fire, sunlight, the smell of a breeze passing over dew-wet grass, the sound of water at low tide softly lapping to its demise upon a beach—were transfixed by the cart trailing a tower of water vapor as it was wheeled to the end of the row of beds. The older nurse would tell the younger to stop at a particular bed. There they would wrap the patient's legs in the hot blankets.

When they came to the boy, the older nurse, without speaking to him, took hold of the top edge of his blanket and pulled it quickly down to the foot of the bed. His only clothing was a pajama top and a pair of baggy rough cotton shorts supplied by the hospital to each child—boy or girl. The younger nurse lifted one of the scalding-hot blankets and tossed it up and down in her hands to avoid burning herself as she handed it off to the other nurse. The older nurse, her hands seemingly impervious to the heat, slowly wrapped the blankets tightly around his legs. The blankets were not full blankets. They were, in fact, tattered pieces of blankets and fabrics, some were blankets that would otherwise have been discarded, some were donations to the hospital, some were old threadbare bath towels, some were little better than rags. She worked each one carefully around a leg, and when one blanket came to an end, she began the winding again, now with a new piece of cloth. Soon his limbs were encased with hot wet tubes of wool.

When the nurse put the first steaming piece of cloth on his leg, he screamed out. She ignored him and continued to add piece after piece of the fabric, winding them around his leg.

His legs felt as though someone was pouring boiling water over them, but it was more profound and deeper than if this had occurred. He felt his scalded skin shrink from the wrappings like a living thing trying to escape harm. Layer upon layer pressed and trapped the heat deep into the core of his limbs. The flesh of his legs—now raw—was no longer a protection against the pain, but rather its conduit into his muscles and bone. When she was done, she turned to him and said, "Well, that should make your muscles nice and loose."

After a bit, the intensifying pain became the cause of its own demise, and he became numb to it.

As the blankets cooled, they became cool and clammy, an irritation against his raw flesh. The nurses did not remove them for several hours, and when they finally did, the bed was wet from the wrappings and remained so the rest of the day.

As the years passed, the coiled snake of memory stirred, and he always felt uneasy at the smell of wet wool: organic and faintly fetid like the scent of a dying animal.

> *"When a leg is completely useless— i.e.,*
> *when it cannot be swung forward and*
> *backward—it is better to amputate it through the*
> *thigh." FDR's Splendid Deception*
> (Contemporaneous medical text, Gallagher)

* * *

After the war, Augustus Stein's family migrated to America from

Austria. His father was a successful butcher in Vienna and remained untouched by the Great War that was supposed to end all wars, but was, in fact, the template for future wars: the first part of a European civil war that twenty years later was resurrected, engulfing now the entire world.

Stein senior had hoped his son would follow in his profession. "A butcher should be proud of his trade. He always prospers. In good times, people want steak, lots of steak, and when times are bad, then there are sausages to be sold, and if things get worse, there are the parts of the animal that you would throw away when people have money to buy good meat . . . you never saw a butcher or his family hungry . . . or skinny." He usually followed this little speech with a jovial laugh and a few pats on his ample stomach.

Stein and another Austrian—a sausage maker—opened a butcher and sausage shop on East Eighty-sixth Street, New York's "Little Germany." The business prospered, and the Steins moved to the suburbs, in fact made several successive moves, each one further north from the city and each new town more socially acceptable than the prior one. Augustus spent his Saturdays in the shop mostly watching his father butcher the large slabs of beef that were to be sold during the following week. His father worked quickly, using a razor-edged large curved knife, only stopping to sharpen the knife with brisk downward slashes against a round metal rod held in his other hand. Augustus would sit on a high stool, watching his father trim the fat from a side of beef and whittle down what was left into steaks and chops. Augustus would ask his father to let him try but his father would say, "You are not yet ready. This is only for experts. The meat is too valuable to be wasted." Often he watched his father cut the meat into fist-sized pieces for his partner to make into sausages, but here also, he would not allow his son to try to do it.

When the topic of Stein's occupation came up with the neighbors, he no longer described himself as a butcher. Now, he was in the "food supply" business. When Augustus was of college age, his father decided that being a butcher was not to be his son's occupation. Augustus was to be a "Professional."

After two years of college, Augustus attended New York University's medical school at a time when the most important qualification for entry was a family able to pay the tuition. He was a good student, applying himself to his studies while many students devoted themselves to becoming active participants in the Jazz Age with all its areas of proficiency and profligacy from clothes to haircuts, slang, bathtub gin and each new dance craze. Augustus, who now peered at the world through thick glasses, never was comfortable with the girls and retreated into his books and cadavers. Small talk was an alien art to him. He who had spent his Saturdays watching his father cut up a side of beef could not toss quick-witted words back and forth with young men who had spent their Saturdays watching polo games. So, it was back to the dissection of the muscles of organisms long past feeling—uncomplaining flesh—whose voices were long past the ability to speak, the spark of life having fled and its ruins preserved in the permanence of formaldehyde. He became as adept in the anatomy and dissection of the human form as was his father with animals.

When Augustus graduated medical school, he decided that he would specialize in orthopedics. At that time, once a person graduated medical school and was licensed to practice medicine, he had but to choose a specialty, and he was by self-denotation a "Specialist." The local hospitals welcomed having an attending "Specialist" on their staffs, particularly so since he would usually treat only indigent or clinic patients and those, always without pay.

Augustus was brusque and officious to his nonpaying patients, not looking at them while spewing medical advice with all the concern of a person spitting on a sidewalk. He was not tolerant of a patient's questions and often would simply walk away in the midst of their questions. Often, he mumbled his medical advice to his patients with a lack of clarity and with a speed that precluded comprehension. His patients, not having the ability to pay, lacked the ability to complain. It was a symmetrically perfect relationship: an abuser and a compliant abused.

Augustus became affiliated with several local hospitals in the area of the affluent suburb north of New York City in which the family lived. After several years, he had few patients, but had a thriving nonpaying practice in the local hospitals. The butcher shop on Eighty-sixth Street continued to prosper so that Augustus' father was quite content to subsidize both Augustus and his medical practice—at least what there was of it.

* * *

At early evening, the two nurses sat at the desk next to the double swinging doors that entered into the ward. The younger one turned to the older who was making entries on a chart. "How does he ever get the parents to agree to it? He *does* get their agreement, doesn't he?"

"People trust doctors. Even creeps like Stein. And besides, what else can they do? He says it's in the best interest of their children. So what choice do they really have?"

"What does he do with the, the, you know?"

"The legs?"

"Uh, huh."

"God only knows."

* * *

The night before he was due to make his rounds, the patients were abuzz with talk of his next morning's visit. Andy turned to the boy.

"Look, I'm telling you I got it beat. I been here for five of his visits, and he never picked me. What you got to do is make believe you are asleep. He never picks anybody who is sleeping."

"It doesn't make sense. What does sleeping have to do with it?"

"I still got both my legs, ain't I? You just do what I say."

* * *

The next morning, the patients awoke earlier than usual. Some had not gone to sleep the night before. There was an unnatural quiet in the ward. Children, frightened, lay silently in their beds listening to the sound of their own breathing. The two nurses seemed to glide silently by as they performed their morning tasks. There was an unexpected tenderness as they ministered to the children: brushing one's hair back, adjusting a pillow, tucking in a sheet, patting a cheek; the small reassuring things that pass between adult and child that smooth a sick child's troubled journey through life.

The boy looked at the bed to his left, its occupant still staring silently at the ceiling. He turned to Andy.

"He's not going to be able to pretend he's sleeping."

"Don't matter. Steinpus ain't never going to pick him."

The swinging doors opened, and Doctor Stein came in with two young doctors behind him. They all wore white coats and carried clipboards.

Andy turned to the boy. "Steinpus! Quick! Now's the time. Pretend you're asleep."

Doctor Stein had a round face and wore round, thick, rimless eyeglasses. He was bald with a fringe of gray-flecked hair. His brush of a mustache, wide as the width of his nostrils, was the same color as his hair. His eyes, distorted and enormously enlarged behind his glasses, made his face look like that of a housefly's in a closeup photograph: a featureless face existing only to support the black domes of its eyes. He wore a stiffly starched white shirt with a black necktie under his white cotton laboratory coat. His necktie was held tight against his shirt with a gold tie clip bearing his initials and a caduceus—a gift from his father, the butcher. His eyes glistened, and his narrow lips were moist. He frequently ran his tongue over his lips.

He walked down the rows of beds, stopping at one, picking up the chart affixed to the foot of the bed reading it over, whispered something to one of the young doctors and then would go to the foot of the next bed. At some beds, he would look at the charts, point to the patient, nod "Yes" and whisper something to one of his assistants who, in turn, would whisper to the nurse. When he arrived at the foot of the bed to the left of the boy, he picked up the chart and quickly nodded "Yes," hardly looking at the occupant lying on the bed with his unblinking open eyes.

He then went further down the row to the boy's bed, glanced at his chart, saw that he appeared to be sleeping, and said, "Yes" and turned to whisper something to one of the doctors. They laughed, and he then walked by Andy's bed, not stopping, making a motion with his head toward Andy and calling out to the doctor following him, "Yes."

* * *

She had just returned to their apartment and was in the process of unpacking her bag. It was noon, and the women who did not have lunches to prepare sat outside buildings on folding chairs or leaned on windowsills looking out at the sidewalk's noontime activity that slowly throbbed its way into a summer's afternoon. Rudy's luncheonette was filling up with the regulars for lunch, and yesterday, Rudy could have told anyone who asked what each person would have for lunch the next day or for that matter, every day of the next week.

The apartment was dark and cool, the windows open, a slight breeze drifted through the still air, and then the phone rang.

"This is Doctor Stein from Peekskill General."

His voice was matter-of-fact, cordial and even warm. It gave her no reason for alarm nor did it have the tightness as would one that carried bad news. Her immediate thought was that by its very ordinariness, a discussion of the outstanding bill was about to take place.

"Yes, Doctor?"

"I'm the orthopedist immediately in charge of your son's treatment, and I would like to discuss with you the course of our treatment—or, rather the suggested course of treatment."

She stiffened. Was it usual for a doctor to call to discuss a treatment plan? Didn't doctors simply do what was best for the patient?

"Any problem, Doctor?"

"No ... but yes. I just want to get your approval for what I believe to be the wisest course of treatment. Naturally, it is what is in the boy's best interest."

"Yes, Doctor."

"The body rejects any part of it that is nonfunctioning. In fact, it treats it as a foreign substance that may do it damage."

"I don't understand what this has to do ..."

"Let me finish. For instance, if one eye no longer functions, we remove it and replace it with a prosthetic device—a glass eye—because, for reasons which we don't understand, if one eye ceases to function, it often affects the other. So, to protect the patient. we remove the useless eye. Now, your son has legs that are ..."

"What are you saying? Are you mad?"

"I believe once you think it over, you will agree to my suggestion and see that it makes sense."

"You are crazy. Don't you dare touch my son."

"I bear the responsibility for his treatment and must do what I believe to be best."

"I am coming up there to take my son to a proper rehabilitation facility."

"But ..."

"If you touch him, I will sue the hospital and make sure you never practice medicine again . . . or anything else."

"I think you are overreacting and . . ."

"I will be there before evening to remove him. You are not to go near him."

She put the receiver down and in a fury, tossed her things back into the suitcase and fled from the apartment. She walked quickly to Broadway looking for a cab to take her to the bus station. Crossing the Williamsburg Bridge to Manhattan, she remembered she had forgotten to close the windows.

10

NINE YEARS LATER

Man is only a reed, the weakest in nature, but he is a thinking reed. There is no need for the whole universe to take up arms to crush him; a vapour, a drop of water is enough to kill him. But even if the universe were to crush him, a man would still be nobler than his slayer, because he knows that he is dying and the advantage the universe has over him. The universe knows none of this.

Blaise Pascal, *Pensées*

The enemy is time, not memory. Time distorts and jumbles, spilling out the past with a lascivious and wonton disregard of the true sequence of events or their importance, tumbling them out in an indifferent perfusion: marriages and deaths; loves acquired and lost; arguments in the rain and rapprochements in midnight telephone conversations; humiliations both great and slight; proud and inglorious moments; "I should have said . . ." or "The next time I will tell him just what I think of him . . ."; a chance meeting on a street, encounters planned with the precision of an invasion; a babble of transactions and events colliding with each other in no ordered fashion.

Memory, until it fades into gossamer threads of nothingness to exist in another place, is cruel or sweet, but usually certain.

Nineteen forty-two. The contours of the year were circumscribed by the war now fought across the world. In the featureless oven-hot deserts of North Africa, in alien specks of fetid volcanic ash in the South Pacific, in the ancient realms of Europe and Asia, in the unending sky and on and under the sea, wherever men could venture, desperate men fought and killed each other with the engines of war and their own human power.

Nineteen forty-two began ignominiously. Oil from torpedoed tankers washed the beaches of Coney Island. The U-boats used the lights of Manhattan to silhouette their targets, and their captains named this seaborne carnage "The Happy Time." Germany ravaged broad swaths of Russia and bombed British cities night and day with relative impunity. Genocide became an undisturbed and unpunished Teutonic policy of state, and Nazis met in conference at Wannsee to decide the "final solution to the Jewish problem" with the polite banality of choosing a date for the spring dance. In North Africa, the Hun kicked dust in the face of the British lion and chased it across the Sahara until he occupied Egypt. It was truly—at least for a time—*Deutschland über alles.*

Japan's empire spread its corrosive stain across the Pacific Ocean, capturing the Philippines, Singapore, Guam and the Dutch East Indies, invading Burma, New Guinea, the American Aleutian Islands—the first invasion of American soil in 128 years—and was poised to invade Australia. Bataan and Corregidor fell, and General MacArthur's escape to Australia—nothing more nor less than simply a flight to avoid capture—in that dark time of bitter failures was actually hailed as a military success.

There were more battles to be lost, more ships sunk, more lives gone, but by the end of the year, the British had finally defeated Rommel at El Alamein; the Americans had landed in North Africa; the back of Japanese naval power had been broken at Midway and in the Coral Sea; the U-boats lost the battle of the Atlantic; Guadalcanal had been retaken; and the Germans had suffered a humiliating defeat in the snows of Stalingrad.

By the end of the year, victory in the future was sure and certain, but the war, the killings and the atrocities would continue for three more years and for some of its victims, forever.

But in Williamsburg, at 75 Manhattan Avenue, at the end of the hall in apartment 2C, the cataclysmic clashes of great armies were like distant thunder beyond faraway hills. Things went on for us as usual with a frightening and pointless sameness.

It was late in the afternoon. Somewhere down the street, we could hear the sounds of an after-school-before-supper stickball game. The bat was the sawed-off handle of a broom, the ball was a smooth pink rubber Spalding. A home run was measured by the distance in sewers it flew, and the bases were cars or arbitrary objects tossed onto the pavement. Every now and then, we could hear shouts in varying degrees of intensity in proportion to the batter's success. Soon, the mothers would call out of windows for the players to come in for supper.

My brother sat on his bed, the blanket half-covering his folded legs, a notebook with a black-marbled cardboard cover in his lap, his braces and crutches like tired sentries separating him from the rest of the world, lay along side of his bed. On a table behind the head of his bed, inside a battered wooden case, a phonograph turntable spun. The worn needle made the record sound even tinnier, but yet somehow enhanced the flatness and loneliness of the single guitar chords and T-Bone Walker's rasp of a voice.

> *Sunday I go to church where I kneel down to pray . . . Just trying to find my baby, won't you please send her back to me.*

I was sitting in my bed at the other side of the room—everything seemed to be done in bed, homework, writing, listening to the radio, most meals, arguments—when he called over to me,

"Would you go over to Eisenberg's and get me a pack of needles?"

"I have to ask Ma."

"Don't ask her. She won't let you go. It's too far. Here's a quarter, and tell her you're going to Mrs. Rubin's to get me cigarettes."

"Eisenberg's" was a mission that I undertook once a week. In those days, every neighborhood had a music store as well as one or two corsetieres and at least two or three milliners. The milliners made and sold ladies' hats. Women's hats were frilly things; wisps of silk and veils that sat upon their heads like nesting birds and had no functional basis. Their demise was caused by a combination of wartime shortages, changes in fashion and the fact that movie stars stopped wearing hats. Around the same time, corsetieres—stores that made custom corsets and brassieres in the back rooms—were also on the way out. Corsetieres—that for some unknown reason always seemed to be owned by spinster sisters—fell victims to a new age that admired the soft yielding bulges of female flesh over the discipline of whalebones. Unused would then be all the skills a young man accumulated learning to maneuver around and under the garment and unhook and unhinge it from its anchored stockings, not to mention the opportunity for neighborhood boys to go behind the shop and watch the women trying on their garments. Custom-made brassieres were rendered unnecessary by an industrial base that demonstrated a machine could better and more cheaply manufacture a support mechanism for a part of female anatomy that came in a limited number of permutations. And then of course, there were the women who decided—mostly in error—that a brassiere was an entirely unnecessary accoutrement.

Music stores were eventually put out of business primarily by television and perhaps a half-dozen other things both subtle and obvious.

Eisenberg's was on Broadway, just off Graham Avenue (now 60 years later, renamed *Avenue of Puerto Rico*), four blocks from my home. The neighborhood music stores sold sheet music, phonograph records, musical instruments, new and used, things associated with the instruments like guitar picks, saxophone reeds and strings and most anything else imaginable connected with music.

Mister Eisenberg—I never heard anyone call him by any other name and could imagine his wife calling out, "Eisenberg, come in for dinner"—was tall, slender, slightly bent over and Viennese. His voice was soft, and he confused "v's" with "w's" when he spoke. His unruly white hair always made him seem as if he were several weeks past needing a haircut. His suit: wrinkled—except for the warmest days of summer he wore a vest—his shirt: washed, but not ironed. He always sported a narrow, tightly knotted black tie in perpetual mourning for some unspoken loss. Indeed, I never saw him appear happy, but rather, he seemed to be gliding through the last gentle act of a life filled with if not tragedy, at least profound sadness.

He had long, delicate fingers that held musical instruments with the assured and easy grace of a lover holding his lady's hand. My brother told me that Mister Eisenberg had been classically trained and had been the first violinist in the Vienna Philharmonic. I do not know how my brother learned this because he had only been to the store a few times. But misery is fungible, and my brother had a way of bringing things out of people, particularly those who needed a secret sharer. When he came to the store, my brother and Mister Eisenberg would talk on and on, my brother leaning with his fore-arms on his crutches having taken them from under his arms and placed them there. Mister Eisenberg, in front of the counter, leaning over to him, talking softly, his face serious and faintly pained. My brother, staring straight ahead, his face expressionless, hardly speaking, nodding; perhaps to an onlooker, two travelers reminiscing about an old and difficult shared journey.

Many years later, at a time of more dead yesterdays than unborn tomorrows, when the shells around people had hardened, my brother had cards printed to give to people who came up to him that read:

DOC POMUS
I'VE GOT MY OWN TROUBLES

I do not believe he ever gave them to anybody, but I guess it felt good to have them on standby in his pocket.

I entered the store and saw Mister Eisenberg tuning a guitar, adjusting the tuning keys, plucking a string with his thumb and holding it against his ear, listening to the sound. Behind him was the glass booth in which potential buyers would take phonograph records to play, deciding whether to purchase them. Today, if you mention a person in a glass booth, people think of Adolf Eichmann. Then, they were ubiquitous in music stores.

* * *

Across the street from my office, there is a Florsheim shoe store. Forty years ago or more, in an earlier life, it was Liberty Music, an upper-class store that sold records, sheet music and a small variety of phonographs. In the back, hidden away in a small room cluttered with tools and disemboweled phonographs, was a German refugee who wore a doctor's spotlessly white coat. He was the repair department, available to repair any apparatus sold in the store and to give advice about radios and phonographs. Around the top of the store was a half-balcony containing six glass booths, a record player in each.

A potential customer would pick out a stack of records—Liberty specialized in classical music and Broadway show tunes—to be played in the booths before making a purchase. Often on Saturdays, my cousin and I would pick out a stack of records, listen to them and then rapidly leave the shop telling the salesman, "We didn't find what we were looking for." Either the salesmen had defective memories or they believed that our search was as committed and perhaps hopeless as that of the seekers for the Lost Ark.

On one Saturday afternoon, while I was on the balcony to listen to records I never would buy, I saw the first genuine movie star I ever did see. I looked down from above and saw Montgomery Clift— a current cinema heartthrob—with a friend talking to one of the salesmen. A few other customers looked at him in a kind of studied nonchalance. For me, it was disillusioning to see he had a large bald spot in the center of his head.

Next to Liberty Music was Church Shoes, an English men's footwear store. The salesmen wore cutaways and striped trousers. The cutaways have long since gone the way of glass booths for auditioning records or for that matter, Montgomery Clift.

* * *

Eisenberg's major sales items were sheet music. In those days, with a paucity of amusements available, in order to fill time without incurring any significant expense, people looked inward, read, entertained themselves, got drunk, went to the movies—especially on nights when they gave away dishes—rode the Staten Island Ferry, spoke and argued with each other, danced, copulated, listened to radios, fought, raised pigeons on rooftops, played musical instruments and sang. Mister Eisenberg displayed the sheet music for piano together with lyrics of the most popular hits of the day in his store window and also tacked them to a column in the shop. They cost fifty cents and could be used over and over until the paper fell apart.

Mister Eisenberg saw me and put the guitar gently on the counter. Turning to me, he said, "What can I do for Jerry?"

"He needs a pack of needles."

Those days a needle, ideally, was good for one play of a record. However, you could get up to half-a-dozen plays, but after the first, there was increasing damage to the disc. Subsequently, the record companies developed sapphire, then diamond needles and ultimately, the phonographs came with permanent ones that never required changing.

Mister Eisenberg handed me the small tan envelope with twenty-five needles, and I gave him a quarter.

"Wait a minute. A new brand came in. They say they are better than the Columbia's. Here, give it to Jerry."

"But, I only have a quarter … with me."

"That's OK. Tell him to let me know what he thinks of them."

* * *

I made many trips to Mrs. Rubin's for cigarettes. Mrs. Rubin owned a candy store around the corner at the end of the block. Although the store was on the same block on which we lived, other than go there, I never walked in that direction since between it and my home there were a series of vacant stores, dark and forbidding, like ruined carious, yawning mouths, while in the other direction of Manhattan Avenue, toward Broadway, there was all the hurly-burly of commerce.

Mrs. Rubin was a widow, and in that time, survival was a day-to-day matter. So when a husband died, there was usually no inheritance, save whatever small business he and his wife ran. It was the widow's lot to then take over the running of the family's business. This also meant that the widows were fair pickings for my grandfather. To my grandfather, it was any port in a storm as in the case of the super of our building. Actually, she was the widow of the super. She was fortyish and stoutly built, and at the death of her husband, she took over the running of the building—including the tending of the coal furnace and necessary repairs. To me, there always seemed to be the acrid, penetrating smell of coal about her. My grandfather, tall, gray-haired, immaculately dressed, admired hard work—as long as somebody else was doing it. It was not long before he introduced her to a more pleasurable way to expend her not inconsiderable energies. As always, whether because he became bored or in those difficult times, because there was a seeming inexhaustible supply of widows or wives whose husbands were worn thin by the demands of industry, he would move on to the next before things got too serious. In fact, in the case of the super, when he sent her back to her coal scuttle, she found out that he was also carrying on with the widow of a doctor, who unfortunately lived in the apartment next to hers. The two ladies got into a hair-pulling contest over Grandpa, causing him to tell us not to leave the apartment until things settled down. This sort of thing happened on a regular basis.

I believe Grandpa was an altogether good role model for me in affairs of the heart and gave me some of the best advice I ever received in this area. "Stay away from red-headed women with black underwear" or it might have been "Black-headed women with red underwear." I am not sure which. Either way, it was pretty good advice.

Mrs. Rubin, although a widow, was quite a different matter. She was heavy and thick-legged, moved slowly dragging one foot after the other and wore long black, shapeless dresses with hems past her knees. Her universe, it seemed, was circumscribed by the length of the counter behind which she shuffled back and forth with all the enthusiasm of a member of a chain gang going to work on a quarry.

Mrs. Rubin ran a *candy store*, which was a rung down on the gastronomic level from a *luncheonette*. A luncheonette had a soda fountain, a counter with seats, served sandwiches, short-order meals and sodas prepared behind the counter from scratch—and dispensed Alka-Seltzers for those in gastric distress—the man behind the counter juggling the fizzy mixture between glasses with balletic grace. The luncheonettes usually had a few—invariably red—plastic-covered booths and perhaps, a pinball machine or two. A candy store sold packaged candies, cigarettes and ice cream. Ice cream companies would supply the stores with freezers in exchange for selling their product. I am sure they could not have made any profit on Mrs. Rubin's sales, but she was able to obtain an ice-cream freezer out of the deal. She hit upon the idea of tossing chocolate bars and chocolate-covered candy into the freezer. This solved the problem of what she could do with unsold chocolate bars and also did not have to be concerned with the chocolate melting or becoming discolored from the heat. Soon, on our block, Rubin's was the place to go for frozen Milky Ways or Twists.

My brother would give me ten cents and ask me to go to Mrs. Rubin to buy ten Camels. Individual cigarettes—called "loosies"—were sold for a penny a piece with a pack of paper matches thrown in. Rudy's, a true luncheonette in the other direction and closer to us, would only sell cigarettes by the pack.

* * *

It was not yet an age of home deliveries … at least not for people of modest means. Maybe for Williamsburg, it would never be. I never remember anything being delivered to our house except the mail … and of course, in this case, the mailman had no choice in the matter.

My father always was angry: angry at life; angry that his back was not quite right; angry at my mother who moved in increasingly further emotional space from him; angry at my brother for not being able to walk (or at least at the fates for visiting a second physical blow to him by way of his son); angry for not making a proper living; angry that he had to tolerate my grandfather living in his house … angry, angry, angry.

My father would often write to the president to give him the benefit of his views on some current item of public interest invariably also indicating his support of the president. Thus enlightened, the president would send my father a reply, and he would proudly show us the smallish envelopes, bearing in the upper left-hand corner the words, "The White House" engraved in blue capital letters. The letters invariably began "The President appreciates your letter of … and has asked me to thank you for your thoughts." It always ended by a (purposely, I suspect) unintelligible signature.

Once, he actually received a letter on White House stationary signed by A. A. Berle. Berle was one of those not remembered enablers of history. He was very close to the president, closer and more powerful than his title, "assistant secretary of state", would suggest. He was a member of the president's inner circle, involved in implementing the New Deal and the Good Neighbor Policy, best famously remembered by diarists for telling Roosevelt that Alger Hiss was a communist agent, to which the president replied, "Oh, forget it, Adolf."

Apparently, the letter to which Berle was the designated responder was one in which my father had written to the president informing him that he had been a supporter and now he intended to run as a Democratic candidate for Congress. He neglected to say that, in fact, he intended to run in the *primary* election against the regular Democratic organization to be the party's candidate. In fact, he had as much chance of being successful in this pursuit as he had in all of the primaries he entered, fueled more by rage than logic.

I envisioned some attractive twenty-two-year-old girl with long blond hair from Georgia, an in-search-of-a-husband volunteer at the White House helping to sort out the thousands of daily pieces of mail, perusing the letter, seeing the reference to Congress and deciding that it should be tossed into a more prestigious bin for personal response from an administration official.

Characters like Berle drift through history, having for one vaporous second, a sometimes pivotal role and then drift away, forgotten in the fog of time past.

Another such individual was McGeorge Bundy. He was national security advisor to Presidents Kennedy and Johnson and was a central—if not *the* central—figure in escalating American involvement in Vietnam and as such, was complicit in the deaths of many young Americans. After he left government, he was scholar-in-residence at the Carnegie Corporation, which had its offices in the same building as mine. We shared the same bank of elevators where I would bump into him and exchange pleasantries. He dressed in the shabby, unpressed, almost eccentric gentility of one accustomed to parties on manicured lawns, being polite to servants and quiet conversations around a very large dinner table. He usually appeared faintly distracted as if beset by private thoughts or unheard music going their separate ways in his head while he spoke to you, his eyes small and vacant behind plain-framed eyeglasses. He seemed disengaged: a tired man at the end of a journey. After he left the elevator, I would often ask a fellow passenger whether he recognized the man to whom I had just spoken. No one was ever able to identify him although, at a certain time and place, in terms of his ability to affect events and decisions that shaped the contours of history, he was, perhaps, one of the most important people in the world.

Early on in his professional life, my father had that appointment as "counsel" to the transit commission. Since that time, until several years before his death almost half a century later, he left a trail of broken lances and intact windmills.

* * *

And so, each day fixed its feet before the next as we all—except for me, for my time had not yet come—remained trapped in seamless spheres of desperation.

* * *

Yorkville is an area on the Upper East Side of New York City, bounded on the north by Ninety-sixth Street and on the south by Seventy-ninth Street. Today, its buildings are mostly postwar, tall square high-risers, each looking like a box in which the other came, as indistinguishable from one another as are its residents, mostly young, paired and brunch-eating, hand-holding, smiling Sunday strollers. However, at one time, still within the memory of some, these same streets were the scene of vicious street battles between Nazi sympathizers and anti-Nazis. Prior to the war, the central headquarters for the Nazi Party in America, Fritz Kuhn's German-American Bund, was located in Yorkville.

Germans, like other immigrant groups, began their American experience on Manhattan's Lower East Side. It offered a casual acceptance of an alien culture and densely packed, but affordable slum housing. As with most immigrant groups, it was a way station until finances allowed for a move from *Kleindeutschland*, as it was called, to a better neighborhood thereby making room for the next wave of immigrants. The new neighborhood of choice was Yorkville, and the General Slocum ship fire—New York's largest civil disaster prior to 9/11–accelerated the move. On June 15, 1904, more than a thousand, mostly German immigrants, from St. Mark's Evangelical Lutheran Church (Sixth Street), died in a fire on a boat day trip up the East River.

After the tragedy, in the new neighborhood, the survivors and others in Yorkville developed a new community that reflected an idealization of life in Germany: dance halls, beer halls, vendors, brass bands with musicians wearing lederhosen, travel agencies offering package trips to Germany and of course, restaurants. Today, gone are the Die Lorelei, Café Mozart, Bremen House, German newspapers sold at corner kiosks, the German movie theater, the breweries, St. Joseph's Orphan Asylum and the pastry shops on Eighty-sixth Street ("German Broadway"). The 2000 census revealed only 7,075 people claiming German ancestry living in Yorkville. As in any vanished society, if the urban archeologist knows where to look, the footprints of the past can be found. Of course, the obvious: Schaller & Weber (German groceries, heavy on the wurst), the Heidelberg Restaurant, one German church and a few bakeries still exist. As whispers, on the sides of the few remaining three- and four-story walk-ups, there are, if one looks closely, faded painted signs extolling long-forgotten products and merchants—remnants of a gaudy past. Often, signs had been painted over other signs: layered history of disappeared generations.

On the southeast corner of Park Avenue and Ninety-sixth Street, facing Park Avenue, there is a large apartment house built of faded yellow bricks. The building is neither intimidating nor imposing. In fact, it bears resemblance to those that line curbs of the once-prestigious parts of the Grand Concourse in the Bronx or Ocean Parkway in Brooklyn, walkways that have long since made the journey from genteel decay to borderline slums.

Turning the corner of Ninety-sixth Street, looking east toward the river, the building's character abruptly changes to one completely different from that suggested by its Park Avenue entrance. On the side of the building is a row of tired stores with dusty, fly-specked windows that would more comfortably blend with the urban decay of the suburbs than the grandeur of Park Avenue. Two of them, Sings Deli & Grocery and Sandra's & Donath's Florist, were once the workshop of Konrad Hoehler, New York's only bracemaker.

In the late thirties and early forties, Hoehler's establishment was a drowsy, glorified mechanic's shop. The legend on the plate-glass window was simply "K. Hoehler" painted in neat gold letters. There was no reception area. Upon entering, the visitor found himself in a single, cavernous room containing half-a-dozen large tables. One or more white-coated technicians were working at the tables. Each table held several aluminum posts and padded strips of leather that would eventually be put together to form the skeleton leg-support system that enable polio victims to stumble through life. The leather was tan and buttery soft like that used for the seats of expensive European motorcars. There was little noise save for the occasional brief clink of a hammer against aluminum or the hushed exchanges between the workers. It was a place bereft of laughter.

Mister Hoehler was a large, balding man, and whatever hair remained was thin and fair. Behind rimless glasses, his eyes were of a pitiless light blue. He was closely shaven, scrubbed clean and polished in the way of an undertaker's assistant and smelled faintly of coarse soap. He wore a stiffly starched white shirt under his spotless white laboratory coat.

My mother would wrap my brother's brace in butcher's paper and carry it by subway to Mister Hoehler. There, she would unwrap it and point out the problem to him. Invariably, it was a problem with the knee lock. A leg brace is made from four metal strips. There are two lengths on each side of the leg joined at the knee by a hand-triggered lock and wrapped round in various places by leather. The braces hold the leg rigid while walking, but when seated, to prevent the leg from jutting out, the brace is unlocked manually thereby allowing the leg to bend. Just as the knee is the joint in the body most susceptible to malfunction, so, too, was the knee lock the usual cause for the visit to Mister Hoehler. If the leather joining the metal tore or needed repair, usually a shoemaker—preferably one trained abroad who was able to do more than just install heels and soles—could tend to it, unless the straps were ruined because of becoming blood soaked from boils that had burst. In that case, new straps needed to be made and sewn onto the braces: a job for Mister Hoehler.

Mister Hoehler would hold the offending brace in his large, blunt-fingered hands and peer at it, looking up and down over its surface like an art dealer examining a piece of sculpture for authenticity. He discussed the problem and its solution with my mother in heavily accented English, spoken in a musical and smothered voice. After there was an agreement as to work and price, he called an assistant over and directed in a somewhat louder voice, more Wermacht than sibilant, the repairs that had to be made and the time frame for them to be accomplished. These were days before there was private or governmental health insurance, and it remained unexplained to me how we were able to raise money for payment.

We went to Mister Hoehler's shop for many years, and I never saw him in any clothing other than I have described nor engaged in any conversation lasting more than several minutes. Of course, these were deservedly awkward times for German residents of Yorkville—particularly when they dealt with Jews. Never mentioned were the unspeakable atrocities visited upon them by the Yorkville residents' former countrymen of recent vintage nor the state of the world and the galactic battles taking place thousands of miles to the east whose genesis, at least partly, swirled about the collision of our two races.

At the beginning, my mother brought the braces to Mister Hoehler by herself, left them there, and then, when repairs were completed, she returned to pick them up and bring them back home. As I grew older, I accompanied my mother on her trips to Mister Hoehler. She carefully explained the process to me, much in the manner of someone who is teaching a child the family business. Finally, when I was about sixteen years old, she believed it was time for me to make the mission by myself. The problem was the caliper that was inserted in a metal sleeve in a heel broke off and had to be removed: a job for Mister Hoehler.

I wrapped the brace and shoe in butcher's paper and proceeded to take the subway to Ninety-sixth Street, holding my parcel on my lap. It was a long ride, and when I got off the train, a policeman, who apparently was riding on the train, followed me and as I stepped off onto an almost-deserted station, approached me from behind and put his hand on my shoulder. As I turned around, I saw his other hand rested on his revolver. He pointed to my package and told me to open it. I looked down, and starting to unwrap it, I saw that, at one end, the shoe was sticking out of the long package. After I removed the wrapping, he told me what I had already observed: that it looked like I was carrying a dismembered leg. He explained that he spotted me on the train, but he did not want to approach me until I got off because desperate character that I might have been, it was safer done after I had disembarked.

After this episode, I was more careful in wrapping the brace, but I never could quite shake the feeling that my fellow passengers believed me to be a ghoul.

11

THE CEMETERY

It may be that the race is not always to the swift, nor the battle to the Strong—but that's the way to bet. Nothing between humans is one to three. In fact, I long ago came to the conclusion that all life is six to five against.

Damon Runyon

* * *

"He has to do something. He can take the test. An insurance broker can stay at home and sell on the telephone, and once you make a sale, you keep getting commissions. He won't be on the street."

Beth David Cemetery, located in Elmont, Queens, is 15.7 miles and sixty-five years from 75 Manhattan Avenue in Williamsburg, Brooklyn.

"What else could he do? He can't leave the house. Do you want him to be a beggar, end up in an institution?"

Located on ground flat to the horizon, it is an old cemetery, filled with people who lived to be old—for the most part poor, some richer. It is a cemetery of small, time-ravaged headstones and monuments of modest height, so that in one glance, you can see clear across the graveyard from one end to the other. The inscriptions on the gravestones are mostly tracings from sample books in the monument stores located across the road from the cemetery where good deals were had by hard bargaining and eternal memory was for sale at cut rates.

"Don't start with him again. Leave him alone. All you want to do is upset him."

To get to the cemetery from Manhattan Avenue, you have to drive up Broadway, cross the Williamsburg Bridge into Manhattan, turn right to East Houston, drive north on the East River Drive until the Fifty-ninth Street Bridge, then east along the Long Island Expressway until the Cross Island Parkway exiting at Elmont. The second Jewish cemetery on the left is Beth David.

"Upset him? You worry about upsetting him. I have to worry about money for the rent. Nobody works here but me."

"I don't want any more fights tonight. It's bad enough that I can't show my face during the day. Everybody knows!"

The arguments are over.

My brother's grave is a short walk from the graves of the people who argued over him.

My mother's grave is pink marble, a bit taller than those around it. The top of the stone is rounded. It is carved into a three-part tower of two lengths in height, the center one higher than those on either side, its curved surfaces making it somehow soft and even feminine, not in the way that great sculptors can do with stone, but in the stone itself, not having to be taken from it by another's hand and chisel, or maybe this is just the way I see it.

One row down is my father's grave marked by a squat rectangle of marble. In the time between my father and mother's death, the rules of the cemetery had changed, and tall monuments were no longer permitted; a fact, I'm sure, that would not have been unwelcomed by my father, who never wanted to stand out from the crowd.

12

THE BLIND DOCTOR

In 1952, if you were Jewish and lived in a neighborhood such as mine, the parental aspirations of the neighbors were identical. Most important would be the ability of a parent to utter the holy words "My son, the doctor." Next, in the hierarchy of bragging rights would be a lawyer, then came a dentist, and if the child was not so bright, he could always be an accountant.

Medical schools rightfully gave preference to applying veterans. Coupling this with the unspoken of, but fairly deserved, preferences afforded blacks, Hispanics and women, it was a bad year for Jewish students with indifferent records. Had I been an albino, bisexual, transvestite, Penobscot Indian and had resurrected myself after serving time in a juvenile-detention facility for being a pedophile, I would have been among the first to be accepted. However, not falling into such a category or any other to which the perception was that reparations had to be paid, I had to search elsewhere for a medical

education. Added to this mix was the fact that America had insti-
tuted a draft of young men for one or another of the various wars in
which we were engaged after the war that took place after the war
that was promised to be the end of all wars. Medical students were
exempt from military service, thus, for some, creating an additional
reason to go to medical school.

It was commonly believed you had to "know somebody" to get
into medical school. My mother took me to meet a man who could
definitely get me into medical school … for a price. We met the gentleman in Garfield's cafeteria located on Church Avenue, Brooklyn.
Apparently, the cafeteria served as his office, and the stains on his
shirt and cuffs were mute testament to the many meals he must have
enjoyed there. Immediately after finishing his meal (for which my
mother paid), he told us his price, which for us, was too steep. We
left him as he started his main course, and at least, since this was a
cafeteria, my mother did not have to leave a tip.

My mother, through her work with charitable organizations, was
friendly with Abe Stark, the future borough president of Brooklyn.
Stark was a carefully groomed older man with wavy and meticu-
lously coifed white hair that played off well against his navy suit.
He always wore navy-blue suits. He had become wealthy by owning GGG Clothes, a men's clothing store, located on Pitkin Avenue.
Virtually every politician and successful hoodlum in Brooklyn was
a customer. Baseball fans across the country knew him because he
paid to have a sign placed at the right-field fence at Ebbets Field,
home of the Brooklyn Dodgers which read "Hit sign. Win suit." The
problem was that the sign was painted on a narrow strip at the bottom of the wall and, in order to win the suit, the batter had to hit
the sign without a bounce—an almost impossible feat. The sign was
further immortalized in a George Price *New Yorker* cartoon depicting a frantic Abe Stark in front of the sign, standing behind the right
fielder, wearing a catcher's mitt ready to stop any ball that got past
the outfielder before it could hit the sign.

Stark had some sort of relationship with Chicago Medical School, but there, too, a donation to the college was necessary and for us once again too pricey.

We then were referred to a Doctor Sklar, who purportedly had connections with European medical schools. The most we could find out about the doctor was that he was a chemist in his late sixties. Though he was not listed as a present or past faculty member of Columbia University in any of their publications, he lived at Butler Hall, a faculty residence of the college.

Whoever set up our initial appointment neglected to tell us that Sklar was blind. When we arrived, we met Yula, the doctor's seeing-eye dog, at the door. Unfortunately, Yula had chronic gastric problems.

After about half an hour in the apartment, the smell became unbearable, and we were forced to make excuses to leave. Additionally, both the doctor and the dog had toilet difficulties. The doctor, perhaps because of his eyesight, left a puddle around his toilet, and the dog, if she so chose, was free to use different parts of the apartment for her own toilet purposes. On a few occasions, we had to carry on a conversation while ignoring Yula's deposits in a corner of the room.

The doctor's head was closely shaved, and on the top and sides of his head were perceptible scars suggesting surgery, perhaps related to his visual condition. He seemed reasonably trim and was usually dressed in a mismatched jacket and trousers—a not unreasonable state of affairs considering that Yula was unable to pick the properly color-coordinated outfits of the day.

Our visits followed a pattern as carefully choreographed as a Fred Astaire dance sequence. After arriving at the doctor's apartment, he would sit opposite us on an easy chair, Yula at his feet. Several awkward minutes would pass in silence, the doctor's head turned slightly aside, his false teeth clacking. When he spoke, his accent was Eastern European; his voice was guttural and had a strangled quality.

He could see a bit out of the corner of his right eye so that when he spoke to us, he turned his head three-quarters to the left. Looking at some point in space over our right shoulders, he would fling irrelevant and often personal questions to us in demonic English. "Do you have a girlfriend?" "How many bedrooms in your house?" "Do your parents get along?" Clacking his teeth while awaiting an answer. Often he would dictate a semiliterate letter for me to write to some school or academic authority and insisted I write it exactly the way he dictated it to me. Sometimes, it was a letter for him to sign, and sometimes it was "my" letter. If it were meant to be a letter that I was to sign, I would rewrite it before mailing, but was careful to read it back to him as dictated.

He would telephone, on occasion, and insist we come to see him "immediately," and when we arrived, it turned out it was to discuss something inconsequential, and in any case, certainly not urgent. We eventually concluded that he was a lonely desperate man who just wanted company.

At the beginning of each meeting, he would croak, "Allo," and at the end, he would say, "Keep in touch." When I arrived in Switzerland and compared notes with other students (although he had warned each of us not to mention his name to anyone), I discovered some who had similar experiences with him. Some of them or their parents gave him money that was supposed to cover certain "expenses." I was unaware whether my mother ever gave him any money.

We all concluded the doctor had no special access or influence that could help us and believed that letters he claimed he sent were not, or if they actually were mailed, they ended up in a European wastebasket or dead-letter section of the post office.

Later, it became a private joke for we students to say a guttural "Allo" when meeting and to croak "Keep in touch" when parting.

13

ON THE WAY

The SS *United States*, which many believe to be the greatest ocean liner ever built, was launched in 1952. I, in a manner of speaking, was also launched then, the year I walked through the dirigible-sized assembly area for passengers embarking that afternoon on the *United States* bound for Southampton.

Taxis and limousines disgorged hundreds of people with hundreds of pieces of luggage at the entrance to Pier Six on the Hudson River. On the north side of the pier was the SS *United States*, a vast, tall structure so large that it was impossible to take it in from one angle. A mighty metal behemoth sleek as a steel knife in bright red, white and blue paint. Endless streams of baggage handlers flowed out of the pier to carry the passengers' luggage into the building. In 1952, people still traveled with large and many suitcases and wardrobe trunks as big as closets. The porters handled these with a dancer's grace as they rapidly carried them from curbside to the reception area's long wooden tables.

My parents had not come to see me off. Saying our goodbyes at the pier, I believed, would only bring up bad memories from their last sea experience when they embarked on a transatlantic voyage from Europe to America and were dumped into steerage.

There was no public transportation to the piers, so we asked a neighbor to drive me to the dock. Upon arriving, I removed my leather suitcases—purchased after much haggling at an Orchard Street discount store—from the trunk of the old Chevy—Fords were still shunned by Jews because of Henry Ford's anti-Semitism—ignored the waiting porters and carried my two brand-new suitcases into the pier's vast reception area. It was as if a theater curtain had been raised upon a tableau of hundreds of people going about in apparent confusion. Entering the hall, there was suddenly a cacophony that assaulted my senses. Many years later, I had the same experience when I was part of a ticker-tape parade as it entered the canyons of lower Broadway.

There were long wooden tables upon which the baggage was placed, tags affixed and then tossed by laborers onto growing mounds of luggage behind them to await porters who would load them onto the ship. Once on board, the bags were sorted and ultimately, delivered to the cabins of their owners.

The university in Bern recommended that, prior to our departure, we register with the Swiss Students Union in New York. I went to their offices in Rockefeller Center and left with an armful of pamphlets and the names and telephone numbers of other New Yorkers who would be starting medical school with me. I made the telephone calls, and we arranged to take the same boat, and rather than share the tourist cabins (the 1952 equivalent of steerage) with strangers, the six of us from New York would share two cabins.

I walked past a tired-looking six-piece marching band playing on the pier, climbed the gangplank and walked onto the ship. A group of smartly dressed officers stood at the foot of the gangplank, one collecting my ticket, another giving me directions and the remaining three smiling and looking nautical. I followed directions and was soon wandering through windowless corridors, stopping every few minutes to ask directions again from white-jacketed ship's personnel and always it seemed, going deeper and deeper below decks. Finally, I arrived at my cabin. My two traveling companions, with whom I had spoken with on the phone, but never met, had already arrived.

Melvin Rudnick was short and had hands that trembled ever so slightly when he was in an excited state. His sunburned face was oily and had the bumpy smoothness of treated acne. He spoke rapidly in nervous bursts and had just placed a picture of his parents on a metal night table between the two bunk beds in the room. All the furniture was made of aluminum, and indeed, to reassure those concerned about fire at sea, the brochures that advertised the ship grandly claimed that the only piece of furniture found on board that was made of wood was the piano.

Melvin was also an alumnus of Doctor Sklar and after we knew him better, gave a wicked impression of the doctor. Melvin, I learned, came from the Bronx, was an only child and the first in his family to travel out of the country. He smiled at me, shook my hand and pointing to a young man who was looking in the mirror, combing his hair, said to me, "Did you ever meet Marty Kaplan? He was smart enough to walk out on Doctor Sklar after one visit."

Marty turned to me. "We sort of divided up the beds so that the only one left is the upper one. If that doesn't work for you, we can flip for the beds."

"No, that's fine with me."

Marty returned to the mirror and combing his hair while Melvin went to the bathroom that was similar to those found on airplanes, but with enough additional room for a shower. After a few moments, Melvin shouted from the bathroom, "Wouldn't it be great to come back with an English accent."

Marty called back, "Why would we return with an English accent if we are going to Switzerland?"

"Well, the boat docks in England. I'm just kidding. But, it would be great anyway. One thing I don't want is a Swiss accent."

Marty, still combing his hair at the mirror, turned and said, "There's no such thing as a Swiss accent."

Melvin now out of the bathroom sat on the bed opposite me. "Did you ever see anything like this boat? You need a compass and a map to find your way."

Marty sat down next to me on the bed. He had a large square face, long forehead and nose so long that the horizontal slash of his thin-lipped mouth and receding chin occupied the small remaining space from the tip of his nose to the bottom of his chin. The most remarkable thing about his face was the abundance of wavy brown hair that began low on his forehead.

Marty put his arm around my shoulder. "Did you get a look at some of these girls that came aboard?" Before I could answer, a beefy, red-faced man of early middle age, wearing a short white jacket, knocked on the open door and stepped inside the cabin. "I'm Ernie, your daytime steward. If you need anything, just press the buzzer between the beds."

Melvin asked, "You mean just like in a hospital, you'll come if we call?"

"Yeah, [laughing] just like in a hospital, I *won't* come. Listen, this is tourist class. On the day shift, I got to service this whole part of the deck ... forty cabins ... a hundred and twenty people."

He started to leave and turned back. "And, oh yeah, only when you leave, take anything you like—they figure that in with the price of the tickets—even some towels, and they won't say nothing. Just don't take the water pitchers. They cost seventy-five dollars whole-sale, and there will be hell to pay, not to mention being embarrassed if you try to make off with them."

That was the first and last time we saw Ernie on the voyage.

* * *

When I am in a strange or new place, I make a point of visiting bookstores. Bookstores are the same anywhere in the world. I wander through a store in a new town until I find a book that interests me, pick it up, get the heft of it, flip through it. The book for me is an object, separate and apart from its contents; each offering a newness and separate set of pleasures. The smells are the same, handling the books give the same familiar pleasures except that which lay inside the books are different: the language and the places where they were printed are different. I have found pretty much the same to be true about women.

In my life and travels, women, and the rituals attendant to them were interchangeable constants. In a new town, to me, they were the equivalent of what the popular gastronomic writers call comfort food. And the sea was the strangest of new towns to me.

I met Emma on the first night out on the slab of deck and sea air available to tourist passengers. She was a young English woman returning home for a visit. Her chin was a little too large, her hair a little too teased, and her eyes a little too dull, but nevertheless she possessed a coarse prettiness in a country maid kind of way. We were there under an endless pavé star-studded night sky, the salt smell of the wind blowing over us, and best of all, her cabin mate never met the boat, and she had the cabin to herself. I remember my first and the almost last words we spoke. "Emma," I thought that was the name they gave heroines in Victorian novels. It goes with long white dresses and gazebos in country gardens." Her almost last words: "My husband would crown me if he knew."

My cousin Maxie, ten years older than I, had told me about married women; their casual availability when separated from their husbands whose lust had worn out and been replaced by habit and pride of ownership. His philosophy, or at least my perception of it, was that married women were like domesticated wild animals that had been fed raw meat by their masters under a carefully rationed allowance. All a man had to do when the master was not around was to wave some meat or its metaphorical equivalent under their noses, and it would set off a series of unstoppable neurological events terminating on a bed behind a locked door. Maxie, of course, was quite mad, but like most lunatics, went about undiagnosed and unrestrained, self-validating his madness and ultimately, dying a miserable and lonely death.

To this unprincipled lunacy, I brought my own character weakness that remains with me to this day. I avoid confrontations, especially when ending a relationship, even if it involves something as simple or ordinary as firing a messenger. In that spirit of calculated cowardliness, the next day, when I spotted Emma in the dining room, I simply walked right by her without even a nod of my head. The effect of this sort of sex-directed cravenness usually left a victim confused and reeling in a paroxysm of inexplicable rejection; the perpetrator, paradoxically, becoming even more attractive. But, such was the unfeeling cruelty or at least, insensitivity, of youth.

On the evening of that day, I sat in a large, comfortable leather chair in the soulless and windowless room that was the tourist-class library. The business-class passengers enjoyed a reading room with windows or portholes, and the first-class passengers were rich enough not to need a library.

There were a few overstuffed leather chairs placed about the room. The books were on built-in shelves with aluminum railings across each shelf meant to remind the passengers that they were still on a ship and not in a second-rate library in a down-at-the-heels small town. Even today, when I enter a restaurant without windows, I look around and usually remark that it reminds me of an ocean liner. The people with me either patently do not know what I am talking about or they remain silent in the hope that by their silence they would seem knowledgeable, even if they were never a member of those remaining few who were part of that ocean-traveling fraternity.

By day, when most of the leather chairs were taken out of the room and replaced by a row of rather dainty wooden chairs of faux bamboo painted the color of gold that were placed in a row and lined up against a wall, it became the tourist-class lounge-cum playroom. In its playroom incarnation, the tourists could dance to the music of a phonograph. A small bar would be rolled in, and drinks could be purchased that were charged to one's cabin. Sometimes, a screen would be set up for movie viewing.

That night, a night that could have changed my life, there was only one other person in the room. I did not notice who sat in a chair behind me. My eyes were fixed to a novel. I read the same page over and over again trying to drive away the thoughts of an ordered past and an uncertain future, in short, the amalgam of homesickness, when a voice from the large leather chair set back to back to mine said, "What's the point of buying the book if you only read one page?"

Her voice was low and gentle, but even in its modulation, she was able to make it unpleasant. It seemed to be its owner's engine designed to convey dismissal and consignment to the garbage heap of people one meets on a voyage. It taunted; it mocked.

Since our chairs were placed in this manner I could not see her face. My first thought: How was she able to see what I was reading? But then I realized that there were two large mirrors on each side of the room, but since she was slouched down in the chair, I could not make out much about her. The second: that she was simply trying to get me to move to the other side of the room. Better still, I would leave the library, and she would have the room to herself. It made me think that such arrogance and nastiness must have had its genesis in a self-assurance borne of great beauty. I half rose out of the chair and turned around. I observed that she was not a great beauty and perhaps, was not beautiful at all. She was thirtyish, her long, dark-brown hair fell about her shoulders, her nose straight and thin-bridged. She wore a black sweater and grey skirt, her legs tucked beneath her. I could not see her eyes since, in apparent disdain, she had already turned away from me.

I half-thought of simply getting up and sitting in another chair or not answering her at all. Instead, without turning toward her, I responded, "The book is like a piece of music or blank canvas for my thoughts."

Still not turning to face me, she said, "The book that you're not reading is not the point. The point is *not* what you say. The point is, when you admit it to yourself, that it has nothing to do with music or art. The point is that there is nothing as lonely as a crowded ship on an empty ocean. If you want music, you should buy a phonograph or wait until you get to Paris. Plenty of canvas there."

She fell into silence, put her book down on her lap, half rose and turned to look at me. She simply stared at me for a moment or two, eyes wide, her face dispassionate, without emotion or animation, appraising, measuring: a tailor's "It is 41 long;" a bloodless doctor's "The test, unfortunately, is positive;" a mechanic's "The car needs a new transmission."

"You want music?" she asked. "Listen . . ."

> *"Stand on the highest pavement of the stair—*
> *Lean on a garden urn—*
> *Weave, weave the sunlight in your hair—*
> *Clasp your flowers to you . . ."*

"I forget the rest."
I continued:

> *". . . with a pained surprise—*
> *Fling them to the ground and turn*
> *With a fugitive resentment in your eyes:*
> *But weave, weave the sunlight in your hair."*

"You may think from my accent that I come here by way of Andover and Exeter, but actually I grew up in a New York slum. When I would come home on the subway, I immersed myself in reading any-thing that would drown out my surroundings ... the more remote and disconnected from it the better. And so came the poetry."

She remained silent, still looking at me, bemused, her unpainted lips in a half-smile. I continued, "After the train stopped at the Lorimer Street station, while walking to my home—particularly when returning late at night or early in the morning—I would recite poetry to myself. For me, it was sort of my mantra of pro-tection against all the evil things that could befall me during that three-block walk. *The Song of Solomon*, two short Robert Burns' and a bit of Byron would just about do it."

"Lorimer Street? I must have missed it in my visits to New York."

Her name was Susan, and we talked and talked until everyone had left. She had been to Europe several times in the last few years and was now en route to Vienna on some kind of art grant. She was from somewhere—to me—*out there*—the alien land west of New Jersey, from there to the Pacific Ocean, a land filled with *real Americans* with blond hair and houses—one to each family—and dinner all together with the father sitting at the head of the table and convert-ible cars and martinis and crab grass and Rotary clubs and Christ-mas trees and snow that does not turn to dirty mush and homes without screaming and where no one ever dies.

We talked and talked until even the attendant had left and there were almost no sounds but the liquid sighing of the ship plunging forward and until the room lights were turned off. We remained in the blackness until the sea dawn that pounced rather than crept upon us as it would on land.

When I returned to my cabin in the morning, the other students were gathered together waiting for me. They were concerned that I had fallen overboard and were about to report a possible accident to the ship personnel. I lied, for the first time in my almost-adult life about something that had to do with women—at least as far as the direction of the lie was concerned, less rather than more—and told them I had simply fallen asleep in the lounge and only just had awoken.

I showered, changed and went down for breakfast. I saw Susan again that midmorning, and we walked the deck chatting. Her roommate was an older infirm woman whom she helped to the deck each day. The woman remained in a deck chair swathed in blankets. The chair had toggles on the bottom of each leg that attached to the deck thereby preventing the chair from sliding when the boat rocked. We made sure to tighten the toggles. A steward would bring her lunch and afternoon tea, and Susan would bring her back to their cabin in the late afternoon. This arrangement allowed us the privacy of the cabin most of the day.

On the last day out, Susan and I did not notice that there was a squall at sea. By the late afternoon when we realized the change in the weather, we ran upstairs to the elderly lady. We found her, still lashed to her chair, her hair askew, somewhat damp, but aside from this, none the worse for wear. She told us about the storm and how exciting it was to be alone on the deck amid the turbulence. At one point, she said, a steward unsuccessfully urged her to allow him to unlatch her and take her down to her cabin.

On the last day of the crossing, I sat with Susan in her cabin watching her pack. She seemed almost in a frenzy, her fingers flying over her clothing, folding and pinning things into place as they were put into suitcases. We exchanged addresses and made elaborate plans to see each other in Europe, all the while she avoided looking at me, almost as when we first met.

I was sincere and she probably less so, or not at all, but at any rate, my letters to her were unanswered, and my last memory was of her fluttering hands, packing, pinning and her not looking at me. I guess she had the same problem ending relationships as did I.

14

PARIS IN THE FALL

I love Paris, why, oh why do I love Paris?
Because my love is near.

"I Love Paris" from *Can-Can*, Cole Porter

Holding our own suitcases, we stepped off the train into the airplane hangar-sized station and headed toward the entrance, joining the streams of people indifferently flowing this way and that like hungry guppies in an overcrowded tank. Marty held a map of Paris over his head and looking up, studied it as we pushed him forward through the directionless crowds toward the station exit. Having heard that the Paris taxi drivers cheat Americans, he wanted to make sure that we were not driven to our Left Bank hotel by way of Czechoslovakia.

We walked out of the station into a warm fall morning raucous with the blaring of automobile horns, policemen's whistles, the roar and throb of traffic and an assault of bright clashing crayon colors that painted the awnings, storefronts, taxis and a hundred billboards.

We piled into the first taxi on the line—a shiny Renault of prewar design that looked as if it had been stamped out of tin. The European custom was to tell the driver your destination before entering the car while standing on the sidewalk. But having come from New York, we did what New Yorkers do to avoid being refused passage by cabbies: we jumped into the cab, sat down together with our luggage *before* we told him where we wanted to be taken. Marty, our navigator, handed him a sheet of paper upon which he had written the name and address of our hotel. The driver, obviously unhappy with either our destination or his passengers, drove in glum silence to our hotel while Marty, in similar silence, traced our route on his map with his forefinger.

Arriving at the Left Bank, the city tableau changed. Rows of tiered three- and four-story houses huddled against each other, resting as tired sentries lining the narrow pavements. The cobblestone streets curved and turned aimlessly, some marching upward, then dipping and twisting out of sight. We passed several men hosing down the streets, and at one, a woman in an apron, pail beside her, scrubbed a sidewalk in front of a bar. At a few curbs, drivers in shirtsleeves and suspenders were unloading deliveries to stores from the open rear platforms of ancient trucks. Running arguments, accompanied by energetic hand movements and exaggerated facial grimaces, were flying back and forth between the drivers and the proprietors of the stores receiving the deliveries.

The hotel was a four-story building. From the ground to the first floor, the exterior was constructed of large granite stones and the top three floors of red brick suggesting, perhaps, that in another, earlier life, the building had been an apartment house with a commercial establishment on the street level. On the pebbled-glass paneling of the twin entrance doors, there was elaborately painted gold lettering that had begun to peel. In front of the hotel stood its apparent proprietor, slowly smoking a large cigar, his eyes traversing the landscape of his domain, a dirty white apron spread across his ample belly. Next door was a bakery, its scents of newly baked bread drifted seductively over us as we untangled bodies and luggage from the taxicab.

Marty, because of his guidebook studies, believed that a taxi fare was an appropriate subject for bilateral negotiations and tried to convince us of this proposition. We huddled for a strategy session a few feet away from the cab and discussed the subject while the driver looked on. Melvin's position on the subject was to pay the demanded fee, but beginning this day if, during the entire time we were in Europe, we were to deduct 10 percent from any tip we paid, by the end of the year we would accumulate enough money to pay for our fare home.

The proprietor puffed his cigar, now and then removing it from his mouth to ponder the accumulated ash at its tip and observed the scene with obvious bemusement. The cab driver looking at the proprietor shook his head and raised his eyebrows in silent unflattering commentary, if not on tourists as an entire class of humanity, at least on us in particular.

We entered the hotel carrying our own luggage unassisted by the proprietor who remained outside, puffing his morning cigar, continuing to contemplate the fate of Western civilization. Inside the hotel, the lobby's only furnishing was a tiny desk to the left of the entrance behind which stood the proprietor's wife. We later learned she was actually the owner of the hotel by virtue of inheritance from a deceased husband whose cigar-smoking replacement now stood in front of the building. She was a tiny birdlike woman of an indeterminate age—somewhere between forty and sixty-five—who spoke twittering singsong English and told us that we had the entire fourth floor—consisting of three rooms and a bathroom—to ourselves. Glancing down at our luggage, she made a clown-sad face and said, "But unfortunately, ze elevator is *hors service*—out broken—so you will be obliged to carry your valises up yourselves." I had the feeling it had been *hors service* since the German occupation. She handed each of us a large key of the type used to lock a closet door and attached to each was a fist-sized, pear-shaped wooden object obviously designed so that its size and heft would remind guests not to walk off with the key. The number for the room for which the key was intended was written in large India ink letters on the wood. My room was 4A.

Picking up my two bags, I climbed the old, sagging stairs up stairwells that smelled of sin and cedarwood and the burnt coffee of too many dead mornings. I arrived on the fourth floor out of breath and pushed upon the flimsy unlocked wooden door with the 4A on it. Once inside the room, I tried to kick the door closed with the back of my foot, but the board-thin wood was warped, and I was only able to close the door partially. I tossed the suitcases onto the wafer-thin mattress and turned around to look out the window.

The scene was Paris in a bottle. Off into the distance, as far as I could see, was the zigzag pattern of the tops of houses—and a few steeples—against a flawless and endlessly empty blue sky. Laundry lines of twisted cotton cord were strung between houses, and hanging from them, shirts, underwear and bed linens were gently billowing in the mild autumn breeze, chimneys, mostly at rest, a few exhaled thin wisps of rising white smoke; narrow round metal smokestacks, some placed over square brick chimneys, topped by onion-shaped tin bulbs with diagonal slashes in the metal to catch the wind, slowly turned in the breeze. Pushing the suitcases aside, I threw myself on the bed and luxuriated in the thought that this was the first time I ever had a room to myself.

That night, I disengaged myself from Melvin and Marty, who wanted to see Paris nightlife. I told them that I wanted to nap and would probably be ready to go out when they were returning to the hotel.

Evening came and brought through my open window the night sounds of the Left Bank; arguments in the unintelligible spewing of a dozen different languages; the tintinnabulation of cloyingly sentimental music from cheap gramophones; the whine of a lonely cat; the smashing of glass; church bells and guttural shouts ending short and angry arguments; the animal kabuki dance of dominance; a passive partner, a gesticulating, threatening aggressor and sometimes the argument carried into the next room, lights turned off and the belly-up act of ultimate submission.

Through my open window drifted the night smells of the Left Bank courtyards: cooking and cabbage; garlic and garbage; and from further off, whispers of the faint scent of night-blooming jasmine and the river.

I turned out my light the better to see unobserved. Acted out in the lighted room across the alley from mine, a one-act play; a table, a wife seated on one side, on the other side, her husband in an undershirt and wearing wide red suspenders, a bottle of wine without a label between them. They shared a silent one-course meal under the pitiless cone of light from a single hanging bulb. Behind them a crib: an unseen baby. The ruminations of a novelist: What destiny, what amalgam of past events could bring these two people together? A wedding in a country church, an angry father —blacksmith, farmer, laborer, humble, profane—angry at a daughter pregnant and unrepentant, defiant; a confrontation; harsh words flung like javelins at the ghosts of not-forgotten wrongs and events twisted by time; the boarding of a midnight mail train to Paris, a note left propped against a rough wooden kitchen table.

At midnight, I closed the window, went downstairs past the proprietress sitting in an armchair, gently snoring. Soundlessly, I placed the key and its wooden attachment on the counter, closed the door behind me as quietly as possible and walked toward the river until I was able to flag a cab to take me to Place Pigalle.

Place Pigalle was to me, living in Brooklyn, the distillation of Paris. For me, it was further than far away: tendrils of the remnants of a half-forgotten dream when awakened from an after-dinner sleep, and here I was, sitting in the backseat of a taxi, hurling through dark Parisian streets to Pigalle.

Arriving, I stepped out of the cab into a harsh electric daylight. Colored kaleidoscopic lights painted garish advertisements for palaces of pleasure that offered seductions without crescendos or at least ones, silent and nasty. Here, a two-story, highlighted windmill turned by an unseen electric hand; there, outlines in neon lights of the disembodied legs of cancan dancers slowly kicking up and down under ruffled colored skirts. The names of the nightclubs that lined the streets were written in every kind of lighted script. Outside some of the clubs were unenthusiastic rummies with painted sandwich boards draped over their shoulders that described the pleasures unique to the advertised establishment: mute testimony to the fact that the price of a man's dignity is a few shots of cheap whiskey.

In the doorways of the clubs, hawkers, like housewives at a poultry market picking out chickens to be slaughtered for the evening meal, sized up the men strolling past. With a skill honed by survival in the gutters of life's back alleys, in little more than a glance or two, they were able to divine the country from whence the tourists came. They walked beside them for several feet, being careful not to tread beyond the invisible boundary marking the territory of the next club. In a conspiratorial manner, they would sidle up to the tourist, keep pace with him and talking to him in his native language, in whispered intimacy, address his perception of their sexual proclivities and insecurities, probing and touching these secret things with a dirty blunt finger.

In the darkened doorways of the side streets, prostitutes displayed their wares. It became cruelly obvious why GIs six years earlier had, in the callousness that soldiers share with adolescents, named the place "Pig Alley."

In the first doorway, a woman, broomstick thin, her wrinkled skin draped loosely over her exposed bosom and arms. She hoisted her skirt and smiled at me; her mouth carious with ragged dark spaces where once were teeth. With the same facility as the hawkers, she ascertained that I was an American and shouted out to me in accented English. I smiled back, but tried to focus my gaze past her, on the doorway behind her, so that by not meeting her eyes, I avoided becoming a participant in the madness that was her life.

Further down, in another doorway, I saw a fat woman—two hundred or more pounds—wearing a bright red dress, sitting on and overflowing a stool, her legs splayed apart, exposing above her dark stockings pale thighs, their flesh rumpled and dimpled with fat. Her powdered face was a chalk-white clown's mask; her cheeks rouged in red circles; her wide slash of a thin-lipped mouth had at its center a small doll-like cupid's bow of a mouth painted in scarlet lipstick. She ignored me, concentrating her attention on two men in coveralls and rough jackets carrying on a laugh-interspersed conversation with her in rapid French.

Walking down the side streets, each doorway offered a variation of a nightmare of sex-driven abuse of the human condition. Women in shiny black plastic outfits; women half-mad from drugs, screaming at passers-by, offering their services in an angry, hate-filled, confrontational way; women dressed as brides, in tattered white wedding outfits; women dressed as nurses wearing short white skirts, white stockings and little caps pinned atop their hairdo; one dressed in a khaki uniform, casually slapping her riding boots with a rider's crop; and catering to the most depraved of all the customers, a few dressed as little girls wearing short skirts and patent-leather children's shoes.

I walked through the district, stopped at a café for a cup of tea and then retraced my steps. It was now several hours later, and most of the women were gone, their sole proprietorships closed for the night. I supposed this was due to lack of business since the product they sold, being replenishable, was seldom out of supply. The fat woman was still at her post, now talking to a different set of, what appeared to be, local workmen. Her makeup was in as perfect—but bizarre—condition as it had been several hours earlier. Off in the distance, I heard the plaintive wail of a saxophone.

I came back to the place where the cab originally dropped me and looked back at Pigalle. It was now mostly empty of people, but it was still ablaze with colored lights—like a lady that never wipes off her makeup.

The next morning, we left for Bern.

15

THE CITY OF BERN

Sometimes these cogitatations still amaze
The troubled midnight and the noon's repose.

T. S. Eliot, *La Figlia che Piange*

Some journeys begin as effortlessly and smoothly as stepping gently on the accelerator of a twelve-cylinder motorcar after the light changes. Some are like the push-off of a roller coaster going downhill.

* * *

Back in time, before girls took your heart around the block for a spin, before life was a double A battery, there was Bern: squat, ancient, smug, the least likely of cities to begin a journey, a mythical place that thrived on cuckoo clocks, currency and chocolate.

The citizens of Bern, at least the men who ran it, those who caused the blood of commerce to course through its veins, the bankers and corporate leaders with soft, pale hands whose pudgy fingers wore simple gold wedding bands, were invisible. Most lived off in the hills around the city or in anonymous gray townhouses on winding streets in Kirchenfeld. Not surprisingly, Kirchenfeld was in the embassy section of the city where Allen Dulles undoubtedly understood Bern's perfect anonymity to conduct his clandestine war and negotiate the surrender of the German armies in Italy. Others in power in Bern resided along the high, inclined banks of the river Aare that lazily wound its way through the city like a monster overfed snake.

They would come into town each day in their Mercedes, disappear into their banks until midday when they would lunch with others of their kind in small, expensive dark restaurants or wooden-paneled private clubs. Across wineglasses, they would converse in conspiratorial tones, bending across the table to each other, sharing secrets. Then it was back to their offices. Promptly at six, as dependable as a German railroad timetable, they would depart for home.

Daytime, you would see their wives in the Altstadt, under the covered promenades, in their sensible shoes and plain dark dresses, strolling in pairs, solid and sturdy: human barricades, impervious to emotion or the assaults of change.

In the afternoons, after lunch, they would be in the tearooms, a Swiss euphemism for the caloric patisseries. Sitting at tiny round tables, they would eat huge concoctions of whipped cream, butter-laden pastry and chocolate in all of its cloying permutations and combinations laughing, talking to each other, dabbing bits of whipped cream from unrouged lips.

You would never see them or their husbands in the public squares of the city or restaurants in the evenings or weekends as they would disappear like the light that vanishes when a refrigerator door is closed. Vacations would consist of either traveling to other Swiss cities or remaining sequestered in their homes where they would entertain their intimates in citadels of privacy, immune from the contamination of tourists or for that matter, any manner of outsiders. Of course, at that time, I knew none of this.

In 1952, my perception of Switzerland was a land of mountains, cheese with holes, men in short leather pants, blond-haired girls in appliqué dresses, skiers wearing sunglasses and American tourists traveling in packs with cheap cameras dangling from their necks.

Juggling two leather suitcases, I stepped from the slowly moving train into the Bahnhof, one of the European temples of transportation built before the advent of commercial airlines, designed to receive and dispatch trains to and from cities both European and exotic. Its cathedral-high roof of glass panes was covered with the soot from thousands of trains arriving and departing their berths.

Standing on the platform, waiting for the train to grind to a stop, I looked out across the station and saw the first Swiss I ever did see: somber gray men—no women that I could discern in the moving mass of bodies—hurrying in all directions with the grim determination of Chinese food delivery men on a snowy night. Each seemed to have a folded newspaper under one arm and a worn leather briefcase clutched in the hand of the other. Later, I learned the briefcase usually held nothing more significant than that day's lunch.

When the train stopped, I stepped off to join the main flow of human current that seemed to go in one direction. As I approached the exit of the Bahnhof, rapt in the newness of swirling scenes around me, somehow I had lost my companions and turned to see them struggling with their bags behind me in the distance. Alone for the moment, in the synagogue of my soul, I was the only congregant. In my mind, I was an amalgam of my mother's strength against a hostile world that threatened her family, my brother's conquest of his environment by sheer will alone and my father's abiding anger at people whom he believed had betrayed him and the uncaring fortunes dispensed by fate that were directed personally against him. Like any amalgam—or mutt— I should be stronger than my parts. These thoughts were in my mind as I walked toward the exit of the station into a new world, but they were the stuff of my propulsion forward. "Alone" would probably be the ultimate state of my being. It certainly now was the most comfortable one.

Hemingway's character Harry Morgan says, "No matter how a man alone ain't got no bloody . . . chance."

But maybe with some men, it is the other way around. Alone, for them, is the way they should travel—the only way they can travel. Otherwise, they are just passengers on a train and passengers fall, jump or are pushed off, and in the end, they accomplish little at journey's end and die to the cackle of alien laughter.

We assembled in the Bahnhofplatz as the exiting crowd rapidly dissipated, going off in different directions, some taking taxis, some on foot. We all had previously, acting on the advice of prior students or the Swiss Student Union (which was neither a union nor composed of Swiss students as they were all Americans), made arrangements for our quarters while at school. There was no "official" student housing. Most of the new, incoming students would stay in pensions—a Swiss version of a boardinghouse—until they eventually ended up with their own apartments.

Back in New York, there had been a cocktail party given by the Swiss Union for students—both new and old—attending the medical schools. From the ethnic mix, it could have been a meeting of a chapter of the Young Israel—and probably one of the Brooklyn, Queens or Bronx chapters, at that. The students who were already in school seemed vaguely hostile, perhaps even suspicious, like old elephants viewing newcomers at a watering hole. Similarly, they used the opportunity to meet other advanced students who had returned to New York for the summer and exchange class notes or sell and trade textbooks as well as benefit from a free buffet.

The Bahnhofplatz was the main public square of the city. As you left the station, to your left, was the city's largest (and only) department store along with a row of fashionable shops, their entrances all set back from the sidewalk under the building's protective eaves. Straight ahead, but a far distance off, were more stores and nearer than these was a modern restaurant, Mövenpick, part of a chain that ultimately failed as a commercial culinary enterprise everywhere except in Switzerland. In the rest of the world—especially in the Middle East—it became a successful chain of hotels, no doubt aided by Switzerland's meaningful relationship with Arab money.

We walked across the Bahnhofplatz to the terminus where trams were waiting for passengers. The others had never seen a tram, and it became the subject of conversations as we lugged our bags across the square. I had seen trams before—much earlier—but we called them "trolley cars." They were the most common form of transportation in Brooklyn, crisscrossing the borough through all its major thoroughfares. The Williamsburg Bridge run was unusual. At either end of the bridge, once the trolley had made the crossing, there were turntables that would slowly spin the car around so that it could retrace its path. At the other end, the process was repeated to return the car from whence it came. The fare to cross the bridge was three cents and then ultimately ten cents. It remained at that level until the trolley line was eventually phased out.

My Uncle Izzy, my mother's youngest brother, at one point in his career was a motorman on the Lorimer Street trolley. Knowing his schedule, we would wait for the trolley at Lorimer Street and Broadway in order to get a free trip from there to the end of the run at Prospect Park. I know trolleys.

Izzy was a handsome man, in the mold of my grandfather. He was the youngest of four living children and was fussed over and protected by his two older sisters. He had a colorful employment history both before and after his service on the Lorimer Street trolley. In 1945, he owned a diner that was reputed to be a gathering place for hoodlums. The diner was in Brownsville, a neighborhood that was the spawning place of the business that represented the furthest extension of the American free enterprise system: "Murder Incorporated." My mother used to take me to the diner for forbidden bacon sandwiches that Izzy constructed for me piled with bacon to astronomical (at least in the sandwich world) heights.

Al "Bummy" Davis, a great lightweight with a powerful left

hook (*The Ring* magazine listed him as one of the sport's 100 Greatest Punchers) owned a bar next door to Izzy's diner and frequently hung out there. On November 21, 1945, four armed robbers tried to hold up the bar, and Bummy fought with them. That day, his left hook failed him. He was shot dead. My Uncle Izzy sensibly decided this was a sign that neither the neighborhood nor his business had any future, and he closed up the diner. Izzy also, as I found out many years later, had served time in jail as a result of working a gas station during wartime that was engaged in violations of the gasoline-rationing laws. Izzy had an attractive, but physically frail wife, May, who died at a young age. He remarried a woman who his sisters felt was beneath his station (or any other one on the Lorimer Street line).

Izzy ended his days as "Irving," a rabbi in a South Florida retirement community.

All of this had nothing to do with my walking across the Bahnhofplatz on a cool, fading October afternoon in the city of Bern other than the thoughts engendered by the European cousin (or ancestor) of Uncle Izzy's trolley car that I now climbed aboard to transport me to my new home. We had been given directions—complete with the name of the tram line—to get to the pension before we left New York and were carrying a modest supply of Swiss currency to tide us over until we opened accounts in a local bank. We dragged our luggage aboard the Länggassstrasse tram. We were the only passengers in the car, but we attributed this to the fact that we got on the vehicle at the start of its run. We later observed that except for returning home after an evening in town, we were usually the only passengers on the tram—something very unusual for anyone riding the New York subway … at any hour of the day or night. The car was spanking clean, and the seats looked as if they had just been varnished and had never been sat in. On the day I eventually left Switzerland, I realized that in all the time I was there, I had never seen them otherwise.

The tram made a short left on Bubenbergplatz, traveled a short distance, then turned right into Länggassstrasse. Traveling up the street, we passed three- and four-story yellow ochre and gray houses that lined both sides of the street, built of sandstone and devoid of any architectural charm or refinement. At the time, these were similar sorts of houses that one would see in the suburbs of Berlin or Prague or Brussels. It was as if the same talentless architect had left his mundane stain across the continent. The real reason was, I suppose, that there was no building of new housing stock anywhere in Europe during the war, regardless of the side on which a particular country found itself or even if it were a neutral. These styles of modest apartment houses that are still found all across Europe were the least expensive to build and could use available local materials.

After fifteen minutes, we ran into a wall of chocolate-laden air. It was like a solid invisible barrier, its cloying sweetness as sickening as the scent of the perfume undertakers dab on laid-out cadavers: tactile and almost palpable. It was first a caress and then became a smothering skin-clogging essence.

We arrived at our stop, Seidenweg, the home of Tobler, the largest manufacturer of chocolate in Switzerland. The production of chocolate requires that it be kept in a molten state until pressed into the desired form of the final product that would eventually be sold to the public. In order to accomplish this, the warm, viscous chocolate was poured into large metal tubs and then stirred by mechanical means. Twenty-four hours a day, seven days a week, the process had to be continued —never stopping—otherwise the mass would harden and be unusable.

We disembarked from the tram in tandem, each of us helping the one behind him with his luggage as he stepped down into the street. Walking several blocks, we finally reached Gesellschafts-strasse 83—happily a block past the assault of the chocolate smell. It was one of several identical houses painted a dull yellow, each attached to the other and each bordered by a tiny, but well-tended, garden that lacked anything of horticultural interest. In America, similar buildings would be city housing projects. In America, however, they soon would become instant slums. In Switzerland, they merely got old.

The building had a small elevator. When it arrived at the ground floor, it was totally dark until we stepped inside and the depression of our weight on the elevator floor acted as a switch that suddenly bathed us in light.

Pension Beckmeyer, our new home, was on the third floor, a large modern apartment with six bedrooms. Frau Beckmeyer waited in the foyer to greet us, accompanied by her daughter, Gretta, who acted as her interpreter.

There was a somber heaviness about Frau Beckmeyer in her long dark tentlike dress that fell until just above her lace-up shoes. She wore neither makeup nor jewelry nor adornment of any kind. Her hair was black and clipped short. Her face was fleshy, and her double chins caused it to be tilted slightly back so that when she spoke, her eyes were glancing a bit downward. Her skin was smooth, almost waxen, and pale. She held out her hand to shake hands. Her fingers were like small overstuffed sausages, but her nails, that last bastion of personal pride, were long and well-manicured. Her hand clasp was flaccid; her hand warm and moist.

"Grüsse." Her thin lips curved in a half-smile whose corners disappeared in the folds of her cheeks.

Next to her, Gretta, about seventeen, was blond, even featured and big breasted, sturdy without makeup, as solid and wholesome, in a German sort of way, as girls found in a travel poster's photograph advertising an Alpine holiday.

"My mother wishes you a happy stay, and we will have a meal after you pack down your clothes."

Gretta showed us to our respective rooms while Frau Beckmeyer stood behind her making an occasional comment that was translated into more-or-less English by Gretta. If Gretta gave a longer than usual version of a translation, she was interrupted by a quick look from Frau Beckmeyer that silenced her as effectively as a thrust

*My paternal grandfather and grandmother with my father stand-
ing behind them in a photo studio in Vienna. At that point, they
only had two living children, but there were five more to follow.*

Me at one year old with my first and last dog

*My mother, Millie, Jerome, and me at a
bungalow colony in the summer of 1935*

Jerome and grandfather at Haverstraw,
a recuperation center for polio victims

Me—four years old and still happy

The iron lung, a primitive and grotesquely ugly device designed to keep polio victims alive until
they could breathe on their own

1939—Jerome and behind him, my cousin, Bernard Wiseman, who was a New Yorker cartoonist and then a prolific children's book writer and illustrator; his brother, Maxie; and me. I am the only one still alive.

Playing ball outside my house looking down at McKibben Street. I am at bat, my cousin, Maxie, is catcher, and my brother is umpire. The cars are from the early 1930s.

My mother and me at the 1939 World's Fair when the world was on the cusp of war

My father, Morris, and brother Jerome in front of the rather delusionally grandiose entrance to Manhattan Arms in the early '40's

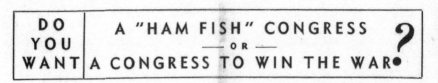

DO YOU WANT A "HAM FISH" CONGRESS — OR — A CONGRESS TO WIN THE WAR?

MORRIS FELDER

Born July 16, 1895 and has lived in this district almost all his life.

Graduated from P. S. 43, Boerum Street, Brooklyn.

Graduated from Eastern District High School, B'klyn.

Attended College of the City of New York.

Graduated from New York University, New York.

Graduated from St. Lawrence University—School of Law.

Ten Years—Chairman and member of Local School Board.

Ten Years—Associate Counsel for the Transit Commission of the State of New York.

Practicing attorney at 66 Court St., Brooklyn, N. Y.

Has taken an active part in numerous charity, welfare and civic drives in Brooklyn.

Member of Marshall Lodge, F. & A. M., Independent Order of Odd Fellows, and many other charitable, fraternal and civic organizations.

MORRIS FELDER

Seeks your support on the following six-point program:

1. Will support our President until the evil forces fighting Democracy and Civilization are crushed;

2. Will do everything within his power to provide the fullest American participation in the Peace settlement and in the international order that will follow this war;

3. Will do everything within his power to strengthen Democracy; to preserve unity; to expose the divisionists and the appeasers, here on the home front;

4. Will insist upon the maintenance at all times of our constitutional rights;

5. Will make every effort to obtain more War Contracts for New York City firms so that all may find employment.

6. Will with all his power and energy, represent all the people of all the district all the time.

VOTE for MORRIS FELDER

For Democratic Nominee For Member of Congress

A handout as voters went to the polls in one of my father's frequent forays into politics

*My mother is sixth from the right (wearing a red cross)
with the group she formed during World War II.*

Grandpa Harris posing in front of our building. Note: my father's fading "Lawyer" sign and the ever-present cigarette

Jerome, my mother, me, and my father at my bar-mitzvah luncheon in my brother's and my bedroom, which was turned into a banquet hall for the event

Another view, now filled with guests, of my brother's and my banquet hall-cum-bedroom

My father and me posing in front of our building with his "Lawyer" sign now made of more imposing bronze

1950—My brother and me in front of the usual photographic backdrop—the side of our apartment house

My father, the perennial candidate, once again tilting at windmills

My brother and cousin Bernard in front of our home, now missing its imposing awning due to my brother burning it down with an accidentally tossed cigarette

My brother in the style of the day—pencil mustache and cardigan jacket

*Duke Ellington with my brother.
Years later, I represented Ellington,
then active in his Broadway play,
Pousse-Cafe, and finally was a member
of the board of directors of the Duke
Ellington Foundation that erected a
statue of Duke in Central Park.*

Me, in London in the 1950s

Me in Munich to master German

My credentials when I was a prosecutor

My brother had well-known Broadway photographer Popsie take this picture of me.

My grandfather in his eighties with my mother

My wife, Myrna, and me attending the Nixon inauguration

My wife and me at a fancy gala

My son, James, and me before we went up for a ride in a B-17

Jerome fixing the photographer with his gaze

Doc Pomus
(June 27, 1925)

and his brother

Raoul Lionel Felder
(May 13, 1934)

invite you to their

121st Birthday Celebration

Wednesday, June 13, 1990
8 p.m. til at least 2 a.m.
at
KATZ'S DELICATESSEN
205 East Houston Street

Come and join us for the finest in food and music

dress: informal   R.S.V.P. Marisa at (212) 832-3939

Invitation to the last happy event before my brother died. About 1,000 people showed up.

Me at the Lincoln Memorial Mall addressing senior citizens from around the country, bused in to assert their rights

A media storm as I left court after arguing Rudy Giuliani's case against Donna Hanover in the best known divorce trial of the day.

Have I got troubles?

My son, James, who now teaches at graduate school and my granddaughter, Millie

My granddaughter, Millie

*Daughter Rachel and
granddaughter Millie*

*Me and Millie with blue eyes inherited from my father (my son, James, also
has blue eyes) while my paternal grandfather had one blue and one brown eye*

from a stiletto. Mostly, Frau Beckmeyer confined her comments to "Gut, gut."

That first day was tiring and eventful. By nine o'clock, all the lights in the apartment were turned off, and I had just fallen asleep when I was jolted awake by chords banged out from a piano accompanied by a loud female contralto, doing scales seemingly in an effort to warm up her voice.

A student who had been on the boat with me had told me that when he thought about the Pension Beckmeyer, he was assaulted with memories of pommes frites and the strange locked door behind which Frau Beckmeyer and Gretta lived.

16

THINGS FALL APART

*Things fall apart; the centre cannot hold . . . and everywhere
the ceremony of innocence is drowned.*

William Butler Yeats

Classes would not begin for a week, hardly enough time to find a
new apartment, hardly enough time to find out how to even *look*
for a new apartment. The Mövenpick seemed to be a likely place
to start. Much to Frau Beckmeyer's delight, once she understood
that I would pay the same regardless of whether or not I dined on
her sausages and potatoes, I foreswore her lunches and dinners in
favor of those at the Mövenpick. In addition to its culinary capabilities, it was the hangout for Americans in Bern, a place to exchange
information and gossip and, sitting in the balcony, looking down at
the bar, an excellent place to evaluate women and girls. It was not
unlike a smorgasbord table where everything looks appetizing and
available.

Americans and anything American had a magic glow about them.
It was only a handful of years before that America had won a world
war that had Europe in its thrall and at the same time, was itself

untouched. If a second-rate American musical group performed in the city, there would be lines around the block. If an American bought something in a store, the owner would race ahead of him to open the door and bow deep enough to steal crumbs from the mice.

I was an American. I was rich. I was Gary Cooper, General Patton, Frank Sinatra, nylon stockings, Al Capone, Clark Gable, a cowboy on a horse, Babe Ruth, the Eighty-second Airborne, Louis Armstrong, the Empire State Building, Joe Louis and a fishtailed car. I was not a skinny Jewish kid from Brooklyn with no money. I was indomitable and irresistible to women.

One evening at the Mövenpick, I looked down from the balcony and saw a woman sitting with one of the older students. She was tall and pale-skinned with large eyes that were the dark blue-green of storm-driven seas. Her cheekbones were high, and her eyebrows were perfectly curved as if chiseled from stone. Her hair was long, silken and black and flowed like liquid down her neck and shoulders. Her cheeks were hollow, her makeup precise and expertly applied. Sitting slumped backward in her chair, she stared intently at her companion who never stopped talking. Although I was never an outgoing person, I happened to have met her companion and felt relaxed enough to greet him and meet her. I walked down to the main floor level from my balcony perch and began a conversation. Her name was Carla Smeisser. She smiled, leaned forward to shake my hand and then slouched back on the chair, her hand holding the gathered fabric of her coat at her throat. As her companion and I chatted, she continued to smile, though it was clear she understood little English. He told me that she was a fashion model who was Swiss and traveled back and forth between Bern and Paris for the shows. After a few more minutes, he announced he had to leave, and in the singsong dialect of Swiss-German, he appeared to ask her if she wanted to accompany him. I understood enough to know that she refused and opted to stay at the restaurant.

After he left, we sat, staring at each other, not able to speak the other's language. I saw that there were small wrinkles at the corners of her eyes, and there was something worn and weary about her. Despite the faint defects, I thought she was the most beautiful woman I had ever seen. She spoke to me in German, and I understood nothing. She repeated it slowly as if speaking to a child. I still was unable to understand her. Finally, she gave up trying to make me understand and tried to speak the little English she knew.

She struggled, "How long you"—she pointed at me—"you have been here, to Bern?"

I pointed at my watch. "Minutes or hours?" She understood this and smiled.

We went on like this, and finally I drew a picture of my face on a piece of paper, drew a smile and pointed my finger at her, "You make me," and I drew an arrow at my smile.

She drew a child's picture of a house, pointed at it and then at me, stood up and said, "Come."

We got into a cab, and she gave the driver instructions.

As we drove through now dark streets, I had no sense of where we were other than that we were in a neighborhood of modest homes and small apartment houses. We stopped in front of a one- or two-family without any lights. Motioning for me to wait, she got out and disappeared into the house.

After about fifteen minutes, she came out carrying a small suitcase and holding a German shepherd on a leash. Once in the cab, the dog wedged itself on the floor of the taxi, stretching across our feet. The heat of the dog's body and the sound of its breathing filled the car. She asked me where I lived, and when I told her, she seemed familiar with the Beckmeyer Pension. While I fumbled with the unfamiliar currency, she had already taken out money and paid the driver. Entering the building, we took the elevator to my floor with a key Frau Beckmeyer had begrudgingly given me. I unlocked the door and led us into the apartment. On tiptoe, we made our way to my room, the dog trailing behind us, apparently unhindered by the fact that I did not turn on the lights.

All through the night, I could hear the panting of the animal and was unable to tell, in the darkness, if the dog was awake or sleeping. Twice during the night, the dog tried to climb into the bed, and twice I pushed it away. Each time, Carla tried to stop me from pushing her dog away. Perhaps she knew the animal too well and feared he would take a chunk out of my hand. In the morning, without Carla issuing a command, the dog padded silently to where she had thrown her clothes the night before, picked them up in its teeth and brought them to her. The dog, unlike me, had obviously been in this situation before.

When we finally left my room, Frau Beckmeyer was outside the door. For a moment, I was convinced she would berate me for behaving in a way that was morally unacceptable to the rules of the establishment. I was wrong. Frau Beckmeyer smiled as she and Carla twittered back and forth in their Swiss dialect. At the end of the conversation, the frau winked at me.

I was as much disturbed by Frau Beckmeyer's reaction as I was at the events of the prior night, and at that moment, all I wanted was to find another apartment. I never wanted to see Frau Beckmeyer or Carla or the dog, for that matter, again.

17

THE ANATOMY CLASS

In a minute there is time
For decisions and revisions which a minute will reverse.

T. S. Eliot

There are some decisions you make that are like falling into a deep hole. Unexpectedly, life forever changes. There are other decisions that you can chew and chew over like a cow its cud, and you make them and end up at the bottom of the same hole anyway. Perhaps it was the German shepherd or Frau Beckmeyer's wicked little smile, or maybe it was simply that I knew deep down that I really did not want to study medicine in Bern. In fact, I realized what I knew all along, that medicine was not my life's calling.

It was seven in the morning and still dark and cold. At that moment, I felt it would never be light and it would never be warm.

The streets of Bern were empty. Walking toward the anatomy building, the cold was like an icicle stabbing its way into the passages of my lungs, chilling the innermost provinces of my body. My breath was suddenly neither warm nor moist, but rather something merely to be inhaled and exhaled in short gasps of cold, alien bursts of glacial air that exited my mouth, before becoming suspended in space and fading into the wind.

A frozen white lace of frost outlined the fences and gates of the buildings. Several times on each block. I would stop and grab hold of a gate or lean against a wall to catch my breath and rest a bit. I could feel the cold metal of the gates through my gloves. It was the kind of cold that in its shock and intensity could be felt as searing hot rather than sharp stinging cold. My brain was numb and congealed, and my thinking was reduced to repeating in my head the same words and phrases over and over again.

I finally arrived at the unwelcoming and foreboding façade of the anatomy building—a perfectly square unadorned red structure, two stories high and from another age, squatting in the center of a small barren lot. A nasty building that meant business, that spoke of epidemics, of pest houses, of the dead. A single, modest sign above the door identified its purpose.

Entering the building, I found myself in a large windowless room lit by a series of bare light bulbs hanging from the high ceiling. There was no furniture, only a large potbellied stove set against one wall.

As I warmed myself before the stove, I entertained the unworthy thought that the reason Switzerland remained at peace with the world through wars and revolutions was that nobody thought the country was worth fighting over. At best, it would be a consolation prize for the loser. I asked myself, "What am I doing here?"

Crazy Lenny came into the room bringing with him a gust of cold wind. He was short and wore a black Melton overcoat that was down to his ankles, a long blue woolen scarf wrapped around his neck, which covered the bottom part of his face, and a blue knitted cap pulled down over most of his ears. The ragged cuffs of his trousers were wet and rested as puddles of fabric on the tops of his scuffed shoes. The only human part of Lenny that was entirely visible were his eyes, large and faded blue that if complemented by a less unusual style of dress might have been striking in their attractiveness. The one thing about Lenny, however, was he knew his anatomy. He had been a student at the prestigious New York Medical College before he was expelled for an affair of the heart.

Lenny, who lived at a university-owned facility, had stolen a heart from the anatomy lab in order to dissect and study it in the privacy of his room. Unfortunately for him, a cleaning lady had found it and turned Lenny in to the school authorities who threw him out. In response, Lenny felt the school had infringed upon his academic freedom, which in turn caused them to diagnose him as "mentally unstable." At the time, New York Medical College, by dismissing him, effectively ended the possibility of him obtaining an American medical education—which all gets back to why Lenny was called Crazy Lenny or just Crazy when he wasn't present. The truth was, despite Lenny's idiosyncrasies, he had been extremely helpful to me when it came to preparing for my first anatomy lab class.

When I arrived in Switzerland, I had brought with me a surplus Army Medical Corps surgical kit that included an assortment of scalpels with disposable blades. One of the first lessons Lenny taught me was that in Swiss medical circles, disposable blades were unacceptable as they were not considered sharp enough. Swiss surgeons and medical students sharpened their own instruments, apparently preferring keenness over sterility. With Lenny's guidance, I spent considerable time learning how to use a honing stone, a skill I have retained to this day.

We were alone in the entrance room when Lenny pulled me over to him and in hushed tones, imparted yet another important tip. When dissecting a body, the Swiss used a sort of layering system, from the skin downward. First, the skin is cut in three strips at right angles to each other, retaining the fourth piece of it untouched to serve as a flap. The fatty tissue under the skin is then cut into the same three-sided rectangle. The dissection then goes deeper into the muscles, cutting them only at one end, while the other remained intact as a sort of hinge, followed by the dissection of the organs, heart, nerves, ligaments, etc.

The final step is to cut to the bone. The trick here, however, was that once the initial flap of skin is created, the Swiss anatomy instructors required a careful cutting away of the very thin layer of epidermis that is attached to the underside of the skin in order to produce what was termed a "pigskin effect." In other words, the remaining skin should, by then, resemble a piece of pigskin. Two thoughts occurred to me. One occurred to me at the time—that while I was grateful for Lenny's assistance, I doubted whether in my future medical career I would be tending to pigs. The other one came to me years later—compared to dissecting a human body, fighting the vitriol in divorce court was as easy as carving a turkey for Thanksgiving.

Other students began congregating in the entrance room. After looking furtively around, Lenny turned to me, lowered the scarf around his face and whispered in my ear, "You're a Jew, I'm a Jew, and we have to stick together."

While I stood there trying to process what he meant, he winked at me and nodded his head, willing me to agree. It was then that I realized that he was quite mad. I thought to myself, "My God, what am I doing here?"

After a half-hour, a man of about sixty, gaunt and stooped, wearing a white laboratory coat, come out of a room on our left. Opening a tall wooden door, he motioned us to follow him.

The room was vast, unheated, with stone walls painted light gray and a ceiling of great height. There were no windows. The only light came from large electric bulbs at the end of long cords that hung from the ceiling. This was a room built for a particular grim purpose.

There were two long rows of cadavers on tables, each covered from head to foot with cheap, gray cotton cloths. At the foot of each table was a large metal wastebasket. On one of the cadavers, the center of the covering cloth was raised to a point, similar to how a portion of a canvas tent rests on a tall center post along with stakes of lesser heights that are driven into the ground.

On top of the cloth covering each body, there was pinned a sheet of paper with two names, indicating the two students assigned to that particular corpse. My cadaver was to be shared by me and a blond Swiss boy who barely grunted a greeting. In the following months, though we shared the same corpse, we spoke not a word to each other, though he seemed quite talkative with other Swiss student who worked at the adjoining table. In fact, he often would go to the other table to do some work on his compatriot's cadaver. Bent over the body, they looked like two pigs at a trough, and it seemed to me that any fair-minded person viewing the scene would think it only a matter of time that one or the other would take a bite out of the poor fellow—or what was left of him—that lay on the table.

Upon entering the autopsy room, we all hung our coats on wall pegs before walking around to find our assigned tables. After a few minutes, Herr Professor Scrank entered the room followed by two assistants. The professor was about fifty, tall, and thin, ramrod straight with sunken cheeks and iron-gray hair combed flat with its part ruler-straight down the middle of his scalp. He was closely shaven, had a precise square black mustache and heavy dark eyebrows. He wore trousers and a vest of heavy dark material over which was a white laboratory coat. In all the time I was there, I never saw him dressed or groomed differently. His young assistants, who also were dressed in white laboratory coats, followed him like scavenger fish behind a shark as he made his rounds up one line of bodies and down the other. When the professor arrived at a body, one of his assistants would remove the cover after which he would say a few words to the students who had been assigned that particular cadaver. The precision with which he inspected the corpses reminded me of the famous photograph of Eisenhower reviewing the airborne troops before D-Day, asking each one, "Where are you from, soldier?"

Interrupting my reverie, Arnie, another American student who had flunked out of an American medical school, muttered, "Jeez, they're white." Later, when I queried him about his remark, I learned that its genesis was in the awful underbelly of American society as it existed back then. In Chicago, where he had attended medical school, all the bodies they dissected were derelicts that had been found on the streets or had been donated to the medical school by the city to save the cost of an anonymous burial in Potter's field, and they were mostly all black. In Switzerland, the people—derelicts or not—who were in that unhappy state were all white.

There were two young women in my class. One was Swiss, stout and square jawed with a man's haircut and rather hairy legs that could support a Steinway piano, who had all the sex appeal of a blacksmith's anvil. The other female student came from the French part of Switzerland. She was slight, had red hair and smiled a lot.

As the professor finished reviewing his troops on the right row, he turned to continue his inspection of those on the left side. The slender female student has been assigned the cadaver covered with the cloth that spiked in the center of the body. When the professor came to her table, he motioned his assistant to remove the cloth. The unfortunate fellow on the table had apparently hanged himself. The noose around his neck created pressure on his cerebellum causing a pooling of blood that resulted in an erection that had now become a permanent part of his remains. Thanks to a combination of rigor mortis and infusions of formaldehyde, it was only surpassed in hardness by the marble one that adorned Michelangelo's *David*.

The professor seemed to spend longer chatting with her than he spent at the other tables, both he and she carefully ignoring the deceased's engorged appendage that was as inconspicuous as a wooden leg on a beauty queen. The Swiss students tittered. I later found out that whenever the school obtained a corpse in this condition, the professor would arrange a similar situation. I guessed the humor lost something in translation.

Nervously, I waited until the professor arrived at my cadaver. The problem was that when he addressed me in his native Swiss dialect, I didn't understand a word. The image of Eisenhower reviewing the troops and the question that he asked, "Where are you from, soldier," came to mind. In response to the professor's words, I smiled and said, "New York." He smiled back at me and nodded his head.

The rest of the morning consisted of a lecture and drawings that the professor had made on a blackboard that one of his assistants had wheeled into the room. Though I didn't understand a word, I carefully copied his diagrams. When the lecture was over, the Swiss students applauded the professor. While joining the clapping, I thought, "What the hell. I clap at the end of an opera, and I don't understand a word of it."

At the conclusion of the morning class, one of the Swiss students who spoke English pulled me aside as we were gathering our coats.

"Why have you done that?" he asked.

"I just followed what the rest of you did and clapped," I answered.

"No, not that. It was the New York thing."

"What's wrong with that? It's where I'm from. Is there something about New York that gets to him?"

"No. It wasn't that. But he asked you if you studied the first exercise, the neck muscles, which is where we will begin tomorrow, and your answer was, New York."

God, how I hated that place.

That night I spent several hours studying an English textbook, memorizing the anatomy of the neck muscles.

When I arrived in class the next morning, a different cadaver was awaiting me. Shrugging it off, I began the neck-muscle dissection.

This new cadaver was a strapping middle-aged man who looked like he might have been a truck driver or longshoreman, except that Switzerland was landlocked and had no shores and boats to unload. His profession remained a mystery though he was quite muscular with strong developed neck muscles.

When I got down to them, instead of the neat, interrelated, flat and easily differentiated muscles that lay upon each other, as I had memorized in my English textbook, the cadaver had a swollen mass of muscle strands bulging out in every which way. It would have been very difficult to do any dissections of the neck muscles and certainly if done, would be totally without value for any instructive purposes.

One of the professor's assistants came by, looked at the neck, grinned and said, "*Kropf*"—which was German for endemic goiter (chronic enlargement of the thyroid gland). The thyroid, located in the neck, directly below the Adam's apple, swollen like that was rarely seen then or now in the United States. Its genesis is a lack of dietary iodine, which, in turn, causes low amounts of thyroxine in the blood. This, then, stimulates another hormone that causes the thyroid gland to become overactive and enlarged. Iodine is found in seafood and the soil of land near the sea. Since the early nineteen hundreds, most table salt is iodized. Between that and the readily availability of seafood (because of improved methods of shipping and storage), the disease is all but eradicated. The only places where it still exists are in mountainous regions not near the sea. Welcome to Switzerland.

The professor had his little joke. As for me, I was rapidly coming to a decision that would result in the world being denied my medical talents.

18

DECISIONS

Language was my problem, or at least one of them ... formal German *in* school ... Switzerdeutsch (the local dialect) *outside* of school. I stopped going to the movies in town, such as *Vom Winde verweht* (*Gone with the Wind*) and *Der Schwarze Ritter* (*The Black Knight*). Although they were shown in English, the subtitles in the three official Swiss languages—French, German and Italian—would be at the bottom of the screen, obscuring much of the images. It was so distracting and annoying that for many years after leaving Bern, I refused to go to a foreign movie with subtitles.

Swiss medical colleges required a proficiency in Latin though Latin was not a required language course in American or British medical schools. It was and remains as dead as the cadavers on the table. The senior American medical students suggested that I sign up for a mail-order course in Latin given by Oxford University. After enrolling, Oxford would mail the lessons and tests to the subscribers.

In what was a sad reflection of our integrity, we all took our tests to the local Berlitz school in town and paid them to supply us with the correct answers. As a result, I have a diploma in Latin from Oxford University—or at least I *had* it at one time, since I had to file it with the school. The odd thing was, even with Berlitz doing the answers, I still only passed by the skin of my teeth.

As the months went on, my studies continued though I never did understand the lectures and was only able to do the actual lab work. Tests were given and not unlike baseball, there was a three-strike rule. If a student failed three tests, he or she was automatically expelled. Fortunately for us, the instructors were lazy, and each year asked the same questions on the tests. The American students who had already proceeded to the next academic level created an underground library of all of the questions on the old exams. The only fee for access to these was American citizenship. With their help and divine providence, I never failed a test. The big one, however, was as the end of two years and required serious preparation. I had no stomach (not to mention interest and enthusiasm) for it.

During the time I attended medical school in Bern, my family supported me. My mother would send me long letters of news at home describing my brother's rising success as a songwriter. He had abandoned performing many years earlier. She would always include a hundred-dollar bill. My father would write even longer letters, usually obliquely telling me all the things that were going wrong and the sacrifices he made in order to send me to school, with the warning that he expected me not to fail or disappoint him. Often, he slipped in a twenty-dollar bill. Later on, my father would talk about the best-selling songs my brother had written, though never failing to mention his disappointment that my brother had not become an insurance broker, working from home as my father had wished.

Days went by, aimlessly, without purpose or commitment and toward no goal that I wanted to achieve. Before the decision was fully formed, I knew I would return to America in defeat. Curiously, neither defeat nor embarrassment really bothered me. What concerned me was the life that stretched before me. I pictured myself striving for mean little things, surviving in an apartment facing a brick wall of an alley in Williamsburg, working at a second-rate job, married to a second-rate wife who hung laundry on a clothes line. I saw myself groveling to bosses during the week and then, in summer, spending my spare time on public beaches after sweaty subway rides, or evenings sitting on the steps of a tenement, exchanging banalities with neighbors. I saw myself having little pride in my children to whom I could impart little culture or knowledge as I struggled to exist from paycheck to paycheck to meet my bills. My dreams would be limited to what I could see at the movies at the Rainbow Theatre on Graham Avenue.

The road ahead was dismal, but still I knew it was time to come home.

19

LAW BY DEFAULT

With no particular enthusiasm other than preventing myself from ending up on life's scrapheap, a prospect that was becoming increasingly likely, I undertook the study of law. I chose applying to a New York law school because I had had enough of traveling, not to mention a lack of necessary funds to attend an out-of-state school. NYU is a national law school, meaning it teaches general American law as opposed to only the law of the particular state in which the school is located. When I applied, it was too late for me to sit for the required LSAT, which was fortunate since I probably would have failed it. Because of my rather varied educational background—in college, I was an English literature major, then I returned to take the science courses necessary for medical school, and of course, there was my Swiss excursion—the admissions people apparently thought I would be an interesting choice and waived the formal entrance requirements. It was rather like choosing a surgeon because he had been a baccarat dealer and had also acquired a working knowledge of Sanskrit. But there it was and here I was sitting in another educational amphitheater surrounded by a lot of rather ordinary young men and three young women. At least, they all spoke English. They approached the law with the competitiveness of a flock of sea gulls fighting over a few breadcrumbs.

I hated law school. The teachers were the kings for a day or at least an hour, strutting and primping before the class, expecting at least mild laughter at their twice-told tales and stale jokes. "Did you hear the one about the female solicitor who dropped her briefs and became a barrister?" I did ... over and over again.

Law is founded on precedent as the basis for arriving at a desired conclusion. It seemed to me at the time that merely because something was done in the past was probably not a good reason why it should be done again and an excellent one why something new should be tried. However, I was there to go through the machine and come out a sausage, and besides, I was running out of professions where I would not have to work particularly hard for a living and I could go to work daily in a clean shirt.

I had to do a great deal of reading of cases stale and dead, and the old devil returned. I would try to concentrate on a case, and my mind would be off on its own path (sometimes two or more) that would play itself out simultaneously with my reading of the material.

I would go to the basement of the school where there were rows of three-sided enclosures called "carrels," each containing a small metal desk and chair. These were intended for study purposes and for students to use books obtained from the library. The carrels were available for students up to 11 P.M., and I stayed there each day from the end of classes until closing. Weekends, I kept the same schedule. Every hour or so, I would put my head on the desk and take a five-minute nap. These were the high points of my evenings. It could have been worse. Raskolnikov had to deal with the Russian winters.

My routine was so regular that acquaintances knew they could find me there and would pay unannounced visits. I had made no friends in the school, and other habitués of the carrels, many of them antisocial misfits, resented my visitors, especially the attractive ones. Their shushes would echo down the line of carrels when I had a visitor.

Between my academic agonies, I was still searching for my Dulcinea. I thought I had found her a few times—once for sure—but they all had the good sense to realize basement life in the reading carrels at the law school did not offer much of a promising future.

I survived the studies and the daydreams, in fact, finishing the course of studies in two-and-a-half years rather than the usual three. I had a diploma and had passed the bar (entailing yet another bout of wrestling with my demons of the textbooks). I then served a year in a different kind of hell.

My father's office at 66 Court Street was small, but it had two windows. The street was named after the fact that its four high-rise buildings housed virtually all of Brooklyn's lawyers or at least those who did not work out of storefront offices. The building was purchased by a Christian Scientist at a giveaway price during the Great Depression and was passed on to his daughters, who practiced the same faith. They maintained a Christian Science reading room on the premises, and it was probably the closest the building's lawyer-occupants ever got to God or whatever deity that religion embraced.

The contents of the office were an ancient desk behind which was a wooden swivel chair, two battered wooden chairs in front of the desk, an easy chair that was covered in brown plastic and a brown metal file cabinet. On one wall, the only decoration in the room, were two framed certificates. One certificate attested to the fact that my father had been admitted to the bar and the other that he had graduated with a law degree from the University of St. Lawrence, a more grandiose name for Brooklyn Law School. The office was on the tenth floor, and in the summer, the windows were opened so that the furniture became covered with a thin film of oily grime: a blessing bestowed by the industrial heart of Brooklyn that the open windows faced. Sometimes, on very hot days, my father would turn on a fan he brought from home, but care had to be taken to weigh down the loose papers on the desk.

My father shared secretarial services with another lawyer in the suite. The secretary was the other lawyer's wife, so I suppose my father got the short end of the deal. In another sense, after seeing her and listening to her, he may have got the best of the deal since she was not *his* wife.

There were three other lawyers in the suite: the suite's landlord, Cohen (the lawyers always addressed each other by their second names) who had some sort of quasi-public position, white hair and his own secretary. He always seemed to be racing in or out of the office. Goldstein, the titled owner of the secretary my father shared, and Rosen, a young lawyer shaped like a soft, over-ripe pear, who had a desk in the open area where the two secretaries sat and who constantly talked about the enormous personal injury cases he had just settled, but who, as I recall, still lived with his mother and somehow, at least when I was there, never made the leap from having his office consist of a desk among the secretaries to his own room.

I came here to work for my father until I got a job. He sat behind the desk, and I sat on the other side. If I received a call, my father would answer and then hand the old Bakelite phone across the desk. While I spoke, he sat, waiting for the phone to be returned to its usual spot.

I would accompany my father to the various municipal offices and courts to file papers. When we met people he knew, he would introduce me, and he seemed proud of me.

These were the days before Xerox machines. If copies were needed, I would take them down the block to a blueprint company and wait in line with the other lawyers to have copies printed. These were also the days of carbon paper, and Mrs. Goldstein was not a great secretary. If she made a small mistake, it could be remedied by an eraser and the word retyped. If the entire document had to be retyped, it would come back, only this time retyped with different mistakes. Then the next retype would have its share of errors, on and on, so that often, one document of modest length could take up a morning's time to be produced.

I used to go with my father when he would have to do a deposition. One day, he seemed to flounder and asked me to take over the questioning. Somehow, I got through it. This was, I suppose, the beginning of his deterioration. Sometimes, it happens in such a seamless way that you look back and ask yourself how did I get from there to here, and sometimes, you are able to find a precise moment in time when things begin to go wrong. My father continued his law practice for several years, but it was never the same. He was hesitant, unsure of himself, depressed and often angry. He was hanging on by just a thread.

All during this time, I would accompany my father to the local Democratic political club near the Williamsburg Bridge. We had, by now, moved to Sheepshead Bay and turned the Manhattan Avenue apartment over to my brother and his new wife. My father kept up the pretense that we lived there so that he could continue his membership in the political organization. Since our new apartment was at the other end of Brooklyn, on Monday nights, we would go to my brother's for dinner, then to the club and finally take a train across Brooklyn to our own home.

20

A FEDERAL JOB

John F. Kennedy had been elected president, and this meant an entire personnel change in the administration of the government down to the local levels. The United States Attorneys and their non-civil service staffs that prosecute federal crimes and represent the government in civil cases would now change.

My father pressed the local Democratic leader to submit my name for a job, and after some interviews, and an FBI investigation, I got one.

My suspicion was that the political hacks did not want the job because it required actually working. There were higher paying, no-show and paper-shuffling jobs that were more desirable. Additionally, the jobs in the U.S. Attorney's offices were usually filled by younger lawyers willing to work the long hours required for trial preparation.

In 1961, I was sworn in by the court clerk and given a fold-over leather ID, the top half stamped "U.S. Department of Justice." The bottom half contained my photograph together with an authentication of my position signed by a Washington official and stamped with the raised seal of the United States Department of Justice.

The Eastern District of New York was different from most other U.S. Attorney's offices. For one thing, it was bigger since its domain was larger in population and size than others, particularly so in population. It had jurisdiction over Brooklyn, Queens, Staten Island, Nassau and Suffolk counties and included New York's two major airports and all its commercial piers.

It was different in another way. It allowed the various assistant U.S. attorneys almost complete autonomy and allowed them to sink or swim on their own with very little, it seemed to me, oversight. Most of the other offices would start the lawyers modestly, and as they proved capable, they would move up the pecking order to the more difficult cases.

After I was sworn in, just before I was to be shown to my new office, several of the lawyers were walking down the hall and told me that I could see my office later. They were on the way to watch "training films" that were about to be shown in the grand jury room and asked me to come along. I went with them. The "training films" were actually movies seized by federal agents because they had been shipped across state lines and were, in fact, simply pornographic movies. The lawyers acted like I suppose young men usually do at a smoker, although I had never been to such an event. This being my first day, I felt uneasy. I had always thought that sex was a private thing and give or take a ribald joke, was not something that was a community enterprise. After it was over, I left quickly and went back to the clerk's office to pick up where I left off. I was escorted to my office. My *own* office!

It was a large room with a large government-issue desk, four or five metal chairs, a sink, a ceiling fan and two windows overlooking a courtyard.

The chair behind the desk was metal, and in the middle of the front aluminum rim around the seat, there was a perfectly round hole about the width of a pencil. The clerk who accompanied me told me that this was a bullet hole made in the course of a bank robbery and that when Robert Kennedy, the attorney general came, he would want to use this chair and might take over the entire room during his visit. She explained that when Kennedy was counsel to a Senate committee and he came to Brooklyn, he liked to use the chair because of the tale attached to it. He enjoyed pointing out the nearness of that bullet to that organ most prized by many men. As it happened, he did, in fact, later visit and told me its history, and I pretended to be surprised. Happily, he did not usurp its usage on a more permanent basis.

The clerk left me in the room and as I pondered my new empire, returned in a few minutes with a small, young black woman with a very large smile who she introduced as my new secretary. I had not previously given thought to the question of a secretary. I had arrived! My own office and my own secretary! She and I hit it off immediately. She was full of energy and had lots of experience having worked both in New York and in Washington and saved me from making mistakes both minor and serious. She told me I could go home and start in a few days. I suggested we get going immediately. Ten minutes later, she appeared carrying a pile of cases high enough to obscure her face. She dumped them on my desk with the proclamation, "Your cases."

She suggested I start with a narcotics case. She told me all the lawyers love these cases. All you have to do is show the narcotics to the jury, and they convict. Everybody hates drug dealers. I learned that when you hear a prosecutor has a record of thirty-five wins and no losses, you can bet your life that these were drug cases.

I saw one file that seemed older than all the rest and had the name of several different prosecutors on it. I asked her about it, and she told me it was a weak and complicated tax-evasion case and was shuffled around from lawyer to lawyer, each one putting it aside until a new lawyer came into the office. I was the last in the line of names of prosecutors on the jacket. I believed that the unspoken design was to let the case age, and then, when the new administration came in, they would drop it claiming it presented prosecutorial problems. I told her that was the one I wanted to try. It was *United States of America* v. *Ahmed Enayati.*

When I read the file, I believed he was guilty, perhaps even probably so, but the case would take a long time to prepare since it involved, at its core, a series of transactions between New York and Casablanca.

In the meantime, I would try a narcotics case while the treasury agents would be doing the preparation for Enayati, making sure that the evidence and witnesses were still available.

21

THE FLYING PITCHER

Anthony Romano was a tough piece of work, dark and brooding, six foot, 210-pounds of hulking anger. He had a narcotics record going back ten years and was reputed to be "...a top lieutenant in the international narcotics syndicate."

Two years earlier, his codefendant, Francis Whelan, had just been convicted and was being led down the corridor to a cell. The courthouse was in an old Sanford White building and at its center was a winding open staircase running from ground floor to the roof. As Whelan was being led away, he broke free of the marshals and committed suicide by leaping over the railing, falling ten floors to the lobby.

Many years later, one Sunday night when I was with then Mayor Giuliani, we were at a new Times Square hotel along with some other people to watch *The Sopranos*. The suite we were headed for was on the top floor and adjacent to a railing overlooking a spiral, open area rising many floors from the lobby to the top floor. I noticed, however, that from the top of the railing to our floor's ceiling there was wire fencing. One of the mayor's detectives explained to me that this was because not long before, a person had jumped over the railing and committed suicide. All of this should suggest that this particular architectural device should be used with extreme prudence by builders.

At any rate, Whelan was not in the forefront of my thinking, and of course, I had nothing to do with that episode that had occurred earlier. But apparently, Mister Romano did not appreciate this.

Narcotics Agent James Attie was my first witness. Attie looked like someone central casting would send if you asked for a murderer. He used his fearsome appearance to insinuate himself into narcotic gangs. Back in the real world, he was a gentle soul who had a graduate degree in social sciences. I thought he and my brother would hit it off. I introduced them, and he soon became one of the regulars at all-night sessions in the lobby of the Hotel Forrest.

Attie just finished testifying that he posed as a dope buyer from Chicago and had bought one kilo of heroin—a little more than two pounds—from Romano and another peddler for $11,700—worth, at that time, approximately $100,000 on the illicit market.

Romano jumped from his chair, pointed at me and shouted, "You're not going to murder me the way Frankie was. You're not going to railroad me."

The headlines of the next day's newspapers spelled it out. "Dope Trial Jury at Ringside as Ex-Con Runs Wild in Court." "Suspect Has Nothing To Lose But His Chains." "Berserk, He Gives Table a Jerk, Then Pitches Pitcher at Judge."

A marshal tried to push Romano back into his chair, but he knocked the marshal to the ground. Then he threw over the heavy oak counsel table and hurled a heavy water pitcher at me. I ducked. It sailed past me narrowly missing the elderly presiding judge, Walter Bruchhausen, and smashed through a large courtroom window.

Five marshals wrestled Romano to the rail that separates the well of the courtroom from the spectator section, bending him backward, shackling his hands and feet. As reported in the press "...the jury of eight men and four women remained frozen."

I suggested to the judge that an adjournment be called.

The next day, the U.S. Attorney called me into his office. There were a group of smiling lawyers with him. The court reporter had had a tape recorder going to assist him, in case he missed anything when he transcribed the minutes.

The recording began conventionally with the witness giving his testimony. Then suddenly, pandemonium. Shouting, screaming, thuds of things hitting other things, glass shattering, cursing and then my voice, rather calm, "Judge, I think we ought to adjourn." Everybody was laughing; I was cool and now one of the gang.

A mistrial was called, and the case was assigned to a tough, no-nonsense judge, Joseph Zavatt for retrial.

Romano had gone on a hunger strike. I was later told that when he could no longer hold out and asked for food, the marshals ordered up a large Italian meal. As they knew he would, by gorging himself after starving, he became very ill. I guess this was the marshals' payback for hurting one of their own.

Romano refused to attend the second trial. Judge Zavatt ordered him chained to a wheelchair and rolled into court. If he did not hire a lawyer, the judge said one would be assigned to him and sit next to him even if the two of them would never speak with one another. It was clear Romano would have his day in court whether he liked it or not, and justice would be done. He was, of course, convicted and was to be a guest of the Federal Bureau of Prisons until old age.

As a result of this case, I received offers for employment from criminal-defense firms. I turned them down. I was having too good of a time.

22

THE STONE KILLER

Shortly after the Romano case, the U.S. Attorney called me into his office and asked me, "Are you rested?"

"Sure."

"I have another case I would like you to try."

"Great."

"It's a narcotics case."

"Oh no. There are lots of people here who love these cases, and they haven't had anything thrown at them. Why me?"

"This is special. The request came from …" and he motioned upward with his thumb. He meant by this gesture not somebody on the floor above, but rather the request came from Justice in Washington.

He tossed a set of photographs across the desk to me. They were from a police crime scene, flatly lit, in black and white and in their artless starkness made the scene somehow even more awful and real.

The photo was of a man dead on the floor of a bar that looked like a stopover on the road to hell. White tile floors, a long wooden bar, some half-filled glasses, a dirty mirror behind the bar, a shelf lined with bottles of cheap liquor: a mean place where overworked men go to at the end of the day to forget.

On the floor, a man lay, a pool of dark blood next to his right ear, a wooden crutch beside his body next to his outstretched right hand. In the background were shoes on the feet of other men, probably homicide detectives going indifferently about their grim business.

"So what has this got to do with us?"

He leaned forward and told me the story.

"William Kearney is a stone killer. One evening, he was in Lemay's Bar in Brooklyn, talking to Michael Benning." He motioned with his hand at the dead man in the photo. "They had an argument, Kearney goes home to his apartment, gets a gun and comes back. Benning is still sitting at the bar leaning on his crutch.

"Kearney walks up to him, doesn't say a word and puts a gun in Benning's ear, blows his brains out in front of four witnesses. Kearney must have thought that in that neighborhood, nobody would say they saw anything even *if* they hung around long enough for the cops. Well, the cops come, and the witnesses are still there, and they give a positive ID on Kearney. They go to his apartment and find him fast asleep. They cuff him and find the murder gun in a closet together with seven pounds of dope."

"So what's the problem?"

"Listen, you'll hear. He comes up for trial before Sobel in state court in August on first-degree murder and the narcotic charge. He is found guilty of manslaughter and gets ten to thirty in Sing Sing. Now Sobel has to deal with the state dope charge.

"Kearney's lawyer makes a motion to suppress based on the fact that there was no search warrant when the dope was discovered. Sobel offers him a deal. If he pleads guilty on the dope charge, he will give him concurrent sentences so he will just have to deal with the ten to thirty, and he doesn't have to worry about our prosecution on the same grounds, but his guilty plea would affect any time off parole possibilities.

"Kearney's a gambler, and his lawyer believes under state law, his motion to suppress has a good chance of success and guesses we would probably do nothing, anyway. Sobel grants his motion."

"He's still away for ten to thirty."

"This kind of guy could do that standing on his head, and with good time off, he will be out in eight, maybe even six years."

"But if he is convicted under federal law," I said, "it only kicks in after the maximum state time is served. He cannot get parole and must serve the full thirty years before he even begins the federal sentence."

"You got it. Now you want to see why we should prosecute, and no one wants us to more than Sobel."

We began the trial, and Kearney's lawyer made the same motion. Detective Thomas Rice of Brooklyn South Homicide testified after learning Kearney's identity as the killer, he proceeded to his basement apartment. He and another detective were let in unannounced by the landlord. They found the defendant asleep on a sofa, awakened him, handcuffed him and placed him under arrest. They asked him for the weapon and "... receiving an unresponsive answer," searched the room. They found a clothes closet with sliding doors. In the corner of the closet, they found a brown paper bag within which was a plastic bag containing a white powder—the narcotics.

On the same evidence that the state court judge heard, the federal district court judge found the search was not illegal since the federal law is less restrictive than New York State law in questions of search and seizure. Kearney was convicted. As he was led handcuffed out of the courtroom, he turned to me and pointed his right forefinger, flexing his thumb up and down, making the universal motion of children playing cops and robbers, or cowboys and Indians, when they shoot at one another.

Kearney appealed. The United States Court of Appeals affirmed the conviction and noted, "While the search and seizure here at issue were conducted by state officials, the admissibility of the seized items in a federal trial is to be judged as if the conduct were that of a federal officer."

Kearney should have taken Judge Sobel's deal.

23

FUNNY MONEY

The front-page headline of the *Daily News* was "Bag $2 Million in Phony Tens, Feds, Cops, Raid Brooklyn House." The rest of the page was taken up by a photograph of the director of the New York Office of the Secret Service and a high police official posing next to a very glum Joseph Maggio, surrounded by suitcases of ten-dollar bills. Some of the newspapers had photographs of me next to the money. There was more to the story than that.

Counterfeiting is far from being a victimless crime. Of course, the recipient, usually a merchant, is stuck with a worthless piece of paper that the Secret Service take from him in exchange for another worthless piece of paper—a receipt. However, its ramifications are far reaching.

The Germans in World War II used concentration-camp inmates who were engravers to duplicate British pound notes in an unsuccessful effort to destabilize the British economy. It is rumored that the CIA did the same thing with South American countries whose governments it wanted to overthrow. History has shown that most revolutions are economically driven. The sequence of events for revolutionists is: create economic chaos, confidence in the government erodes followed by political unrest and ultimately anarchy, and then the governments collapses.

The Maggio raid took place on February 9. Since the prior October, bogus tens had shown up along the entire East Coast and as far west as California. For months, New York merchants were fooled to the tune of $4,000 to $5,000 a week. The Secret Service had issued public warnings about counterfeit bills. Authorities indicated that other major cities had been flooded with these bills. Five separate plates had been used with the designation of the Philadelphia, Boston, Richmond, Atlanta and San Francisco Federal Reserve banks.

Counterfeiters celebrate Christmas more than neighborhood priests. When they have a large sum of queer money that they want to dispose of, they try to do it around Christmas when retailers are busy and money changes hands frequently.

It all started late one evening. Because that particular evening I was on call to authorize arrests, I received one from the Secret Service. The Secret Service had been watching a man for three months who they suspected of running a warehouse for funny money and believed they now had to act immediately because the money was about to be moved. It was in a suitcase in the basement of a home in the Bensonhurst section of Brooklyn. They wanted to search the premises, but the legal foundation for doing this—obtaining a search warrant from a judge—without revealing the identity of an informant, was tenuous. At any rate, a decision was made to seize the money immediately regardless of the fact that it probably would be suppressed as evidence, thereby effectively making the case—lacking the principal item of evidence—impossible to prosecute. To the Secret Service, the major gains would be that millions of dollars of funny money would have been taken off the street, and it was hoped, the counterfeiters would realize the sheriff was not far behind them, and they would close up shop.

I thought it was a good opportunity to observe law enforcement in action. The newspapers, rather grandiosely (and falsely), later explained my presence as saying I "…headed the raid."

When we arrived at a pedestrian row house in Brooklyn, the lights seemed to be turned off. The agents, accompanied by city police, entered the ground-floor apartment. Maggio, a babysitter and an infant were there. Maggio's wife was away at work. The apartment was neat and clean with a new TV playing in the darkened living room.

Maggio worked days at a dirt-under-his-fingernails job as a mechanic/serviceman. Growing up in my neighborhood, I had met lots of men like him. For them, it was always a dark night in a cold year. I could see him after work at a bar, and the guy next to him telling him he has a cousin who has to store something. No risk, just keep it in your basement until it is picked up, and there's five hundred in it for you, and all Maggio's thinking about is the new TV and money left over to take his wife out for dinner.

We went down to a basement bin secured by a large padlock. One of the city detectives took out a lock-picking kit and opened the lock. It was done just the way it's shown in the movies—with little surgical-like instruments poking around in the keyhole of the lock. According to the papers, "…hidden under a pile of empty boxes and other debris, agents found two large airline-type wardrobe suitcases, a valise and two cardboard cartons—all crammed with counterfeit tens in bundles of thousands."

Albert Whitaker, in charge of the New York office of the Secret Service, later told the press "…it [this seizure] will stand as the biggest in the country."

Ironically, one of the cartons wore a label that indicated it originally held a statue of "The scales of justice in white Carrara marble." Another was sheathed in Christmas wrapping.

Shortly thereafter, Maggio, described as "swarthy and stocky," remained silent, downcast. He identified himself as a mechanic/serviceman for a "utility firm outside of New York." His only prior police record had been for disorderly conduct.

His home was used as a drop for the bogus money, which was sold for $200 to $300 a thousand in face value. It turned out that Maggio was aware that he was being watched and made no effort to pass any of the money himself. Maggio, a Navy veteran, basically told us not much beyond his name, rank and serial number. We verified his name, address and occupation before his arraignment.

There was a line of cars going back to New York with the suspect and the money, and since I came in my own car, I followed them. I was able to do something I always wanted to do; I drove to New York at 90 miles per hour on the Belt Parkway and hoped a highway patrolman would stop me, and I, as in the movies, would waive him away showing him my credentials. Just my luck, I was not stopped once. Where is a cop when you need him?

Back at Secret Service headquarters, Maggio was dumb enough to pose with authorities next to the money in photographs that were shown on TV and in newspapers around the country. I was glad his child was still an infant and with any luck, would never see them.

The end of the tale was that the counterfeit money was suppressed under the Illegal Search and Seizure Doctrine, and Maggio walked off a free man, but merchants' confidence in the U.S. currency was maintained.

I was not particularly sorry about the outcome.

24

JAIL VIA PERFUME

I am color blind. Some people think that this means I do not see colors. On the contrary, I see colors and respond to them quite well, but I see them differently. Sometimes, I am virtually overwhelmed or deeply moved by the colors in a painting or in a landscape although I may not be able to distinguish red apples in a green tree or tell certain shades of gray from shades of green.

Similarly, I have a sinus condition—what Jew does not, at least until he leaves his mother's home. Although my nose may often be stuffed, my sense of smell is very acute.

One of the things we prosecutors did was to assist, on occasion, federal law enforcement in their investigations. We would advise them what sort of evidence was necessary for a conviction and lawful methods to obtain it. To assist in investigations, we could also force people to give evidence and supply information by way of grand-jury subpoenas.

Banks are insured by the Federal Deposit Insurance Corporation (FDIC). When you go into a bank, you will see a small plaque that announces this fact. The point is, if you defraud a bank, you have probably violated federal law.

I was assisting some FBI agents in an ongoing probe of phony Federal Housing Administration home-improvement loans. If you get away with doing this, you have, in effect, robbed a bank without a mask or a gun. But, since the bank is insured by a government agency, you have, at the end of the road, stolen from the government. That is where I came in.

In the course of an investigation, I interviewed Mrs. Selina Boston. Her perfume was distinctive, nearly overpowering. To put her at ease, I made small talk and in the process, told her I admired her perfume and asked her about it. She told me it was an expensive French import.

Some time after that, I was looking through some FHA loan applications at a branch of the Manufacturers Trust Company in an effort to work with the bank to tighten up its application process. While flipping through the applications, there it was again. The same overpowering smell, only the name at the bottom of the application was "Mrs. Rita Fane" together with a home address different from that of Mrs. Boston.

I queried the bank officer about the loan, and he told me that actually Mrs. Fane was due in an hour to pick up her check. I waited at the bank to meet her, and sure enough, it was the woman I knew as Mrs. Boston who came in to pick up the check. She was placed under arrest.

The next day's newspaper contained an article with the heading, "Perfume Traps Her" and under that "Home Loan, Sweet Home Loan Rejected."

There were lots of jokes about this in the office, as well as by news commentators, not to mention the girls who asked me what I thought of their perfume.

25

ME AND THE MAFIA

One day, I was told that I was going to receive a promotion. I was going to be assigned to a small group devoted to OCD (Organized Crime Drive). I did not care for this since I felt it was not lawyer's work. It went round and round, and the work product would seldom see the inside of a courtroom. It seemed to me to basically be a centralized intelligence-gathering endeavor involving all the many federal law-enforcement agencies and the NYPD. I read many handwritten transcriptions of conversations the NYPD supplied that they obtained from confidential informants "X" or "Y." These were, in fact, transcripts of illegal wiretaps, and "X" and "Y" were code words not for people, but for wiretaps.

This was all so many years ago, and I suppose this no longer happens, and if it does still occur, it is more subtle and private. None of these sorts of things would have even been remotely admissible in court. There were also the charts with lines drawn between names to show the genealogical relationships between individuals and families that were immediately covered up if a visitor entered the room.

There was also the gentle bigotry of the time. An FBI agent asked me if it was OK to show something to Joe Costa, the chief of the criminal division. The implication was that since he was Italian, he could not be trusted with organized-crime information. I pretended I did not understand the import of the question and do not know if he was ever shown the material.

I rapidly came to the conclusion that—Appalachia notwithstanding—there was really no such thing as organized crime, at least the way it was portrayed on *The Untouchables*. I did not believe that these people were really geniuses who, under different circumstances, could have been captains of industry, successful honest businessmen or community leaders. They were, in fact, just thugs in fancy suits who could never be successful in honest endeavors and had to resort to violence because they could not succeed any other way. Sure, they knew each other and in some cases, were related to each other and went through ridiculous initiation rituals similar to the Masons. It was disgusting to observe them coming in to inform on a lifelong friend or close relative in order to save their own skin.

Bobby Kennedy came to our office, and when it came to my turn to speak, I told him my opinion on organized crime and the Mafia. The next day, I was out of OCD. I was happy.

26

ENAYATI AT LAST

I was now in the office almost three years, and still the Enayati case, the loser that no one wanted to try, rested on a table in my office. Cases are not like wine. They do not get better with age. In fact, the reverse is true. I decided I must go to bat with it. It was now or never.

The case was, at core center, a criminal income-tax evasion case. The basis of the case was that Enayati, an American citizen, made a great deal of money selling heating equipment to a company in Casablanca and never reported the money he made on his American income-tax return.

Enayati's defense was that he had merely devised a scheme to get his own money out of Casablanca, which had currency restrictions and did not allow money to leave the country.

He claimed he opened a dummy corporation in New York and basically sold and shipped virtually empty cartons to himself in Casablanca labeled as "Heating Equipment." He then paid the New

York company (himself) for the shipment, and the money was sent as payment to the U.S. dummy corporation. The end result was that it was his own money that was paid him by his own Casablanca company. He may have violated the laws in Casablanca, but, since it was his own money, no tax was owed in the U.S.

The trial started, and the government paid for Colonel Noir, the now-retired senior police official who investigated the matter, to come to America to testify.

The good part about being the government's lawyer is that the government has no problem spending vast sums of money to prosecute a case.

The colonel arrived. His English was less than perfect, but still understandable. The problem was that no one had informed me he was absolutely blind, and this was a case that relied heavily on documentary evidence.

I thought at the very least, I could acclimate him to the geography of the courtroom and made many dry runs in the empty courtroom with him, all to no avail. During the trial, he had to be led to the witness box, and still, he stumbled over the furniture.

The jury came back with a hung verdict. The judge, Zavatt, was fulsome in his praise for me and hated Enayati.

When I questioned one of the jurors, she said she did not believe the government witnesses because nobody needed heating equipment in Casablanca. Go figure.

It was decided to retry the case. I hated retrials. It was like having to make up with an old girlfriend after you finally had gotten rid of her.

I tried to make up for all the loopholes for the first trial when it came up for retrial. This time Enayati hired David Price, at the time, one of the deans of criminal bar. Also, they now knew the government's entire case, and of course, the colonel was still blind.

Enayati was acquitted, and the judge, Jacob Mishler, soon to be chief judge, was quite kind in his remarks on the record to the jury.

"I might tell you that Mister Felder ... presented it [the case] as well as any case I have seen [a prosecutor] present to a jury. [Turning to Mister Price who had just arrived] I said that Mister Felder was trying the case against one of the ablest defense counsel in this area, and I thought that Mister Felder did beautifully in trying his case for the government, and I might tell you, although I did not tell him, that I thought your summation, Mister Felder, was one of the best I heard."

* * *

Fate does not hand out erasers. Whether it involves portentous decisions by parliaments or by a person sitting alone in front of a tattoo artist, decisions are made that will forever change everything that follows. Human beings seem to possess a genetic predisposition to avoid decisions.

Britain put off painful decisions regarding their empire and kicked the can down the road for two hundred years, but eventually ended up without an empire. People, with their finite, limited span of life do not enjoy such luxury. Sometimes when offered two choices, we try to do both. "I will marry this one, but continue an affair with that one." Whether it is about people or empires, it never works out.

I had a decision to make. On the one hand—the iconic beginning phrase of every self-wrestling decision-making process—I had a job, a respected job that included an intimidating leather ID that said in stamped gold letters, *United States Department of Justice*, a salary, modest but seductive in its constancy and growth. But, no matter what I achieved in salary, in the future it would only provide for a small home located in an area in which I would not live by choice and a carefully prescribed lifestyle that would not allow for the elegance of my dreams. In short, I would not be living in the life of a Fred Astaire movie, but rather, the logical progression of my life would be better than that I enjoyed growing up, in the hope that my children or my children's children would, building upon my life, have better ones. In short, I would be but a way station in an evolutionary socioeconomic journey. This sort of existence seemed not much better than a future of bringing the wash home from the Laundromat and swapping lies with my neighbors sitting on the stoops of tenements.

My briefcase was filled with notes to myself containing columns labeled *Pro* and *Con*. I finally made the decision, but now it was a question of *When*, which was another way of putting off carrying it through.

I began putting my files in order, inserting a memo in each explaining the history of the case, what was done, what needed to be done, what I thought of the credibility of the prospective witnesses, the strengths and weaknesses of the case and the general strategy to be used in the ultimate trial. The object was to give my successor the music of the case that was not evident from the lyrics of the FBI reports.

I still did not turn in my resignation. I was still beset by fears. I was newly married with present and prospective obligations, no money, no family money, no clients and a horizon bleak and unpromising. The only experience I had was in federal criminal cases and would now be relegated to only representing criminals who I would have been only too happy to put in jail, rather than getting out of jail.

Paralyzed by fear and indecision, I still could not bring myself to tender my resignation. I could not have envisioned that the decision would soon be made for me by a songwriter and an Israeli heartthrob.

Most people are like Mister Palomar who, stirred by the birds' singing, describes his life as a series of missed opportunities. That was not going to be me, but perhaps it was always me, since only looking through the prism of time can you tell if choosing one opportunity over another that becomes seemingly lost was better or worse than the moment's choice. My guess is that mine were lost about 50 percent of the time. Batting .500 is great if baseball is the game, but in the real world, it may simply result in a mediocre existence or one much lower on the Richter scale of life or worst of all, simply being ordinary. I was trembling on that precipice.

Trapped, sitting behind a government-issue desk in a government-issue chair, reviewing government-spawned papers was, to me, a one-way ticket on a treadmill to oblivion. But there I sat, staring at another of life's abysses, regretting yesterday's might-have-beens and dreaming of tomorrows if-onlys and making eleven thousand dollars a year.

I waited and waited for my merry-go-round to take me to within snatching distance of the ersatz ring of gold while doing the sovereign's work and taking the king's shilling until opportunity entered my life in the form of the angry ring of a telephone that tore me from my sleep in the early morning hours, eventually transporting me to—at the time—the pantheon of the divorce gods: page three of the *Daily News* and a headline that read "Best Man Kisses, & Tells" together with a photograph of me looking impossibly young and photographs of an unhappy husband and wife (story continued on page ten) with the heading, "Waiter Serves Court Hot Dish of Infidelity."

27

FROM THERE TO HERE

Mortimer Shuman was sixteen years old when he came into my brother's and my (in surrogate fashion) lives. My brother had begun to develop a reputation as a songwriter of both music and lyrics. We had a teenage cousin who lived at the other end of Brooklyn. She had a friend who was known to be a sort of misfit, but who was musically very talented. She wanted my brother to meet him with the thought that perhaps they could work together. Until the end of my brother's life, people both strange and ordinary would come up to him and "My son-daughter-nephew-bookmaker-hairdresser's husband is unbelievable. You just gotta hear his material."

They eventually met and for years were successful collaborators. Many years and many millions of best-selling songs later, Morty moved to France, became an expatriate, acted in some French movies and wrote a hit musical, *Jacques Brel Is Alive and Well and Living in Paris,* ending his days in Europe as a cultural icon of sorts. Although my brother and he had been separated for many years, they died about the same time and although I had not seen Morty for a number of years, ended up giving a eulogy at his memorial service. But I am getting ahead of myself . . .

Morty, at sixteen was full grown, perhaps more than six feet tall. His physique resembled a large sack of potatoes with a belt around its middle. His face was Russian-peasant ordinary with buttonlike dark eyes embedded in the puffy flesh of his face; his voice loud and deep and with resonance that of a much older person; his appetite for food—any food—unending. I remember him being more in the kitchen, gazing into the open refrigerator as a man would a naked supine and willing woman, as much as I remember him working with my brother at the living-room piano.

My grandfather never referred to Morty by any name other than "The Fresser." *Essen* is the Yiddish verb to eat while *Fressen* refers to the feeding habits of an animal, as opposed to that of a human being. But perhaps, my grandfather was annoyed as much by the fact that he and my brother used our living room—my grandfather's bedroom at night—for almost as much time as Morty used the refrigerator in his search for sustenance.

Most indelibilized on my memory is a picture of him sitting at the piano, my brother hovering over him, leaning his left arm on a crutch, his other hand on the piano, sometimes stretching over to press his finger on a particular piano key and then repeatedly pressing it or another key until just the right one was found. Morty would play one phrase or passage over and over again until my brother would signify that it was OK, and then Morty would write it down on lined music paper while my brother picked up a chewed-over pencil and jotted down the line or passage in a notebook that rested on the piano next to his right hand. When the song was completed—sometimes hours later, sometimes it took only a few minutes—Morty played it from beginning to end while my brother softly sang the lyrics. When they were writing on assignment—particularly if

it was for a movie—my brother would sometimes have to do prepa-
ratory work including reading (or pretending that he had read) the
script. On rare occasions, if the movie company insisted, he would
watch the unscored picture, but usually, even for the title songs of
big-budget movies such as Elvis' *Viva Las Vegas,* it was sufficient to
listen to a few-sentence synopsis of the plot during a telephone call
from California. When he scored the music for the movie *Anzio,* he
wrote the theme song, *This World Is Yours,* that was to be sung by the
then-popular Jack Jones, knowing nothing other than it was a war
movie.

As Morty and he became more successful, Morty became increasingly unreliable. Sometimes, he was hours late for a writing session,
and sometimes, he simply did not show up at all, offering telephoned
explanations that became, with time, increasingly more fabulous.
When it would happen, my brother would shrug his shoulders and
say that Morty was just a kid who made too much money too fast,
and then he would change the subject, tossing this problem in the
dustbin of his life's inequities.

* * *

Shana Mayer was an Israeli singer performing at a local nightclub,
Café Sabra, now out of business for many years. Café Sabra, in a collision of a life's memories, was located on the ground floor of an apartment building on West Seventy-second Street in which my brother,
as a tenant, spent his last years.

She was olive-skinned, dark-eyed with jet black hair and had, in
that pre-silicone implant age, a figure that could make women hate
her and be the stuff of pimply adolescents' dirty jokes.

Morty dropped into the club one night, saw Shana, and that thun-
derbolt of emotion that has toppled empires, ruined lives and made
smart people do stupid, irrational and even criminal things, struck
him in one or the other of various parts of his physical or emotional

anatomy. In short, he was smitten, besotted, and the provinces of those parts of his brain that controlled reason and rational thinking capitulated without hardly any resistance. Morty and Shana were soon married.

* * *

In the early morning hours of a chilly January day five months after the wedding, the telephone rang.

"It's me, Morty. Did I wake you?"

"It's all right. I had to get up to answer the phone. What's the matter?" Half-asleep, I was talking on autopilot.

"Nothing's the matter. No. Everything's the matter. It's not working out. It was all a mistake."

"What is a mistake?"

"Shana. Me. The whole thing."

"Did you speak to my brother?"

"I just spoke to him, and he said to call you. You would help."

"Where are you?"

"I'm in a hotel on Columbus Circle. I've checked in, but I can come over."

"Morty, it's three o'clock in the morning. I can meet you after work."

"No. I have to do something or at least, know where I stand. I don't want to wait until tonight. No, I can't wait until tonight."

"OK. Let's meet for breakfast." I jotted down the time and place we would meet.

When I awakened the next morning, I had an incomplete memory of the middle-of-the-night conversation and was not quite sure whether it took place or whether it was all fragments of a dream. I glanced over at the night table and saw my pad with my note reflecting our appointment for a breakfast meeting and rapidly got dressed.

While it was still dark, we met at seven o'clock in a West Side coffee shop and talked for an hour. By the end of the hour, I had my first divorce case. But, there *was* a problem. I was still an employee of the Department of Justice, and as a matter of fact, I had to be at work in an hour. The existence of my daytime job seemed to make no difference to Morty. But back in the real world, I could not take on private clients while at the same time, have the government as a client. I could get away with preparing a will for a friend or even go, without pay, to a real-estate closing for a friend or relative, but this was a divorce case that because of the occupation of the parties, was going to be quite public. I was also sure that Shana and the club owners would want to milk the situation of its maximum publicity value, as well. "White space"—news as opposed to advertisements or column items—is the most important possible placement in a newspaper and is not for sale. I was aware that divorce litigation was a blood sport and things would end up in a very public—perhaps protracted—trial.

On the subway ride to my office, I made up my mind to quit my job that very morning. I had previously decided to strike out on my own and was merely waiting for the proper opportunity now delivered to me by the divorce gods.

As soon as I arrived at the courthouse, I went to the office of the United States Attorney and asked his secretary, Edna, to set up an appointment with him for that morning. I told her it was a personal matter.

* * *

The United State's Attorney was and still is a direct presidential appointment while my appointment was one made by the attorney general.

Joseph Hoey, the boss, was a neat package of a fifty-two-year-old man, steel-gray hair, pressed suit, starched white shirt and unblinking blue eyes that honed in on the person to whom he was speaking like a searchlight on a clear night. He was a veteran prosecutor and was rumored to be friendly with the Kennedys.

Once, a lawyer who represented the prospective purchaser of a manufacturing plant, its equipment and the goodwill of a business that the government was about to close down came into see me about allowing it to stay open. If the business was permitted to remain in operation, it would result in a financial windfall for the buyer. In the course of a ten-minute meeting, he mentioned his closeness with both the Kennedys and the fact that the attorney general had suggested he come in to chat with me, the prosecutor handling the case, and "Bobby" was sure that it could all be worked out. I told him to wait a moment because I had to take care of something down the hall.

I went to Hoey and explained the situation. He said, "Make a memo of the conversation."

"Then what?"

He paused a moment, looked at me and said, "F___ 'em."

He was that kind of a person.

* * *

Around noon, Hoey's secretary called and told me it was a good time to come in to see him since an appointment had just canceled and he had some free time.

When I went into his office, after we exchanged pleasantries, I told him my cases were all in great shape and basically, were stabilized, and I had prepared extensive memos of what had to be done on each individual case in the immediate future. By the time I was halfway through explaining this, he realized that I was about to tell him that I was leaving. He could not dissuade me, and I was no longer in the employ of Uncle Sam.

To my surprise, I discovered that I was now to receive a substantial sum of money from the government. At that time, attorneys who did not take vacations or worked holidays or weekends were entitled to compensatory time. This meant that they had the right to take off from work at a later time to make up for the time they worked on weekends, holidays or during their normal vacation period. In the three years I served, I had hardly ever taken a vacation and usually worked weekends. Upon resigning, I learned that the compensatory time I had accumulated and to which I was entitled, now as a former employee, logically, could not be credited to me in kind. Instead, I would receive a check in payment for my efforts. I, therefore, received a check for three-month's pay, which was helpful in my establishment of a legal practice. It is my understanding that since the time I received my final check, the government ended this practice, and the new rule, quite sensibly, is that unused compensatory time remaining at the end of employment is forever lost.

My next job was to find an office.

It is not particularly difficult to find an office to open a legal practice in any of America's large cities. The starting point is answering an ad in a "legal" newspaper, this is a periodical specifically targeted to lawyers. These daily papers are distributed by subscription to law offices, listing court calendars, reporting legal decisions and most importantly, containing personal advertisements for legal employment opportunities, services for lawyers and available office space for rent. I quickly found an acceptable office at 342 Madison Avenue. This building, ironically, was owned at the time by the same Christian Science people who owned the building in which my father had his office and from which I had practiced in Brooklyn.

*　*　*

Joseph Tiefenbrun was a barrel of a man with a shaved head and a lisp. He had an extensive commercial practice and seemed to be an excellent businessman as well as an accomplished generalist at the law. He had a large corner office, and then there were a number

of smaller offices, each about nine feet by seven, each with a single
window, all situated in a long row down the hall from his own room.
Outside the offices was a receptionist who sat behind a glass window. I found Tiefenbrun quite pleasant and helpful to me. When he
sustained a heart attack, as a matter of professional courtesy, I called
his adversaries to obtain adjournments of his matters for him and
explained his medical problem. I was shocked that more than a few
of them said to me, "Anybody else, I would not hesitate to consent.
But not him." Go figure.

Tiefenbrun rented out the smaller offices and included in their
rent was the privilege of having their phones answered by the receptionist. The monies he received from the tenants enabled him to
maintain his personal office cost free. This was not an uncommon
practice, then or now, in legal offices. Any time a client gets out of the
elevator and there is a large office with either no names on the door
or only a sign with the legend "Law Offices," he or she can bet that
it is not really a law firm, but rather a group of individual lawyers
who are tenants of space and included in the price is a receptionist to
answer their telephone. Conference rooms are booked as if they were
hotel rooms, and the lawyers who interview or meet with clients in
the conference rooms are billed by the hour for their use. Tiefenbrun, however, had no conference rooms since he wanted to maximize
the return on his investment.

In order to inspire confidence in prospective clients, I would meet
them at night when I was alone in the office, and I pretended that we
had to have an evening meeting because I had been busy in court all
day. I would keep the doors to all the small offices closed. While the
client was sitting in my office, I walked down the hall giving imaginary instructions to imaginary people sitting behind closed doors. "I
will be with you in a moment" or "Let's get this out tonight" or simply "Don't" or "Let's think about it." If the client was an important
one, I would use Tiefenbrun's office and sit behind his desk, carefully removing beforehand his personal photographs, diplomas, etc.

I sent out announcements in raised thermographic lettering (I could not yet afford engraved ones) to announce the fact that I had resigned from the government and was open for business on Madison Avenue, together with my new telephone number Murray Hill 7-3432.

* * *

Shana began a divorce action against Morty, and it worked its way up the calendar until the trial began before State Supreme Court Justice Emilio Nunez. Nunez was, at the time, the only Puerto Rican serving on the New York Supreme Court bench. He was a tall, handsome man with a perpetual scowl on his face and gave the appearance of a Spanish grandee receiving tribute from his subjects. Shana had hired Harry Lipsig as her attorney. A diminutive man, perhaps five feet in height, Lipsig was a legendary trial lawyer whose specialty was negligence law. He was enormously successful and led an office of perhaps thirty to forty lawyers.

After the case, we got to know each other quite well, and he referred clients to me steadily. At one point, he recommended a female client to me. After the case was over, somebody told me she was probably his girlfriend, over whose affection he was engaged in a tug of war between himself and another well-known lawyer. While I was representing her, I knew none of this.

Lipsig had a large corner office and perched himself on a high-backed plush chair behind a desk that was only slightly smaller than the quarterdeck of the *Queen Mary*. He once confided to me that he had to have sex at least once a day or maybe it was once a week, but in any event, the remark was a conversation killer, and I didn't pursue the subject with him. At some point, he shocked the legal community by adopting, in his eighties, his adult secretary. He practiced until late in life and in his last years, spoke in limericks.

("There once was a young man from Perth, whose wife was about to give birth . . .")

The divorce trial opened with Shana, clearly amply rehearsed (of course, there is nothing wrong in that having occurred as long as the testimony is truthful, and I assumed it was), telling a woeful story that resulted in the judge treating her sympathetically, even protectively, as if she was a child who was forced to explain an unpleasant experience. I felt the case was going poorly.

One night during the case, Morty and I were sitting alone in my little office, and I asked him once again to run through the key events of the marriage. I learned then that there is always "one more thing" that clients either neglect or deliberately will not tell you, and it pays to always ask that one question—even as late as in the midst of a trial. Going through the events of the marriage for the hundredth time, he, for the first time, described several breakups with Shana. Each time, it appeared that when Shana came back home, a waiter at the Café Sabra who had also been the best man at the wedding, would be carrying her bags. Enter on the scene ex-Café Sabra waiter, Henri Reijnek.

I asked Morty, "Is it possible that Henri was having an affair with Shana?" He laughed and said, "It's ridiculous." I suggested then we would have nothing to lose if he let me call Henri and put appropriate questions to him since Morty indicated he was still friendly with him. Morty again repeated "It's ridiculous." Morty told me Henri was now working as a waiter at Thwaites, a restaurant on City Island—an island off the Bronx.

Before he called Henri, I asked Morty to promise he would say exactly what I asked him to say. He agreed.

He called the restaurant and while waiting for Henri to come to the phone, I wrote out for Morty what I wanted him to say: "Henri, I know you had an affair with Shana, but I want you to know your friendship with me is more important than your affair with Shana."

Morty again said that it was ridiculous. I pointed out he promised to do exactly as I asked. Henri got on the phone and after exchanging a few words with Morty, I pointed to what I had written down. Morty duly repeated "Henri, I know you had an affair with Shana, but I want you to know your friendship with me is more important than your affair with Shana, and I hope we are still friends." Henri replied (I could hear him since I was sitting next to Morty), "I'm glad you feel that way, Mort, because my friendship with you is more important than Shana." I told Morty to tell him to get to the office as soon as he was able to get out of work.

At 1 A.M., he appeared in my office and repeated the particulars of his affair with Shana. Morty was visibly shaken, and Henri turned to him and said in a heavy Dutch accent, "Don't worry Mort, she laid there like a corpse." I served Henri immediately with a handwritten subpoena. The next day, I put him on the stand, and he repeated the story. The *Daily News* breathlessly reported,

> "Harry Reijnek, 22, here from Holland three years, confounded Manhattan Supreme Court Justice Emilio Nunez, not to mention Shana, by his free and frank admissions.
>
> " 'One night she stayed in my apartment,' Reijnek said of the shapely, petite Shana, 32. 'This was …' (One month after her marriage to rock 'n' roll composer Mortimer Shuman.)
>
> " 'The second night I stayed with her at the Coliseum House. I slept with her.'
>
> "Reijnek, who lives at 360 City Island Ave., Bronx, and totes a tray at a City Island restaurant, was led into further testimony by Raoul Lionel Felder of 342 Madison Ave., attorney for Shuman.
>
> " 'Did you have sex relations with Mrs. Shuman from Oct. 15, 1963, to Nov. 15, 1963?' Felder asked.

" 'Yes, at her apartment,' the waiter replied.

" 'How many times?'

" 'Three times,' replied the wavy-haired data keeper.

"At one point in the testimony, Justice Nunez interjected: 'You knew she was married?'

"Reijnek replied he did.

" 'You know you are confessing to the commission of a crime, don't you?' the jurist pressed.

"The handsome swain answered quietly: 'I know it now.'"

According to the newspaper, Shana's last observation in the matter was: "She promptly threatened to have the talkative best man deported to Holland."

Shana was suing for $700 weekly alimony. Shana ended up accepting $150 a week. Morty at the time had co-authored songs that eventually would earn millions of dollars.

In those days, divorce was to law as proctology was to medicine. Many lawyers had divorce cases kicking around that could not be settled, but either because of lack of ability or enthusiasm, they were not anxious to try. While I was in the government, I, of course, dealt with many lawyers and had tried many cases. Directly after the story about Morty's case appeared in the newspapers, I started receiving calls from lawyers I had dealt with in my former job. They all followed the same pattern. "I have this old divorce case that has been kicking around, would you be interested in trying it?" In the first year I made $50,000. Life was beautiful.

28

PRESIDENT CARTER

Sclerotic-shelled, half-buried in the wet sand, ancient waters flow through my flaccid, pulsating mollusk membranes.

* * *

As years go, 1977 came and went and was not particularly eventful. Jimmy Carter was sworn in as president, and in August, Elvis Presley died. In retrospect, the country would have been better off if the reverse had happened. Carter turned out to be a crypto anti-Semite, the cause of lines of cars waiting for gas at filling stations, believing he could solve America's energy problems by turning down the White House thermostat and walking around in last year's Christmas gift of a cardigan sweater. Elvis might not have been a great president, but at least, he would have been an interesting one. Imagine an overweight, stoned president? If nothing else, his talks to the nation, even without backup singers, would have been anticipated TV events. HBO could have charged subscribers and the proceeds used to reduce the national debt, not to mention the possibility of breathing life into a moribund music industry.

Recently divorced women in New York of a certain age and social status, if they feel the need to work, usually do one of three things. They believe that to succeed in these three jobs requires no intensive skill or training other than that with which they have been graced by way of genetics or a self-observed unique personal intelligence, taste or insight. They become interior decorators; try to sell stocks to their friends (until they run out of friends or names in their address books); or in similar fashion, become real-estate brokers and try to sell apartments to these same friends. Usually, they run out of friends before they run out of available apartments. This is similar to recent law-school graduates who lack experience, but nevertheless believe that they have a natural gift for writing, negotiation and dealing with clients. My experience has been that it is *precisely* in these three areas that they are (and usually remain) deficient.

Landlords do not like to rent apartments to lawyers and diplomats. Lawyers, they believe, are litigious and cheap (the former occupationally and the latter perhaps, genetically), given to nonpayment of rent based on nonexistent legal precedents that, even if they do not ultimately carry the day in court, delay the payment of rent to the landlords for many months.

Diplomats are another story. There are thousands of these in New York who are attached or assigned to the UN and since they enjoy diplomatic immunity, cannot be sued. If a diplomat, who back in his home country lived in a straw hut in some fetid jungle, defaulted on his rent for a Park Avenue duplex, the landlord's only remedy would be to write an angry and probably unread letter to our State Department. This sequence of events, quite understandably, has caused a reduction in the number of rental apartments landlords make available to UN people. If they want to find a place to live, the only alternative is for their mission to purchase either a condominium or cooperative apartment to be used by their personnel. This option has an added attractiveness in view of the fact that a foreign diplomatic mission is exempt from paying any property or related real-estate taxes. In a most of the time tough New York City housing market, a diplomat's search for an apartment to purchase becomes an alien journey in hostile terrain.

Doris Diamondo, herself the former wife of an Albanian diplomat, was particularly sensitive to their housing dilemma and came up with a simple idea that set her apart from other real-estate brokers and in the process, made her wealthy. She researched and finally produced a map, distributed to all diplomatic missions, listing the locations of the legations and the addresses and descriptions of all buildings that would sell apartments to diplomats. The map also, of course, listed Diamondo's name, telephone number and the fact that she would be glad to assist them in their purchase. Once a building's board made the decision that it would approve a sale to a diplomat, the deal became easy for Diamondo to close since, in the way of public officials everywhere, they were spending other people's money.

Diamondo's life was ruled by the stars, and in her dealings with them, they were despotic. These intimate conversations with the heavens had as little mutuality as that of a Latin American dictator ordering an execution. They were shared with no one and often resulted in unusual, if not odd, life choices, ridiculed by some, bewildering to others. She hired and fired employees, made or postponed sales of apartments, cultivated or ruptured friendships all as might be dictated by the stars and their relatives "the numbers"—combinations of the number of letters in a person's name, birth date, address, mother's maiden name or husband's occupation. Frequently, as a condition for employment, she would insist that a prospective employee change the spelling of his or her name and, in some cases adopt a new name. There would be a direct relationship between how badly the applicant needed the job and their acquiescence to, what more analytically oriented or skeptical people might consider to be, her gentle insanity.

When she explained her decisions by reference to the "numbers," she did so with the casual self-assurance of a Baptist minister dismissing the theory of evolution. At some point along this celestial road to certainty, the "numbers" revealed to her that a peanut farmer from Georgia would be America's next president, and she should do everything in her power to make sure that this, in fact, happened. This meant, in terms of modern American politics, raising large sums of money.

I was an absolute novice in the way politics was (and still is) played in New York. Traveling in this virgin (for me) territory, I learned that basically the process begins and ends with money. More specifically, it is a game of you-raid-my-pocketbook-and-I-raid-yours, the object being to cause money to make the journey from your wallet to the politician's coffers. Modern politics is a rich man's game or at least, that of a poor man or relatively poor man who has friends who are rich or know how to get money from rich people.

Diamondo had previously recommended a client to me. Therefore, according to the rules of the game, this gave her an implied right to ask me to contribute (albeit indirectly) to a cause of her choosing regardless of my personal feeling about the object of my soon-to-be largess. In this case, it was indirectly the improbable political future of a former governor of Georgia whose ambition appeared to far exceed his ability.

She called me one day and in a bubbly sort of way, told me she was hosting a party at her home for Jimmy Carter and was short money for the liquor bill. She was clearly hitting me up for money (a modest amount, thankfully). Carter had little name recognition and had not yet formally announced that he was running for president. He was, in fact, at the bottom of a long list of wannabes. My answer to her, in view of subsequent events, now seems absurd.

"Jimmy Carter? I think I've heard the name before. What is it?"

I don't drink alcohol, but for some reason I vaguely associated the words "Jimmy Carter" with a brand of liquor—*Jack Daniels*. "Why would you want to pay for another brand to be served at the party?" Clearly we were talking about two different things, but this did not seem to bother Doris. She went happily forward on one railroad track and I on another. Finally, I understood what she was talking about, but she either did not care or was indifferent to what I had been talking about, and so, her brook just kept gurgling merrily downstream. But the liquor cost was modest, and as soon as I could wedge a word in, I immediately agreed, cutting off her explanation of the numerological inevitability of Carter taking up residence in the White House. After earning a fair profit from her recommendation of a client, I had as little choice to turn her down as a pregnant eighteen-year-old to refuse a marriage proposal—from the boss' son.

One of New York's secrets is that there are some very wealthy people who are able to rent apartments for much less—sometimes grotesquely so—than the going market rate. During World War II, the state legislature, in order to prevent landlords from exploiting a dwindling supply of available apartments, froze rents. After the war, there was a reason to continue rent control because of the plight of returning veterans who flooded into a city in which there had been absolutely no building of new apartments for four years. In the years following, rent control continued simply because of the practical arithmetic that there were more tenants who vote than landlords who vote.

Doris lived in a prewar, rent-stabilized building on lower Park Avenue that would have passed for just another elegant condominium or cooperative building as were its neighbors. Actually the building, although it was but a rental building in which dwelt tenants who were paying under-market rents, offered more services than other East Side residences—even swanky condominiums— since another provision of the rent-control law compelled the landlord to provide the identical services that existed decades earlier in the particular building. Thus I found myself riding up in an elevator to Doris' apartment with a live elevator operator, at a time when most other buildings, in a spirit of economy, had fired their elevator operators and made the machines self-service.

There were two apartments on each floor. Doris' apartment was large with rooms that seemed to flow into one another in different directions. The room where the party took place was large and square and opened into a smaller room. In this room was a long table set out as a buffet and a smaller table behind which stood a hired-for-the-evening bartender in a tuxedo with frayed and tired lapels who served liquor, half of which I paid for. I was proud to note that I bought only the most expensive brands.

The larger room, as was the style of the day, contained a number of small, round tables with dainty rented wooden chairs painted gold, designed to look as if they were made from bamboo. Small china knickknacks were placed around the room on every available horizontal surface.

Rich people like to have pictures of poor people hanging on their walls, and in random mosaic fashion, Doris' walls were filled with large and small paintings of peasants toiling in the fields or sitting around a humble fireplace doing what peasants do around humble fireplaces or simply waving beer steins and getting drunk in a local tavern.

Having not attended the course on chitchat at my finishing school, I always feel uneasy at parties, and as the party progresses, an empty closet begins to have an unnatural attraction for me. Luckily, the room usually fills up with people to the degree I can fade away in unnoticed fashion—the trick being not to come with a coat thereby allowing me to ooze away.

Jimmy Carter came to the party proceeded by two muscular men with earpieces who appeared to be bored, though it was hard to believe that whatever they were listening to on the earpieces could have been duller than that which they were witnessing. Carter wore bluish-gray trousers and a blue blazer that looked like it came from the best shop in town, but sadly, the town was Plains, Georgia. He wore thick-soled brown shoes, and aside from the sartorial sin of brown shoes with a blue outfit, the shoes looked like they were designed to cross Georgia ditches rather than Doris' threshold. His face was a celebration of banality. His teeth, too large for his mouth, made him look as if he borrowed a set of someone else's dentures; his nose curved and unduly protuberant, somewhat displaced from the centerline of his face, reminded me of the proboscises floating this way and that in *Les Demoiselles d'Avignon*. He could have been another tourist in Times Square, a cheap camera in his hands, looking up at the buildings; a person you would walk past and neither see nor remember.

Carter stood next to Doris in the doorway between the larger room and the smaller one containing the buffet table. I stood to one side holding a glass of wine, smiling, hoping no one would talk to me. I was not disappointed. People walked by Doris and Carter, some smiled at them, some shook hands with him on the way to the food. There was a lot of smiling in the room.

Soon, Doris, standing as proud as a parent beside her son at a bar mitzvah, tapped a glass with a fork, and asked everyone to pay attention. Doris then introduced Carter as he stood beside her in an embarrassed bridegroom pose, hands clasped demurely in front of him. Most of the people in the room were standing, juggling a drink, a plate of food and a cloth napkin. The scene had all the grandeur of the reading of the treasurer's annual report to a ladies knitting society.

Carter's voice, thin, high pitched and whiny, hardly carried over the room past indifferent listeners to those seated in back, talking to each other, paying scarce attention to him.

"First, I want to thank Doris and all of you fine people."

He droned on passionlessly, his delivery: monotone without any rise or fall for emphasis; his accent: B-movie Southern belle—this speech obviously made a hundred times before. It was divided into three parts. The first dealt with the things that were wrong with the country. This fell on particularly nonreceptive ears since most everyone in the room prospered *because* of the things that were wrong with the country. The second movement of his verbal symphony was an explanation of what he would do to fix the first. But since most of the people present did not accept his first premise, and additionally, believed that in the future, the only things he would be in a position to fix were outhouses in Georgia, or perhaps a stray dog, his audience began to delicately nudge their way around him to get at the food on the table behind him and the drinks served at the bar next to it. He did, however, have an attentive audience in the rented bartender with wilted lapels whose attention was in an inverse proportion to his ability to understand English.

Third movement: Carter ended his peroration with the declaration that he would always tell the truth—which elicited as much interest as a lecture on chastity at a nudist's convention—and they (the guests at the party) should go home, wake up their children and call their friends to tell them that they had met Jimmy Carter, the next president.

There was a polite titter from the few people still listening to him since it was their perception that the bragging rights for meeting him should be his, not theirs. He smiled in return, believing that their trace laughter was an acknowledgment of his little joke, that he did not mean that they should actually wake up their children when they arrived home. The telling of their brush with history in the person of Jimmy Carter could wait until morning.

By the time he had completed his little talk, most of the guests had slipped away, unable to say their goodbyes to Doris because she remained rooted next to Carter while he spoke. When he finished, Doris, decompressing in the postorgasmic glow of Carter's oratory, thanked her remaining guests for their expected financial support.

When I had arrived at the party, I spotted a woman who lived nearby and was a person of substance and some achievement—an island of seriousness in a sea of pretenders. Although I searched for her, I did not see her again at the event and later discovered in the course of my professional activities, that she spent the evening vomiting in the bathroom, that being her first sign that she was pregnant. Shortly afterward, I learned she aborted the child without informing the father (a close friend of mine), who at the time, unfortunately, was married to someone else. Again, I could not but later think the future might have been better served if, that night her choice of terminating her pregnancy and Carter's choice of pursuing the presidency might have been reversed and a new human being with all the unknown talents he or she could have been possessed were loosed upon the world and Carter returned to picking peanuts.

In the next weeks, Doris was unrelenting in her telephone calls to me, asking me to call clients in the pursuit of raising money for Carter. I tried to accommodate her and hit up a few wealthy clients for donations, and a few of the few actually came across. As in the case of women chasing, it is only the successes that are public, and the number of failures required to achieve those conquests remain a private matter. I soon realized that it was not actually the amount of money I was able to raise that kept me in the game as a player, but rather, from Doris' perception, it was a happy confluence of my "numbers" with those of Carter or a combination of mine with the name of Doris' cat or something of that nature.

A few weeks later, I began to receive and accepted a series of invitations to Carter-related events at fancy homes, which surely represented a handsome return on my modest original liquor investment. At most of them, Carter appeared—at one, his wife came in his stead—and they, more or less, followed the pattern of the initial one. At these homes, it was the hostess—in an unspoken protocol, it seemed it was usually the lady of the house who spoke, or perhaps Doris only made her contacts through prospective hostesses—who introduced Carter with Doris standing to one side beaming, in her best mother-of-the-bride mode. As time progressed, the homes became more elaborate and the dresses more elegant as it began to be more of a possibility that hosting a party might be a precursor to an invitation for an overnight stay in the Lincoln Bedroom. Most of the hostesses were of an age when if they spent the night at the White House, it would no longer be possible to bestow ultimate bragging rights upon future children: that the arrangement for their stay on earth was made in the Lincoln Bedroom. Of course, this was all many years before Clinton turned the White House into a Holiday Inn.

By now, I was considered a regular at these events. After he finished his brief talk, Carter would go about the room talking to the guests, exchanging a few words and answering questions. At the initial parties, holding my glass, half-filled with white wine—which was happily now paid for by someone other than me— I would join a group of people gathered around Carter. When he paused as he worked the room, I would bend forward, nodding sagaciously to the questions and listened intently to Carter's answers. At the later parties, I became more audacious and put forth questions or variations of questions that had already been asked at prior parties. Like Fred Astaire who on each retake of a movie scene repeated it precisely down to an insouciant gesture of a hand or the arch of an eyebrow, Carter repeated his answer precisely as he had given it at a previous party.

Soon Carter began to recognize me, and at the end of one party, by chance, we rode down in the elevator together. He shook my hand, looked earnestly into my eyes and thanked me for all my help. It was unclear to me if he was thanking me for the liquor I paid for at the original party or for the softball questions I had just asked. Whatever, the graciousness of my mumbled response was only exceeded by the sincerity of the comment that it engendered.

Years later, I learned that politicians in office have an unusual relationship with both elevators and toilets. If they want to avail themselves of either convenience, it is held vacant for their exclusive use. In the case of elevators, it is only shared by bodyguards and selective guests, and in the case of toilets, they are only used by the official in lonely splendor. That is except for Lyndon Johnson and Louis XIV who frequently used the venue to conduct affairs of state.

Business was bad for bookies when Buster Douglas fought Mike Tyson in Japan for the world's heavyweight championship. In the bookmaker's economic world, it resulted in the equivalent of a "market correction"—the euphemism that stockbrokers use to keep the suckers coming back after a disastrous day on Wall Street. There was simply no Douglas money out there since nobody was foolish enough to bet on him, either to win or at least to leave the ring in substantially the same condition in which he entered it. The fight announcers confined their on-air comments to a discussion of whether Douglas would survive the first round.

As the fight progressed, the announcers traversed the verbal land-scape from almost schoolyard IQ-level sarcasm concerning Douglas' prospective use of the ring as a mattress to a hysterical "This is the greatest upset of all time." In similar fashion, over the next months, the political pundits' opining turned from professional skepticism into guarded surprise and progressed to unabashed amazement. Carter's simple image of clodhopper integrity allowed him to do well in the Democratic primaries.

Armed with all sorts of difficult-to-obtain passes (I was still reaping benefits from my liquor donation), I attended the Democratic convention in New York, which had all the gentle ambience of a rock concert (perhaps an oxymoron) for middle-aged residents of Middle America.

To the public, Carter's awkwardness seemed to translate into an earthy righteousness and was the antithesis of the other politician-candidates' images, burnished and polished by media-savvy consultants and pollsters and rubbed shiny by the big-city bosses.

Because of the elective primary process, Carter won the nomination going into the convention with many states already in the bag. In the general election, he additionally benefited from the fact that his opponent, Gerald Ford, had assumed the presidency by succession, not election. After Richard Nixon resigned one step ahead of the sheriff, Ford's first act as president was to pardon him. The popular perception was that a deal was made to allow a criminal to avoid his just deserts, regardless of whether he had already received his just deserts—as well as the whole meal.

After Carter was elected, the telephone wires were abuzz with congratulatory calls to and from all the people who were at the parties. With the election behind her, Doris was able to go forward with an elective surgical operation and told us of the excitement at the hospital when they received a call for her from "President-elect Carter." This call, I imagine in her mind, assured her of the nurses responding to her before her discharge or possible relapse, as well as her having a surgeon with a reasonable degree of sobriety.

A thick book was circulated listing all presidential appointments. I was told that I should make note of any that interested me, but that I had to return the book by the next morning. Barring an argument with myself—I was self-employed—I was insulated from being fired. Even so, I was reasonably certain that directorship of the CIA was not available, not to mention that my finances did not allow for an ambassadorship to an exotic island. I took a pass at this gluttonous feast of the victors.

Shortly after his election, Carter passed through New York and again arranged for a series of meetings with his early supporters to be held at a hotel opposite Madison Square Garden where the meetings were held to celebrate his nomination. The streets around the hotel were closed to traffic and the sidewalk closed to pedestrians. A pass was needed to enter the hotel, and names had to be submitted in advance to the Secret Service to obtain a pass for entry to the floor where the meetings were to take place.

Once I arrived at the floor, an agent led me to "my" particular meeting room. I was the first to arrive, and the agent stopped me as I was about to enter and said, in a quiet voice, "You may want to kill some time downstairs. Once you enter, I have to ask you, for security purposes, not to leave. The president will not arrive until everybody is here and seated, and as of now, he is running late." I indicated I would wait, and he pointed out the adjoining bathroom and an array of bottled waters and sodas on a sideboard. As we chatted, another agent placed a chair in the hall next to the doorway, and I was told if I needed anything to speak to him.

The meeting room was, in fact, the large living room of a suite in which all the furniture had been removed and replaced by a sideboard and three long tables arranged in a U with five chairs from the hotel ballroom behind each of the tables. At each place, there was a white cardboard sign containing in large black letters the name of the person to be seated at that particular place, and behind each sign was a yellow legal pad and a pencil. Most of the fifteen names were prominent local people familiar to me by reputation or from prior Carter-related events. There was one name, however, that caught my eye, Elizabeth Taylor, the iconic, not yet faded, queen of the cinema who was to be seated next to Carter. I poked my head out the door and looked up and down the empty corridor. There were only clusters of agents standing about, along with the one posted outside the door. He faced outward and was tilting dangerously back on his chair. Certain that no one could see me, I went back into the room and moved the cards around so that now, Taylor sat between me and the president-elect.

When we were all assembled and hushed, Carter arrived with two Secret Service agents in tow. Before he began speaking, one of his early supporters, a Holocaust survivor and regular at the early parties who had become successful in New York's rough-and-tumble real-estate market, and who Carter had courted not only for his monetary contributions but, I believe, also for his Jewish networking connections, went up to Carter. In halting English, he made a graceful little speech noting that on his—sometimes terrible—life's journey, he carried, and often hid, his Bible. It was beyond his imagination that he would ever stand next to the President of the United States. He held out the Bible to Carter, who at this point appeared to be impatient and had a fixed smile on his face, with the request that it may have its final resting place somewhere in the White House.

Carter accepted the book and thanked him. I could not help but notice that with the faintest whiff of disdain, barely touching it, he passed it seamlessly to the Secret Service agent standing next to him. The gesture, I thought, was one of a potentate receiving birthday gifts from his subjects; his expression not one of disdain, but rather of an indifference trembling on the brink of boredom.

Carter then stood in the center of the U formed by the three tables, thanked the group for their support and asked if anyone wanted to ask him any questions Most of the thirty guests simply congratulated him, but then Elizabeth Taylor, turning her perfect face and huge violet eyes toward him, asked a question beginning with the words, "I'm British, you know …" No one in the room knew this—and to this day, I don't know if she is or ever was British. Years later, when I represented her husband in a divorce case against her, I should have asked him the question.

We were all told to remain seated until Carter left the room. Apparently, this is the protocol with dignitaries. Sometimes, it is carried to extremes. I was at St. Patrick's when the Pope paid a visit. A thousand people had to remain in the overheated church until the pontiff left. The only trouble was that the pontiff was not leaving that quickly. He stopped to chat, shake hands, give blessings, allow his picture to be taken, etc. A thousand busy New Yorkers began looking at their watches acting as busy New Yorkers do, faces reflecting the journey from boredom to anger. It was a display of the triumph of impatience over religiosity.

I waited until everyone filed out of the room after Carter went on to his next meeting down the hall. Alone in the room, I slipped the cardboard plaque with Elizabeth Taylor's name in big black letters into my inside jacket pocket. Afterward, I showed it around for a while, but in the miasma of time, it has gotten to that place of lost things and joined pocketknives, photographs of dead relatives and love letters to people now old or gone.

29

985 FIFTH AVENUE AND THE GOVERNOR

On October 18, 1977, Reggie Jackson blasted three home runs in a single World Series game that resulted in the Yankees winning the Series. Jackson and I lived in the same building, 985 Fifth Avenue—only five or six subway stops from Williamsburg, but a seemingly unattainable dream for me as a kid. Even though I was not a sports fan, I could appreciate the magic effect of the three home runs in one game on the sports-loving public. While he became a *national* hero, here in *New York*, he dwelt among the gods in the Pantheon—assuming that is where they hung out. That night, by chance, we rode the elevator together— I, in order that he would feel some privacy in his own home—avoided him and intensively studied the building department's small poster posted on the wall next to where the elevator operator stood. Jackson was involved in an argument having something to do, I believe, with his girlfriend's mother's sofa, thereby giving living evidence of Kipling's line, "The Colonel's lady and Rosie O'Grady are sisters under the skin."

I had one other dealing—perhaps, I should say "instructive life lesson"—with Reggie Jackson. I had rented a spare room in my office to Bill Goodstein, a lawyer, whose principal professional value to the stream of lawyers who visited him seemed to be his access to judges. This didn't accomplish much in the way of justice or produce income for him, so he decided to become a sports agent. Somewhere between his journey from lawyer to sports agent, in the course of pursuing the latter endeavor and attempting to cultivate baseball players, he hooked up with Reggie Jackson. Goodstein had invoked the ire of Yankee owner George Steinbrenner because he hung out in the Yankee Stadium parking lot hoping to sign up players for his new business. Steinbrenner referred to him—when talking to a sportswriter—as "The Stalker." This was reported in the press, and the sobriquet stuck, or at least that is how I would, at times, address him.

At some time after the World Series, Jackson was sued by a lady claiming he injured her when he threw her to the floor of a local movie theater. In truth, what happened, as Jackson described it to me, was that the lady, who he did not know, simply, without invitation, sat herself down on Jackson's lap. He stood up to release her from his lap, thereby propelling her to the floor.

The case came on for trial, and since it was to be a jury rather than a judge deciding the case, Goodstein's access to judges was to no avail. Goodstein, because he was unsure of himself, asked me to help pick the jury for him. The fine print of the request read that I would pick the jury while he read the sports pages.

Trial jurors generally, in the New York State Supreme Court, are chosen in the absence of a judge from a group of randomly chosen jurors. This happens in small rooms on a floor apart and separate from where the trial would be held. The litigants observe the process while each lawyer takes his turn asking questions of the prospective jurors in the panel, rejecting some and accepting others as qualified to serve, until the membership of a complete jury is agreed upon.

The judge is only involved in this process if some difficulty arises. And, in this case, some difficulty did quickly arise.

As soon as Jackson walked into the little room, the prospective jurors crowded around him asking for his autograph. My adversary was appropriately outraged, and he lodged a complaint asking for the presiding judge to come down to deal with the situation. The judge came, wiping the remains of some chicken salad from his chin, and lambasted the prospective jurors. He explained to them that in the American court system, each litigant is equal, and they must comport themselves in an impartial and dignified manner. They promised to do so, and he then angrily left the room to attack the rest of the chicken salad. After a pause, the jurors, hardly missing a beat, charged out of their seats again asking for Jackson's autograph. My adversary was well counseled in agreeing to a settlement. The case was never tried.

In court, Jackson was wearing colorful cowboy boots and saw me staring down at them. Actually, I thought they were in atrocious taste, but he misinterpreted my gaze and asked me if I liked the boots. I answered, "They are really remarkable." He then asked my size. Out of politeness, I told him. He said he was getting me a pair of boots as a gift. After six months went by, and not having received the boots, I told the story to Goodstein. He reminded me that Jackson was a TV spokesperson-pitchman for Panasonic TV. He added that he was still waiting for the Panasonic TV set Jackson promised him.

Nine Eighty-five Fifth Avenue was an interesting building in a great location between Seventy-ninth and Eightieth streets facing Central Park, one of the few rental buildings remaining on Fifth Avenue. It had a colorful roster of tenants, including the great trumpet player Miles Davis, who I once had to help into his apartment because he could not get his key to work—although there seemed to be nothing wrong with either lock or key. The problem seemed to be Miles' mechanical ability—at least as far as locks were concerned.

His one-time wife, the Emmy-winning actress Cicely Tyson, still lives there. I bumped into her one evening when I returned home after spending a day having great difficulty in memorizing a few lines at an audition for a movie to be directed by Susan Seidelman. I told Cicely of my inability to even remember the few sentences involved in the audition. Cicely graciously offered to help me memorize lines using certain acting techniques. I did not get the part, and so we were both saved an ordeal.

The director or producer wanted me to try out for the part since the role was that of a lawyer. When I eventually saw the movie, they used an actor rather than a real-life lawyer even though Ms. Seidelman had striven for verisimilitude in her casting. It was obvious to me then that actors make better lawyers than lawyers.

At one point, Mel Brooks moved into the building with Anne Bancroft who was then, I believe, appearing on Broadway in a limited run of a play about the same time I represented Brooks' ex-wife in a dispute involving their prior divorce agreement. The building is a small, one-elevator building with two apartments on each floor. On several occasions when I saw Brooks walking into the building, I would walk around the block to avoid any sort of confrontation.

Brooks was brought up in Williamsburg, too. While the case was ongoing, Brooks had a private showing for friends and family of his most recent movie, *Young Frankenstein*, as I recall, at the now-gone Sutton Theatre at Fifty-seventh Street and Third Avenue. His ex-wife invited me to the showing. They may have had children together— I don't recall. Spitballs were flying around the theater, people were talking to each other and making noise. I had not seen a bunch like this since I left Williamsburg, which shows, I guess you can take the boy out of Brooklyn, but not Brooklyn out of the boy.

On another occasion, I represented a lady in a divorce, and she and her husband lived directly above me at 985. Every time they argued, I not only heard it, but she would bang on my floor, and on other occasions, she told me it was her husband who would bang on my ceiling (their floor) simply to annoy me.

The building was owned by Bernard Spitzer, the father of the future governor, Eliot Spitzer. The governor was then a private lawyer, and occupied—probably rent free—the penthouse apartment in the building. He seemed to be a driven individual, monodirected and jogged daily with the grim determination of a guy who was part of a lynch mob—and had an equally unhappy look about him. Sometimes I used to chat with him. Eventually, years later, we became adversaries when he tried to have me removed as the chairman of the State Commission on Judicial Conduct threatening a lawsuit under the Public Officers Law to force my removal because of a book I had written. Believing that there still was a First Amendment, I invited him to do so. Shortly thereafter, he became embroiled in a suicide confrontation that he had no chance of winning with the majority leader of the state Senate calling him a "senile piece of shit." His resulting Watergate-style cover-up of another incident caused his approval numbers in the polls to fall to approximately 30 percent—only a few months after he won the gubernatorial election by a landslide. I thought I made a mild joke with no basis in reality in a press interview when I said, "I may be chairman longer than he is governor."

A short time passed, and then Spitzer was caught with a prostitute. The FBI had a wiretap recording of his making the necessary arrangements for the $4,000 hooker. He sounded like Eisenhower plotting D-Day. He told her what train to take, exactly when she must arrive, that he would pay for the train and exactly what she could spend at the minibar in the hotel. He even explained that, since he had slightly overpaid her, the overpayment should be credited against her next house call. Jackie Mason had the final comment. "What can a $4,000 hooker do that a $3,000 cannot?" The governor was forced to resign, and oh yes, as far as my boast, my term as commission chairman ended on March 31, 2008. I was chairman fourteen days longer than he was governor.

The governor's father was actually a good landlord when I lived in the building. But, I have my own feelings about landlords that are akin to those I have of bedbugs.

A landlord—theoretically, any landlord—is the ultimate thief in our society. He has produced no product to help his fellow man, has created no intellectual idea or work of art that would ennoble or elevate man either intellectually or spiritually. All property in New York, if traced back far enough, has its ownership in property being stolen or conned by white men from Indians. A real-estate owner is nothing more or less than a receiver of stolen property and in a normally honest society, would be considered simply as a thief.

30

THE DANCE BEGINS

KOCH MAKES A BID TO BE MAYOR
AND JOINS HANDS WITH MISS AMERICA

The trajectory of our lives is often determined by people with whom, gently or violently, we collide along its path. Each collision changes and deflects our life's course, and each interception affects the next, causing our final destination, for better or worse, to end up at a different and unexpected place. I started out the journey believing that my destiny was to be a neighborhood doctor, married to a woman who would grow ugly with time, but with dignity, who would be the mother of my two children, well-behaved kids who would do passably well at a local public school. We would own a two-family house in an indifferent, but not violent Brooklyn neighborhood with a tenant living upstairs, which meant my family could live rent free, affluent enough to buy a new car every three years. Fortunately or unfortunately, my life became a road with unexpected twists and turns and along the journey of my mortality—Andy Capasso intersected with Judge Gabel and she with Miss America and I with Rudy Giuliani and a hundred ineluctable other permutations.

* * *

In 1977, Ed Koch was a liberal Congressman representing Greenwich Village (could there have been any other kind of Congressman spawned from the geography of those twisted streets?). Koch was a man in search of another job—not just *a* job, but *the* job; mayor of New York City. New York mayors were often political hacks or fools; some were knaves—of greater or lesser degrees of evil—and one, John Purroy Mitchel, who forgetting to buckle his seatbelt, was even dumb enough to fall to his death out of an airplane flying upside down.

Everyone wants to be the mayor, a position that because of the very ordinariness of most of its occupants seems attainable in the ambitions of many local two-bit politicians and even those whose worth is of a somewhat lower denomination. New York's mayor has great power, but not the power of a public official who can command an army or affect the destiny of his people. Actually, though the mayor does not have an army, he does have his police force. But even more important, the mayor of New York has patronage power. He can appoint every new criminal and family-court judge and replacements for civil-court judges whose terms expired and also appoint people to hundreds of positions, both paid and unpaid, as he oversees a vast municipal budget with opportunities to reward friends both corruptly and legitimately.

From the day a mayor is sworn into office, and sometimes even earlier, other politicians both great and small begin to imagine themselves as candidates for the mayoralty in the *next* (albeit four years hence) election. In order to become the Democratic Party nominee—which, usually is tantamount to being elected—Ed Koch had to battle Abe Beame, (a former mayor), Mario Cuomo (an Italian-American and later governor), Herman Badillo (a Puerto Rican New Yorker), Percy Sutton (an African-American) and Bella Abzug (a former member of Congress) in a primary. After the initial primary vote, there would be a runoff between the two candidates who had received the most number of votes.

Koch began his campaign with name recognition of fewer than 30 percent of the voters and actual support from the polled voting public of a dismal 6 percent.

In a breathtakingly close first primary round, Koch with 20 percent and Cuomo with 19 percent were the two victors.

After he won the right to a runoff with Cuomo, Koch, a bachelor, had another problem. The battleground seemed suddenly defined by the repulsive underground slogan "Vote for Cuomo, not the homo." The slogan's truth or falsity did not affect the damage (or hurt) it caused.

In those days homosexuality did not sell well in New York—even among homosexuals, most of who lived inside closets whose doors remained mostly unopened, if not locked. The answer to Koch's problem was Bess Myerson. By 1977, Myerson had become a household word having been Mayor Lindsay's consumer affairs commissioner and a TV personality by virtue of enjoying an ongoing role on a popular quiz show.

Myerson certainly had her share of stormy heterosexual relationships—and one stormy very public divorce—but there was also sly, half-stifled questions about her sexuality in the "come sit here beside me if you have something bad to say about so-and-so" set. Koch and Myerson were not exactly a match made in heaven, but rather in the calculated cynicism of campaign managers.

31

CAPASSO AND THE BESS MESS

The chair across from me was burnished by a hundred bottoms, some sheathed in layers of silk garments gently sliding in almost-sighs against each other, some in crinkly cotton dresses calling up summer nights and ferry rides and girls whose long brown hair blew in the wind, drifting in and out of the dreams of half-forgotten memories or some in denim jeans worn rough by wear and rubbing of laundry soap and those that were made to seem so by limp-wristed designers. The chair welcomed the bottoms padded with fat and others thin flesh over bone; bottoms of the tired and beaten down and the ones with the $30,000 pocketbooks whose profession was "doing lunch" and favorite port of call was the plastic surgeon for "just a little off from here, but not so anybody would notice."

The strumpet chair welcomed with indifferent embrace the grifters, the greedy, the confused, has-beens, wannabes, the victims, the scared who had good reason to be scared—and of those even some who ended up murdered—the women frightened of losing Park Avenue apartments or Hampton homes—death by real estate—and those who were simply frightened of life itself: the beaten, battered, pampered, lied to, deceived; the purveyors of rehearsed, overtold stories, told so often that the self-deceiver becomes a true believer; the seducers, the angry, the hate filled and the seekers of reparations for all the wrongs and inequities visited upon them like Ahab heaping upon a whale's hump, "All the hatred and rage that had been in his race since Adam down."

Nancy Capasso sat facing me. She was tall, perhaps five feet, ten inches in height, not dainty or elegant tall, but big-boned tall—unlike fat women of a certain generation whose mothers would say, "My daughter isn't fat, she is big-boned." There was an impatient heaviness about her as if under her fashionable brown suit, her body contained a restless energy: a locomotive building up steam. She had a small nose, closely cropped blond hair capping an even-featured face, little brown eyes that within the course of a few moments traversed the landscape of my office, assessing and valuing its furnishings. During our conversation, they widened in anger or disbelief and squinted at me through lids narrowed in confrontation. She had a way of turning her head to the side, but continuing to stare at me in a fixed gaze with a kind of "*You* mean to tell *me*" skepticism when I told her something she did not want to hear.

She let fall names of gangsters, public officials and almost-celebrities, her eyes challenging me to react. I did not. She peppered her conversations with wisecracks like a sort of latter day Jewish Texas ("Hello, Suckers! Come on in, and leave your wallet at the bar") Guinan. Under all of this, it was clear to me she was a frightened little girl from Queens who had been playing out of her league.

She tilted her head, and with a half-smile, asked, "What's a nice Jewish girl like me doing in a situation like this?" I did not respond. She waited a moment, lowered her gaze, and with another half-smile, added, "I ... suppose you know about my situation."

Even though this was like asking me if I knew that today was Tuesday, I shook my head from side to side and said nothing. I thought, "Only in New York would it be called a 'situation.'" Of course, I knew the story. Even guys too cheap to buy a newspaper read the headlines on other people's papers and knew about it. Housewives sitting under hairdryers in Queens knew about it, as well as every shyster this side of the Hudson who sat in a one-room office behind a door peeling with paint knew about it. But the idea was to get her talking. Most lawyers are barely listened to by adults outside of the various people who need their money—children, secretaries, clergymen and hookers—when the listening is part of a financial transaction. Lawyer-listening is an art. A lawyer must be interested, but not judgmental; caringly sympathetic, but not slushy sentimental; sensitive, but not weak.

Nancy was about to tell me about what the newspapers had named "The Bess Mess."

"OK. This nice Jewish girl has five children and a husband who ran off with Bess Myerson. She became Miss America the same year he was born."

She paused. After a few moments of silence, I said, "That's it, or do I have to know anything else?"

She smiled, nodding, "Very funny ... very funny. I need a lawyer, not Jackie Mason."

"OK. Let's start. Take a deep breath ... the beginning ..."

She was now at ease and began talking. I did not take notes, since notes distract and friends—particularly friends who are nonjudgmental—do not take notes. Doctors take notes as you talk to them so that they can later cut you up in a more informed fashion or prepare a defense if sued for malpractice. Teachers jot down demerits in anticipation of a session with the principal. Cops ask you questions and write down the answers when they give you a ticket or after a night of questioning in a small room that smells of sweat and cigarettes. I wanted her to talk to me as she would a concerned friend.

The important things I would retain in my head, and the details I could fill in at the countless meetings that would undoubtedly follow. For now, it was the music that I wanted to hear, not the lyrics. I watched her as she spoke. This would be an audition for a possible future drama to be played out in a shabby downtown courtroom.

When clients tell you about their predicament, they always start with the things that to them, are the most important, so I already knew it was the age thing along with the other woman—maybe it was more the age thing than there being another woman—but also, there was the fame of that woman.

On a summer's day in July 1965, Nancy, married with three children to a successful businessman, looked out her suburban window across her lawn at a street whose pavement shimmered in the heat. The street was being dug up for a new sewer line. A young man, shirtless, his body as if oiled, wet and glistening from the shadowless sun, labored with a shovel. He saw her at the window and then came to her house and asked her for a glass of water. They chatted, and within several days, an affair began. Nancy was twenty-five-years old, and she later found out by looking at his driver's license, Andy Capasso was nineteen.

Digging ditches for the installation of sewer lines was Andy Capasso's business and that of his father and his father's father and barring an extraordinary confluence of events would, undoubtedly, have been the business of his children. Teaming up with Nancy was the first of these sorts of extraordinary or at least, unusual events that propel people awash in banality along if not extraordinary, at least, unexpected paths.

Andy had the face of an unsuccessful hoodlum. His mouth usually hung open, lower lip moist, his voice husky and without refinement. His eyes were vacant and without luster, dark and smoldering behind drooping lids; his nose short and flat, the product of genetics or an angry fist followed by poor doctoring. Looking at him, one might reasonably assume that the high point of his career would be as the driver of the getaway car or more likely, the guy who has a daily route picking up numbers collections.

Andy swept Nancy off her feet or vice versa. A marriage ensued followed by the birth of two children as quickly as nature and fecund female anatomy would allow. Andy's fortunes in the sewer business rose with inexplicable rapidity and provided sufficient money to support a Fifth Avenue duplex, a Park Avenue apartment, an estate in Westhampton Beach, a separate condominium in Westhampton Beach and two Palm Beach apartments.

In March 1983, Andy's company was awarded a $5.5-million contract to do work on the Brooklyn rail yards and in the following month, won a $53.6-million contract to rebuild a sewage plant. This was all perhaps due to his warm relationship with advisers such as Matty "The Horse" Ianniello and a handful of subsequently disgraced or jailed politicians (in one case a politician committed suicide while under investigation), or perhaps, it was due to his ability to master the proper business model in his chosen industry. He described it, and was subsequently quoted by writer Shana Alexander, as "a pay-off business. You gotta pay off everybody. There are blacks; we gotta pay off blacks. There are women; we gotta pay off the women."

Andy's business practices ended up in a collision with New York's federal prosecutor, Rudolph Giuliani, who intended to clean up what Time Magazine had called "The Rotten Apple." Giuliani had the face of a de' Medici and the reforming zeal of a Judge Samuel Seabury, whose investigatory commission led to the downfall of New York Mayor Jimmy Walker. Andy was road kill for him, and he soon indicted him for evading $1.5 million in income taxes.

Andy Capasso pleaded guilty, was fined $500,000 and in the finest hoodlum tradition, remained closed mouthed, serving twenty-one months of a three-year sentence in Allenwood Federal Penitentiary.

Ironically, if Andy *had* actually paid off blacks and other minority groups, he might not have landed in prison. Andy's company, in the course of its business, did pneumatic drilling, pounding, digging and other activities that were not only disturbing to the people living nearby, but also, because of vibrations created on occasion, did do actual damage to property. Claims would be made for these damages, and Andy's company, like companies engaged in similar businesses, would try to settle these claims before they rose to the level of litigation. Payment in settlement of the claims was a legitimate business tax-deductible expense.

The IRS noticed that Andy's company was paying more in settling these types of claims than its competitors. Either his company was sloppier in its drilling or was unduly generous in its settlements, but at any rate, they determined that the subject deserved a closer look.

When IRS agents tried to interview some of the claimants, they discovered that these people were nonexistent.

Andy had a simple, but profitable scam going. If he worked in an Italian neighborhood, he drew checks to nonexistent people with nonexistent Italian-sounding names in payment for nonexistent damages. If the work was done in a Polish, Jewish or African-American neighborhood, there would be checks drawn with corresponding ethnically named payees. White Protestants were not included since in New York, there are virtually none. It was Andy Capasso, with the help of a banking officer who perhaps looked the other way, and some other colleagues, who cashed the checks and pocketed these tax-free monies.

Included in the ultimate indictment was also the matter of Andy charging off $1.3 million as a business expense for renovations he did on his family apartment at 990 Fifth Avenue and at his love nest with Bess Myerson at 563 Park Avenue.

Bess Myerson won the Miss America title in 1945. The usual trajectory for a plastic-faced Miss America then as now was to make appearances (of a noncontroversial sort) at public events, theaters, corporate boardrooms, appear wholesome—you can look, but you can't touch—being not too bright and eventually winding up with a rich husband from the Midwest.

Bess Myerson broke the mold. She was a Jewish girl from the Bronx. Ambitious and smart, she had no intention of dwelling in the reflected glory, wealth or power of a spouse. She found no attraction in leading a comfortable life, but rather chose to embark upon a journey filled with chaos and turmoil.

By the time Capasso and Myerson crossed paths in the incestuous Manhattan social scene of money, politics and mob-driven power, she was already a celebrity. Recognized by anybody who ever bought a newspaper or owned a television set, Myerson was one of the most visible figures in New York City.

In 1969, Mayor John Lindsay appointed her as the head of the Department of Consumer Affairs. This, in turn, gave her instant access to the media each time she discovered a bar of soap that cost ten cents less than any other bar of soap. In diaries that her then-husband attorney, Arnold Grant, claimed were hers, she described her sponsor Lindsay as being a "lousy lay," though given her penchant for exaggeration, Lindsay may have been in her head rather than in her bed. The truth was that her private life was a shambles. She had left a trail of broken bodies and unhappy love affairs. It wasn't a pretty picture. Myerson had been arrested for shoplifting, stalked a former lover and on two occasions, been suspected of leaving bags of feces outside the unfortunate recipient's door as well as sending a barrage of anonymous letters.

The former Miss America hooked up with the hoodlum—Andy Capasso, who supplied money to fuel her activities in return for his social entrée into respectable society. Myerson supervised his wardrobe and coached him in the art of chitchat. She could only do so much. At the core center of his being, Capasso remained a second-class ditch digger in a first-class suit.

Bess worked the party circuit with Andy in tow. Her friends and the regulars on the scene were beguiled by the earthy directness of her mouth-breather on a leash as he accompanied her on her nightly rounds.

As for Mayor John Lindsay, he hoped that his good looks and New York credentials would carry him to the presidency, and to achieve that elusive goal, he was prepared to convert from a Republican to a Democrat. Then, as now, an important early hurdle in a presidential quest was Florida, a state with a heavy population of retired New York Jews. Bess—who later anointed herself as "Queen of the Jews"—was enlisted to help with this voter pool. Her role as "Queen" was to travel to Florida with Lindsay and to walk with him among her subjects, letting them know she had bestowed her blessing on him. Without notice, Bess canceled the scheduled trips, and Lindsay's hopes, because of the indifference of retired Jews preferring to play pinochle in condominiums rather than flock to meet the hopeful candidate, were dashed on that sunny coast. Lindsay ended up broke, unable to pay for his own medical bills until, many years later, he was rescued by then-Mayor Giuliani, who appointed him to ceremonial posts so that he was eligible for health insurance.

As it turned out, when Myerson ditched Lindsay, she already had other plans, and Andy Capasso was in her sights to supply the money to realize them.

32

THE BATTLING CAPASSOS, THE FRIENDLY JUDGE, HER DAUGHTER AND MISS AMERICA

As would be expected, the pen is usually partisan to the hand that holds it. Sometimes (though mostly not), it is also loyal to the truth. In wielding it, I will attempt to do the latter, as both selfish and attractive might be the former. Everything written has been revealed through my version of events. And in my view, it is far more responsible than what has been written in the press or recounted by irresponsible guests at a myriad of Manhattan social events. More often is the case that a person who dwells within an event and is a part of its molecular structure has a vested interest in presenting a one-sided or distorted picture. While in the matter of Rudy Giuliani, the pearls might be spread out upon the table for all to see, I am one of the very few who can choose the most flawless pearls to make a perfect necklace, tossing the rest into the dust heap of innuendo, gossip or mean prevarication.

This tale has a fine texture, a warp and a weave. It is complex and stretches out over several years, and as far as my involvement is concerned, it began tangentially with a judge corrupted by love, who was then charged by the federal government with perjury and obstruction of justice and ultimately, while acquitted of criminal charges, was forced to resign. It involved a former Miss America and her thug-lover who became a convicted felon and traversed the landscape of the governance of America's premier city, culminating in events that became nationally significant.

In 1983, Justice Hortense Gabel was seventy-one years old; at least that was the chronological age of her body. She was at an age and particularly in a condition where, in a certain kind of woman, who knowingly allows her body to retreat into a lumpy androgynous mass best suited for the formless wraparound housecoat, but was not a coat and usually worn by women who did not live in houses—unless a walk-up, third-floor tenement apartment could be referred to as one's *house*.

She would smile at those she spoke to, but because she was cross-eyed, it was difficult for the recipient of her discourse to discern whether it was the listener or some distant sunset or other object more deserving of her smile that may have come within her purview. This effect was intensified by her eyes peering from behind simply framed glasses of enormous thickness that made her eyes bulbous like those of mutant goldfish. The newspapers later described her as being blind—but that may have been because her defense lawyers believed it would play well to the jury.

In 1983, Hortense Gabel was a justice of the Supreme Court of the State of New York. Bear in mind that her court was really not the *supreme* court of the state, since two *appellate* courts were superior in authority, and as far as *justice* was concerned, in at least one matter, her court had little to do with the dispensing of it. Judge Gabel presided over Special Term, Part V, room 300 of the New York State Supreme Court located on the third floor in the courthouse at 60 Centre Street. In this large room with high windows rusted

shut, counsel tables scarred by gauges and scratches made by generations of keys in nervous, angry or bored hands, were funneled all
of the matrimonial cases in Manhattan. Behind the judge's bench
was a large and faded mural of Peter Stuyvesant signing a scroll, surrounded by stoic, iron-faced Indians (are there any other kinds?),
perhaps contemplating the fact that they probably had just signed
away their birthrights in exchange for a trunk filled with trinkets.
In the background of the mural was a group of smiling Dutchmen
who had just picked their pockets. The mural was painted in the
nineteen thirties by an unnamed WPA artist who was unable to
paint the seated governor with his right leg in reasonable juxtaposi-
tion with his left. Whistler also had a problem painting legs, but
with this, the artistic similarity ended.

Also in the same year 1983, President Ronald Reagan proclaimed
it to be "The Year of the Bible." Aside from being used as a script in
houses of worship, the other two places you always find Bibles are
courtrooms and second-class hotels. The latter two places, and one
might even include the first, are unfortunately, too often not temples
of truth. A cynic's argument could be made equating the truthful-
ness of girls in the proximity of Bibles in second-class hotels with
that of witnesses under oath in courtrooms, resting their right hands
on a similar tome.

The Greek chorus in *Agamemnon* chanted, "Good prevail, prevail."
But in 1983, there were not too many Greek choruses around —at
least not in Manhattan —making it a mixed year for the "Good"
prevailing. Musgrave and Peterson performed the first Space Shuttle
spacewalk. Men had now permanently replaced monkeys in space-
crafts—good for the monkeys, but the jury is still out as far as the
men are concerned. A suicide truck laden with explosives in Beirut
killed 241 US servicemen, and *Stern* magazine announced that it
acquired the "Hitler Diaries," which turned out to be as phony as a
waterfront hooker's kiss on the last day of Fleet Week.

At 11 A.M. on March 17, on Forty-fifth Street and Fifth Avenue, the St. Patrick's Day Parade was winding its way up the avenue. Some sidewalk onlookers paused on their way to somewhere else, politicians stood in the street, shaking hands, exchanging occasional perfunctory hugs, as the parade, accompanied by growing crowds of marchers fueled by breakfast beer, stormed its way north up Fifth Avenue. As they passed St. Patrick's Cathedral, they received the benign blessings of the cardinal. Continuing on, the parade passed the reviewing stand and stationary television cameras on Sixty-eighth Street. There, privileged spectators who believed they did not need the political benefits of being participants in the march or because they had physical limitations that prevented them from marching themselves, but nevertheless believed themselves, seated in hurriedly constructed viewing stands, too important to be relegated to the sidewalk with the vast unwashed public, who also viewed the procession. By the time the parade reached Seventy-ninth Street, it had lost its steam, and the bands were, for the most part, silent. Martial music wafted down from further south on Fifth Avenue from still energized and marching musicians. The crowds had splintered off into clumps of three or more people for the usual communal activity—getting drunk before sundown.

In 1983, I still lived at 985 Fifth Avenue. Although the parade ended at Seventy-ninth and the building was set back from the street by a driveway, past experience with the parade caused the management of this building and most others that had glass fronts to board them up, protecting them from the aftershock of the marchers' exuberance. Indeed, what passed for the celebration of an event of arguable religious significance often lasted until the next morning—or, at least until the liquor or money ran out. In more recent years between the exhortations of the former cardinal and a bolder Giuliani police force, the parades became tamer, at least to the extent of limiting the use of the streets as public bathrooms and vomitoriums.

Early in the afternoon, as the first part of the parade was dribbling to its death at Seventy-ninth Street, I exited my building for a brief stroll. The doorman looked up from a small black-and-white television and said, "Mayor Koch just mentioned you on television."

"You're kidding."

"No, no, I heard him."

"Well, what did he say?"

"I dunno, but he was at the parade."

"You can't remember anything he said?"

"He was wearing a white turtleneck, Irish-styled sweater."

Returning to my apartment, I called several people, but found no one who had been watching the parade. I chalked the incident up to doorman delusion, a condition common to all of us who sit too long in one place with nothing to do, becoming half-awake and half-asleep: disconnected thoughts and perceptions colliding in skewed and inaccurate combinations.

The next day, I asked people in the office if they had heard Koch mention my name on television. One secretary said her mother, who lived in Queens—my guess is that no one in Manhattan watches the parade—called her. Her mother could only remember that the mayor said something like, "Even Felder had no problem with her."

She did not know what the mayor was talking about. I did. I realized I'd been snookered.

* * *

The State Supreme Court building, perhaps neo-Greek or neo-Roman or a bit of both with a soupçon of neo-WPA architecture thrown in, was, nonetheless, an imposing structure. The long flight of stone stairs leading to an impressive pillared column portico has been used as a backdrop for many movies and television shows when it was relevant to show actors entering a temple of truth to play a role in justice dispensed or denied. The driving principle in having this and similar public buildings constructed during the Depression was to have as many people as possible engaged in public-works projects. This included architects, so that the ultimate esthetic result was a compromise of conflicting visions. And because the object was the *spending*, not the *saving* of public monies, the end result was often overblown, if not borderline tasteless.

Since, presiding over the construction, there was no profit-driven entrepreneur demanding cost-effectiveness and a maximum utilization of space, the result was a circular building with all offices and courtrooms radiating as spokes in a wheel off corridors that banded around the structure, leaving a vast open unusable rotunda in the center of the building. This is unusual since in the heart of downtown New York, rent is charged by the square foot in astronomical figures, and builders scheme to make bathrooms, hallways and lobbies as small or narrow as possible to maximize the rent roll.

Surrounding the inside of the rotunda, there is a mural, several times restored, depicting all the great lawgivers of history. During one of the recent restorations, an artist who was working in another part of the building, struck up a conversation with me. As we chatted, we looked up at a portion of the mural depicting Abraham Lincoln. He pointed out that at Lincoln's feet was a little black boy, arms apart and outstretched, hands empty. He explained that originally the child had a watermelon in his hands, but with changing times and sensibilities, during one of the restorations, the watermelon was painted out of the picture. This seemed to me to be a reasonable decision.

Immediately outside Room 300 where divorce cases were heard, there is a marble water fountain affixed to the wall. It had long ago, either by failure or purpose, lost its capacity to produce any water. Along the semicircular lip extending out from the wall, there are small vertical burn marks where dead generations of lawyers had placed their cigars before going into the courtroom. After they finished pleading their cases, they would pick up their cigars—mute testaments to cigar smokers' frugality and ability to distinguish one half-smoked cigar from another.

It was "Motion Day" that sunny morning in 1983, and the room was filled with lawyers and a few litigants. The lawyers came in a variety of sizes and permutations that would daunt a Daumier. There were lawyers—particularly those who brought their clients with them—who were scrubbed, freshly shaved, wearing their best suits. Others wore wrinkled jackets, fat bellies spilling out over their belts, some balding with strands of hair plastered down on greasy scalps, papers sticking out of jacket pockets; angry, mean little pygmies of the law.

There was a sprinkling of female lawyers, usually dressed up in outfits as close to what a woman who wants to get dressed up as a man could achieve before it changed from a fashion statement to one of sexual preference.

The lawyers were mostly all Jewish—the law being primarily a genetic disease—at least in New York City.

As in a play without a curtain, one by one, the participants arrived on the stage: attendant lords taking up their positions in anticipation of the sovereign's arrival. First a court officer, grim and armed, presumably to protect the judge against a Jewish lawyer not cast to type or sufficiently inflamed to do something more physical than merely mumble after the judge made an adverse ruling.

The officer spoke to the assemblage. It was like the angry voice coming from a tenement window on a summer's midnight, shouting down to boisterous kids gabbing on the steps of the building. "Aw right. No talking in the courtroom. If you have anything to say, take it out into the corridor."

The officer's announcement silenced the court for a few moments.

Then the clerk came out of a door beside the judge's bench carrying a stack of files representing the cases on the day's calendar and walked to her desk at the side of the room. There was a door on each side of the judge's bench. At the side of one of the doors stood a court officer who pounded his fist on the door three times, shouting, "Hear ye. Hear ye, Hear ye. Special Term, Part Five is now in session, the Honorable Hortense Gabel presiding. No talking in the court-room. Put your newspapers aside, and wait for your case to be called, and then come up to the bench without clients."

The judge entered the courtroom helped up the few steps to the bench by her law assistant. Because of her spine problems, she held a large pocketbook by its handles in front of her so that it would pro-vide a weighted counterbalance for her troubled back as she walked to the bench. She mumbled "Good morning" to the assemblage, and the clerk began to call the day's cases.

The lawyers listened for their cases to be called with the judicial equivalent of an anticipation that was somewhere between waiting to be called to the Torah and being next in line for the dentist's chair.

The case of *Capasso* v. *Capasso* was called. As I started to come for-ward, the clerk said the judge wanted to have the case heard at the end of the second call. After all the motions are called once, there is a second call of the calendar to give the lawyers who were late an opportunity to be heard. Finally, at eleven thirty, when the court-room was empty except for myself and my adversary, the case was called.

People tend to read into other people's smiles what they want to see. I look at the Eisenstadt's iconic photograph of Doctor Goeb-bels scowling at the camera, and I see a satanic grimace: evil incar-nate. The citizens of the Third Reich viewed that same thin-lipped, twisted mouth as a symbol of resolute intensity.

On the wall of my conference room hangs a drawing commis-sioned for me as a gift by a client who had just won her case that I had tried before Judge Gabel. It depicted the judge smiling down from her throne-bench tossing out judgments like floating rose petals with only slightly less the majesty of Michelangelo's God hovering atop the heavens, looking down upon his creation. Even the losing party in the case reflected on my wall would not have, at the least, described the judge's smile as a sneer. Back in real life, the judge was, in fact, a corrupt individual, albeit corrupt for reasons one might say are noble, as perhaps might be the case of the person who steals food to feed his children or commits a crime or does violence on behalf of his country—a troubling shifting of standards between good or evil to suit a particular person or situation.

I stood before Judge Gabel. She smiled down at me.

"Mister Felder, I could not help but read in the papers about Bess Myerson's alleged relationship with Mister Capasso." She was referring to the scandal that had for weeks dominated the tabloid press as *The Bess Mess.* "I want you to know that my daughter is employed in some fashion by the Cultural Affairs Commission." This said with a dismissive downward wave of her hand indicating that her daughter was one of numerous and nameless employees of a vast city agency headed up on high by Bess Myerson, the city's cultural affairs commissioner. She continued, "I believe you both know me and know that this would not affect my judgment. But if either of you feel I would not be fair, I'll recuse myself."

What Judge Gabel had just said was a lawyer's worst nightmare. If not a nightmare, then in the grand scheme of things, excluding those involving sex and money, arguably potential professional suicide.

What is a lawyer to do? If the lawyer opts for recusal, then he is basically saying to the judge, "I cannot trust you to be honest and fair," which of course, is supposed to be the reason for the judge's existence in the first place. There is also the question that if a judge is forced to recuse herself, she may wreak retribution against the lawyer asking for her to step down in his other cases—cases in which there could ostensibly be no valid reason to seek recusal.

If a lawyer chooses not to seek recusal in a particular case, then his or her client may be in peril at the hands of a prejudiced judge. There is also the school of thought that since the situation would now be on everyone's radar, the judge would bend over backward to be fair. The latter was a posture that became evident, over the next months, would not occur even if the judge did not have back problems.

I also believed that to ask for the recusal of this elderly judge would embarrass her in the legal community, particularly since she already indicated she would not be affected in her decisions because of her daughter's coincidental employment. In addition, in all my previous experiences with the judge, she had ruled in an appropriate manner. Therefore, I said that I had no objection to the judge continuing in the case.

It was a grave mistake on my part, which gets me back to what Mayor Koch said on television during the St. Patrick's Day Parade—"Even Felder had no problem with her." Now I understood. This began a journey in Judge Hortense Gabel's courtroom that led me to Rudy Giuliani.

33

DEATH BY LITIGATION: CAPASSO V. CAPASSO

A JUDGE CORRUPTED BY LOVE: A FEDERAL CRIMINAL TRIAL

PIKUL V. PIKUL: A HOMICIDAL MANIAC ALMOST SUCCEEDS

I AM ACCUSED GIULIANI ENTERS THE SCENE

The choreography of a lawsuit is as rigid as that of the last reel in a B Western movie. In some situations, however, one of the actors or the director decides to improvise, and then things can go wrong, terribly wrong.

The anatomy of a matrimonial case is simple and transparent. Papers are exchanged—Summons, Complaints, Answers, Counter-claims, Replies—accusing one of the parties of doing thus and so, the other party says he or she did not and never would do such things, and then, the fight begins about the real core of the case. It could be the children: who gets them, who visits them, who can twist their minds in the future, who hates the other spouse enough to use them as weapons. Though usually, it is really all about money: money real or imagined, money in banks, stock certificates, under mattresses, ensconced in pension funds or deposited in tiny, one-room banks on second-floor offices in exotic Caribbean islands; money borrowed or lent, or the monetary value of "things"— homes, cars, jewelry, grandma's wedding presents, mortgages, furniture, art, trading-card collections. Like Annabel Lee who was "…loved with a love that was more than love" to some people "…money is money and loved with a love that is more than love." It is the force of life. They will covet it as they would a neighbor's wife, steal it, caress the thought of it, hide it and easily lie about it under oath in divorce cases.

For the most part, drama or at least the stuff of drama no longer exists in civil (as opposed to criminal) litigation. Because of discovery procedures, there no longer can be trial by ambush. Before the parties enter the courtroom, each party knows the specifics of the other's case. Each party can be made to answer written questions from the other, produce documents and suffer forensic experts going to their place of business to examine books and records. Ultimately, they are questioned under oath by their spouse's lawyer in his or her office, their answers taken down by the machine of a court reporter: a grandiose title for a public stenographer who is paid by the transcribed page and whose employer has figured out how to maximize profits by filling up a page with a minimum number of words. Some states, like Connecticut, allow questioning on all the dreary and often sordid facts that comprise the parties' married life, and others, like New York, in the hope of keeping the emotional temperature at a bearable range, limit the subject matter of depositions to finances. Given the intimate and profound relationships many people have with their money, the latter approach usually does not achieve its goal.

If arguments arise during the deposition, the lawyers either call the judge for a resolution or make note of the problem and reserve its resolution for a later court meeting.

All of this sounds pretty routine, wonderful and orderly. The problem is, however, what is a wife, or worse yet, a wife with children, to do during the anywhere from eight months to a couple of years until the case is finally tried and then presumably she will receive everything to which she is entitled and even sometimes everything she deserves or does not deserve?

There is something called *pendent lite* relief. The wife's lawyer comes to court and says, in effect, "Judge, you have no real way of knowing if what I say, in terms of my client's needs and her husband's income, is accurate or if the other lawyer's version is the truth. But, this wife and these children cannot wait eight months [the time that will usually elapse until the trial is held] to eat, pay the rent and all the other family bills that have and will accrue in the interim. We, therefore, ask you to render rude justice on an emergency basis until, some months later, when you hear all the evidence and witnesses, you can do perfect justice." In some states, this application for temporary relief is made orally, in others, it is made based on skeletal papers and in some, by detailed motion papers, supported by affidavits and documentary evidence.

While the Capasso case wended its way through the court system, Koch's new commissioner of cultural affairs carried on a public affair of an altogether different nature—and one that could hardly be qualified as being "cultural"—with Andy Capasso (putting aside the fact that it is the ultimate oxymoron to, in any fashion, couple the words "cultural" with "Andy Capasso" in the same sentence).

Andy was quite generous with Bess, building her a $5,000 fireplace and a mirrored bathroom in her apartment, installing a tennis court for her use at the Westhampton family home, paying for a Caribbean vacation home and buying a $1.6-million (all cash) Park Avenue love nest. The problem was that he was not as generous with his wife and children. A motion for temporary support was in order.

On behalf of Nancy Capasso, admittedly in a triumph of exuberance over realistic expectations, I made a motion before the State Supreme Court Judge Hortense Gabel seeking an interim $6,000 a week in temporary maintenance and $2,000 in child support. Much later, in the context of a federal criminal trial, the behind-the-scenes process of making temporary awards was revealed.

Five years after the matter of the interim award was put to rest, across the street from the State Supreme Court building, in Room 318 of the federal courthouse, before a jury with the one and the same Judge Hortense Gabel, however, on this occasion sitting in the defendant's dock, the issue was resurrected. Prosecutors working for the United States Attorney, Rudolph Giuliani, explained that the two law clerks who reviewed the temporary support papers, and whose duty it was to recommend to the judge the amounts of the awards, recommended $2,000 a week as interim alimony, $350 weekly child support and a direct to source payment of $6,000 monthly maintenance for the couple's home at 990 Fifth Avenue, all to be paid by Mister Capasso. There were also ancillary amounts suggested to be ordered such as accountant's fees, etc. The recommendations of the law clerks were usually, as a matter of custom, rubber-stamped by the judge.

Unbeknown to any of the actors (at least those on my side of the stage), twelve days before the interim award by Judge Gabel, there had been a private dinner party at the judge's home at which she introduced her daughter, Sukhreet, to Bess Myerson. The seeds of her employment with Bess, if not then planted, were, at least, strewn. Later, on the same day that the recommendation for temporary support was made, the judge in her own hand crossed out the recommended $2,000 alimony figure and wrote in its place $1,500. This overruling of the law clerks' recommendations was most unusual, and particularly so as it was apparent the judge had never read any of the papers and in fact, because of her disabilities, probably lacked the physical ability to read the large number of materials presented to her even if she had so desired.

From there on, things began to spiral downward for us. Andy had retained Sam Fredman, a tall, fat man with an onion-shaped bulbous body. His eyes, nose and mouth were compacted together in the center of his large round head. His skin was taut and his face closely shaven; his hair, what there was it if, was plastered neatly atop his head, a solid oily mass. He reminded me of one of those pink pigs who are laid out on banquet tables with an apple in their mouths. He could have been the president of a Midwest Kiwanis Club ... if Jews belong to Kiwanis Clubs. His booming voice originated somewhere deep in his intestines and rumbled its way upward in its tortuous course to freedom.

Sometime early in July, I had seen him in the courthouse, and passing him the lobby, he nodded and smiled. Since his personality was one of limited complexity, the smile was strange enough that its memory stayed with me. At the time, I assumed that he knew nothing about the private events that had transpired regarding the Capasso affair and the judge, though in my experience, it would be a thick-headed lawyer not to know or suspect something of the scene behind the scene, particularly where events were so extraordinary. New York City, however, is full of thick-headed, insensitive lawyers, so I believe Mister Fredman to be guiltless, and he receives the benefit of my belief in his ignorance of what had transpired. This is a belief that was shared by the government prosecutors.

After the initial decision against Capasso, Fredman had brought on an order to show cause asking the judge to reargue and reconsider her decision. Since he was basically telling a judge that she had made a mistake, this type of motion usually has as much chance of success as Osama bin Laden would have had showing up at a bar mitzvah (even without a bomb). What usually happens in such a situation is that, at the very least, the judge will not redo his or her order until there is an evidentiary hearing or at a bare minimum, only after listening to arguments from both sides on the merits of the motion. If there is truly an emergency, the judge simply makes the order to showcase returnable at a very near date so there could be an exposition of both side's position as early as possible. This did not occur.

After reading Fredman's moving papers, without notifying us even of his application—and certainly, one would be hard put to imagine any dire emergency that could have been explained in the documents—she immediately reduced the maintenance from $1,500 to $750 a week and child support from $350 to $250 a week—all without the benefit of hearing from us at all. Surely, at this point, Blackstone must have been turning over in his grave. To compound the damage, she then placed the matter on her calendar for argument not days later, but rather *months* later.

It was painful to explain to Nancy Capasso what happened and my judgment that the majesty of the law was less majestic in her particular case.

Fredman's expression, which I interpreted as being smug, was perhaps his belief that he must have been the reincarnation of Justice Cardozo. After all, he had apparently convinced a judge merely on papers—without hearing the other side of the story—to substantially overrule her own prior order. Fredman was ultimately elected to the New York State Supreme Court and happily, because of the fact of my relationship with him had deteriorated, no case of mine would have appeared before him. It was easy to understand why the federal prosecutors thought the judge was bought and paid for by Andy. The currency was not money, but rather employment for her problematic daughter. Nancy Capasso was the price for solving Judge Gabel's parental dilemma.

In federal court, the prosecutor explained:

"Two days after the judge cut Mrs. Capasso's support payments in half, the judge telephoned Bess Myerson. Judge Gabel left a message for Ms. Myerson to call her at home. For the remainder of the summer, Judge Gabel delayed making the final decision on the issue of how much money Mister Capasso would have to pay ... The possibility that the maintenance payments might be further reduced remained an open question."

There were other calls from Myerson to Judge Gabel's line in the courthouse, a private number previously reserved only for her husband. When asked, Myerson sometimes identified herself as the "commissioner" and sometimes as "Mrs. Robinson."

On August 24, Sukhreet was officially hired by Myerson. A cynic might say that once Judge Gabel performed her part of the bargain, Myerson now did hers: the hiring of the daughter. At least that was how the federal prosecutors would later view the situation.

Sukhreet was an "odd" young woman. Actually, she gave new dimensions to the word. Years later, she again drifted across my professional landscape when, in the midst of an awful and very public custody trial, she arrived in court to testify on behalf of one Joseph Pikul, telling the judge basically that he was an OK guy. Back in the real world, Pikul was a homicidal maniac who, shortly after his custody trial, was convicted of first-degree murder. Pikul had brutally murdered his wife and while awaiting trial for that particular crime, he was also defending a custody case brought by my clients, a young professional couple who were the cousins of the two children whose mother had been murdered by Pikul.

The trial was going poorly for us. The presiding judge, Kristin Booth Glen, apparently believed that merely being *indicted* by a grand jury for murdering his wife as opposed to actually being *convicted* of the murder represented no particular impediment to his continued custody of the children. This was an amazing conclusion in that the allegation was and the evidence introduced during the homicide trial proved that after strangling his wife, he stuffed her body in a car trunk and dumped her in a ditch in upstate New York. Even more telling was that Pikul, when arrested, happened to be wearing women's panties and a brassiere under his clothes.

Apparently, his proclivity for wearing female undergarments also did not seem to disturb the judge. In fairness to her, however, she did seem uncomfortable when I played a video he had made of himself masturbating, dressed in a bride's outfit while a tape played an orchestral rendition of "Here Comes the Bride."

During the custody trial, Joseph Pikul remarried. True to form, he attacked his new bride with a knife. This caused the judge finally, albeit I suspected begrudgingly, to award my clients custody.

During the trial, based on the fact that Pikul, after he was arrested, told his cellmate that he contracted AIDS, I asked the court to have Pikul submit to an AIDS test. The judge denied my request. My reasoning was that if Pikul, indeed, had contracted AIDS, given, at that time, the knowledge or lack of knowledge of the disease, he risked infecting his children during visits with them. Even more dangerous was that given his mental state, if he felt he was facing certain death, he might bring about a *Götterdämmerung* (Twilight of the Gods), killing his children along with himself.

It turned out that the judge's decision to deny my request for Pikul to be tested for AIDS was a question of putting her view of the law above common sense. Three days after Pikul was convicted of first-degree murder, he died of AIDS in a prison infirmary.

Judge Kristen Booth Glen subsequently was appointed as dean of New York Law School. Though the press claimed she was less than stellar in that position, she was, nonetheless, rewarded by New York City voters when she was later elected to the surrogate court, the highest possible elective judicial post in the state.

The Capasso case continued its downward spiral. Months later, there was another round of oral arguments pertaining to Judge Gabel's reduction of support for the Capasso family. At least this time, we were allowed to be heard, though we were still unable to change the judge's mind. She simply reserved decision. Translation from legalese: Nothing changes until you hear from me (the judge) again.

Three months after the oral argument, the judge further reduced Nancy Capasso's maintenance from $750 a week to $500, while child support was also further reduced from $250 to $180. The judge also held Nancy in contempt for not turning over a valuable Cy Twombly painting to Andy.

Mother love being as compelling a tyrant as romantic love, the judge had tossed aside all pretense of impartiality and sailed forward in arrogant disregard of consequences or even an appearance of impartiality. Since dignity and any sense of embarrassment had become irrelevant to the judge, we were forced to play a game that, fortunately, I had seldom encountered in my career. The judge would render decisions, we would appeal them, and the appellate courts would reverse her decisions. This happened in a series of decisions on financial matters and in the affair of the Cy Twombly painting. To make matters worse for the judge, the entire story became public property beginning with an exposé in the *Page Six* column of the *New York Post* that also revealed the Bess Myerson/Andy Capasso connection.

The New York State Commission on Judicial Conduct began an investigation. Years later, I became chairman of this commission. Back then, my first exposure to the commission was as a subpoenaed witness in its hearing to remove Judge Gabel from office. The proceeding was held at the Association of the Bar building on West Forty-fourth Street in an overly ornate room reflective of an age when the legal profession was suffused with a sense of its own regality. The contrast between the extravagantly carved wooden walls bedecked with large formal portraits of long-dead leaders of the bar and Judge Gabel, facing the forces aligned against her, was startling. Seated alone at one end of the along table in her ill-fitting black dress, one eye looking at me, the other wandering off somewhere high and to the left, a fixed smile, resembling a cross between that of the Mona Lisa and a mentally challenged child was both comical and terrible.

The odds against her were lousy. When I was called to testify, I volunteered nothing, merely answered honestly all questions asked. Indeed, I knew very little (other than that which was already public record) since in a sense, I was the person from whom the true backroom machinations were intended to be hidden. When the commission was done with me, I left the room, but before leaving, wished the judge luck. She thanked me much the same way that someone on death row thanks his lawyer who assures him he had done everything possible and still the governor has denied his stay of execution.

The hearings droned on. Judge Gabel resigned her office before the commission could render its inevitable verdict.

This was hardly the end of the matter. Rather, it was but the end of the beginning. Rudolph Giuliani, then U.S. Attorney for the Southern District of New York, had begun a major investigation into The Bess Mess. It could hardly have been otherwise since the press carried regular front-page stories, reporting on the revelations du jour. The story had two elements: There was the underlying "fix" in the Capasso case, and then the unspoken question, "What is to be done about it?" The only person who was in a position to do anything about it was Giuliani. If a call had been made to God to send an actor to fill the role, no one would have been more perfect. The only thing missing was Martin Scorsese to direct. And even that would have been problematic as I had represented his wife.

Giuliani's ascent in the criminal-justice system was rapid, and later, as even his enemies would be forced to acknowledge, was based on his ability and not on wealth, influence or connections.

Giuliani, the grandson of Italian immigrants, was born into a working-class family in Brooklyn. Flirting with the idea of becoming a priest, he attended local Catholic schools: Bishop Loughlin Memorial High School in Brooklyn and then Manhattan College. Eventually he went to New York University Law School, graduating magna cum laude. Following the usual trajectory of students who do well in law school, after graduation, he clerked for a federal judge in New York. When a young lawyer signs on to clerk for a federal judge, there is an agreed commitment, usually one to three years, after which the clerk moves on, either to one of the white-shoe law firms or to the U.S. Attorney's Office.

In 1970, Giuliani became an Assistant United States Attorney for the Southern District of New York. There were more than over a hundred Assistant U.S. Attorneys in the district. Usually young lawyers become lost in this homogenous mass, swim around anonymously for a year or two and then move on to large law firms. Not so on both counts for Giuliani.

By the time he was twenty-nine, he was named chief of the narcotics unit. The narcotics unit was highly desirable because usually, narcotics cases were slam-dunk situations, enabling the prosecutor to end up with an enviable record of convictions, much as a fighter can establish a great winning fight record by fighting a string of carefully selected pushovers. As mentioned earlier, in narcotics trials, the prosecutor would leave the evidence on the counsel table and while the case was being tried, allow the jury to gaze at the package of poison. All the while, the prosecutor did not hesitate to remind the jury that drugs were the cause of all society's ills from crime to disease to murder. The jury usually came back with a conviction before they would have enough time to go out for their free lunch.

When I was in the U.S. Attorney's Office, I once tried a narcotics case involving a large amount of cocaine. The cocaine was contained in a glassine bag. To emphasize the large quantity of the drug, which had an astronomical street value, during summation, I held it up to the jury and let it fall on a table in front of the jury box. I hoped it would make a loud thud to emphasize in an auditory manner the amount of the seizure. When I did this, the bag, which was loosely fashioned, opened, and a cloud of cocaine blew out of the bag over me as well as the jurors seated in the first row. I couldn't help thinking that this must have been the happiest jury ever assembled.

Giuliani rose in the ranks of the office to become Executive U.S. Attorney, a quasi-management position. By 1975, he was recruited to the Justice Department in Washington as Deputy Associate Attorney General. By 1981, he was Associate Attorney General, the third highest position in the U.S. Justice Department. In that capacity, he supervised all the U.S. Attorneys Offices, all federal law-enforcement agencies, the Bureau of Corrections, the Drug Enforcement Agencies and the U.S. Marshals.

Romance or love or whatever name that can be affixed to this hormonal tornado is the great deceiver of men. Unfortunately or fortunately for Giuliani, that tornado entered his life in a career altering way. Giuliani met Donna Hanover, a local newscaster in Florida. During their courtship, she was hired as an anchorwoman at a New York television station. For a reporter, simply working at a New York station is tantamount to a ballplayer getting drafted into the major leagues. Working anywhere else in the country, except Los Angeles, is strictly minor-league stuff. A news anchor is like the star pitcher or at least number four in the lineup. Hanover was not about to pass up this opportunity, and Giuliani was not about to embark on a commuter marriage; he in Washington and his wife in New York. To remedy this situation, Giuliani was willing to take a demotion to become U.S. Attorney for the Southern District of New York.

While U.S. Attorneys are presidential appointments, they are actually selected by or at the very least must have the approval of the senator from the state who is a member of the same party as the president. Federal judges are chosen by United States senators. The senator representing the party in the White House has two picks to every one from the senator representing the party that is not in power.

In order for Giuliani to obtain his appointment to the New York office, it was necessary to enlist the Republican senator from New York, Al D'Amato. In 1983, Giuliani, with the help of D'Amato, was named U.S. Attorney for the Southern District of New York.

Giuliani and D'Amato remained close for a while and indeed, there was a famous published photograph of D'Amato and Giuliani, both wearing knock-around clothes, jumping out of an automobile trunk to assist in the arrest of drug dealers. Later, they had a falling out. They both seemed to agree that Giuliani came to D'Amato, explained his dilemma and sought his help in moving back to New York. From this point, the stories differ. D'Amato had his version of events, and Giuliani his. D'Amato claimed that after Giuliani had a successful career as U.S. Attorney, he wanted him to run for U.S. senator from New York. There was, however, a price involved. Giuliani says that while D'Amato wanted him to run for the Senate, he also wanted, as part of some arrangement, to have the right to hand pick Giuliani's successor. At that point, there were several serious investigations that were ongoing in the U.S. Attorney's office. Giuliani believed that these investigations could be compromised under D'Amato's handpicked successor, or at least, his successor would not be supportive of the young attorneys handling them. D'Amato countered by saying that he was willing to have a committee recommend Giuliani's successor—much in the manner of how panels chose candidates for appellate judgeships. Giuliani's position was that this committee would simply be window dressing composed of yes men appointed by Senator D'Amato, and it would have the same result as D'Amato directly naming the successor. The dynamics of the situation were explained at different times to me over dinner by each of the men. I offered at one point to have both of them come to dinner, and we would try to resolve the differences. If this were a divorce case, it would be a meeting to attempt a reconciliation—something with which I have considerable experience. D'Amato was willing—at least that is what he told me, but Giuliani was not—at least that is what he told me.

In a relatively short time, Giuliani became the most celebrated prosecutor in the country, attacking organized crime—in fact literally destroying the Mafia as an institution—drug peddlers, white-collar criminals and Wall Street. In a celebrated case—*The Pizza*

Connection Trial—Giuliani tried the case himself, moving to a motel in Connecticut (the venue having been changed because of potentially prejudicial pretrial publicity). Giuliani as chief prosecutor built an unmatched record: 4,152 convictions, as opposed to 25 reversals.

At the beginning of World War II, German submarines were able to torpedo ships off the American mainland virtually at will. I remember as a boy going to Brighton Beach and seeing ship wreckage washed ashore on the oil-slicked sand, as well as an occasional mines—large black iron spheres with metal spokes dotting surfaces like spines on a porcupine. The police would chased everyone off the beach, the people in near-panic dragging blankets and towels behind them. No wonder the German submariners referred to this as "The Happy Time."

Similarly, when Giuliani was the U.S. Attorney, it was "The Happy Time" for criminal-defense lawyers. Indictments came fast and deadly, and there was no shortage of work for these lawyers. In fact, after Giuliani left office, these same lawyers would talk of Giuliani's reign as "the good old days."

Parenthetically, in one Wall Street prosecution, a stockbroker was handcuffed to a chair while awaiting arraignment. As it happened, someone in a grotesque act of graffiti drew a swastika in chalk on the wall in the U.S. Attorney's office. The swastika was within a reasonable distance from the defendant who coincidentally had been a Holocaust survivor. He claimed this was a vicious act, designed to particularly hurt him. An investigation ensued by the U.S. Marshals and the FBI, and it was determined that the scribbling was done by a person or persons unknown and had no connection to the defendant or to Giuliani or to his office.

Years later, when I was with Jackie Mason in Hollywood to perform on his TV show, *Chicken Soup*, the California papers carried major stories of the swastika event in relation to Giuliani's subsequent mayoralty campaign.

Giuliani as U.S. Attorney had morphed into a larger-than-life fig-

ure—Savonarola in a business suit with a law degree. The lure of
the Capasso-Gabel-Myerson case must have been irresistible to him.
Years after the event itself, the criminal trial in federal court began.

Long before the criminal trial, I represented Sol Goldman in a
highly publicized divorce case. Sol was the largest owner of real
estate in the city of New York, other than the city itself, and the
Archdiocese of New York: arguably, at least in part, as far as the archdiocese is concerned, the only real-estate fortune ever built on ped-
erasty. Since there had been an ongoing housing shortage in New
York, and rent control was still in effect, rent-controlled apartments
were harder to find than a kosher butcher at a Klan barbeque. The
statute that allowed for rent control made it possible for there to be,
in the same apartment house, a person paying $3,000 a month for a
two-bedroom apartment, and on another floor, under rent control,
a tenant paying $75 a month for substantially the same apartment.

Goldman hated lawyers and particularly judges as tenants. Lawyers' stock and trade is litigation, and perhaps no litigation is as
attractive to them as that which would save them spending their own
money. For this reason, if at all possible, Goldman avoided renting
apartments to lawyers. To him, judges were even more undesirable
as tenants. He told me of one judge-tenant was able to adjourn his
nonpayment of rent case so many times that Goldman simply gave
up. It was not worth the trouble and expense to have one of his lawyers repeatedly going to court only to have the case adjourned. So he
allowed the judge to live rent free in an armed truce with Goldman.
Goldman never seemed particularly angry about this, but rather it
seemed to me that he considered this one more example of the inequities one faces in a corrupt world.

Parenthetically, other landlords were only too happy to rent to
judges, feeling that this gave them some additional favor in court.
Indeed, the late Lou ("I Love New York") Rudin's organization
owned a magnificent building on Sixty-eighth Street that would be
hard to differentiate from a high-end co-op. It is occupied by judges,

former judges, at least one former police commissioner and one former mayor, all paying rent at the reduced stabilized rate.

Because Goldman owned so many apartment buildings, I would frequently receive requests from people hoping to obtain a rent-controlled or rent-stabilized apartment at a less-than-market rate. When I received these requests, I would simply pass them on to someone in the Goldman office, and there they would dwell on a list, probably forever, never to be called. Sometimes, I would tell the people to call the Goldman office directly and ask for the person handling the list. I never spoke to Sol or any member of his office requesting any special treatment for these people. One reason being that I could not have cared less if these people were able to obtain an apartment or not. Perhaps, the main reason the people on the list never got anywhere was because of the way the rent-stabilization law was constructed. Each time a tenant moved to a larger apartment in the building, an additional rent increase could be charged. Virtually everybody who called my office seeking help wanted at least a one- or more often, two-bedroom apartment. From the landlord's perspective, this would not make economic sense. The landlord would usually want to rent out a vacated studio apartment, obtain an increase when it is rented, then move the tenant from the vacated apartment up to a one-bedroom and obtain another increase and yet another when the former one-bedroom tenant then moved into a two.

I remember at some point a particular judge, who I didn't know and had never spoken to, called me and made it clear to me that he wanted an apartment for his girlfriend. He, too, went on the list to nowhere. At any rate, Judge Gabel, long before I met even Sol Goldman, became a tenant in a Goldman building that had at least one other judge as a tenant. The other judge apparently also was a habitual complainer and consistently withheld rent.

Which brings us back to Judge Gabel's criminal trial. According to testimony, Sukhreet Gabel asked her mother to try to get her an apartment in a Goldman building. The mother answered, "I don't know Goldman, but I know a lawyer who is a friend of his, and I will speak to him." I was that lawyer, though I had absolutely no recollection of the event since I was basically a conduit when these calls came in—if indeed she ever made such a call to me in the first place. When this nonevent came out in the criminal trial, there was the gossamer suggestion of some sort of payoff from me to Judge Gabel in the guise of a rent-stabilized apartment. The illogic of this seemed to escape the defense lawyers. Besides, all else, why would I pay her off or reward her with *anything* when she was involved in an apparent criminal conspiracy to hurt me and the client I represented?

When asked about this situation via a phone call to me from one of the prosecutor's assistants, it impelled me to go to Goldman's office and ask them to search their original records and find out how the apartment situation came into being. After everybody in Goldman's office went into a tizzy to locate the records, my recollection is some record was eventually found that made it amply clear that I had not made any call asking for preferential treatment of any sort. This was my first contact in a professional capacity that I had with Giuliani.

All the defendants in the case were eventually acquitted, I believe because much of the case rested on the testimony of Sukhreet Gabel. The jury did not take kindly to her taping and then testifying against her own mother.

34

ADVENTURES IN THE ART GAME

THE MOM OF POP ART AND THE
MULTIMILLION DOLLAR COIN FLIP

THE BRIDE OF WILDENSTEIN

THE SUPERMODEL AND BILLIONS OF DOLLARS

PABLO PICASSO DRAWS A GET-WELL CARD

People love to sit around the campfire and tell tales about money. Mostly, it is about other people's money, seldom their own, unless their comments begin with "I almost ..." or "I could have ..." Usually the numbers are as inflated as a Macy's Thanksgiving Day parade balloon and their versions of their "almost" financial ventures just as filled with hot air.

In this bantering, usually by the have-nots of the world, numbers are flung back and forth by them like participants in a demented ping-pong game. But, in their financial blustering, real-estate fortunes remain undiscounted for illiquidity or marketability, and stock-market fortunes that are often, at core center, merely pencil writings on restaurant napkins and just as disposable and erasable, yet, in these boardrooms of braggadocio are treated as realities.

However, in the world of art, particularly in its commercial transactions, the numbers *are* real—although based on mostly smoke and mirrors. In that world of specialized commerce practiced by the few and very few, it may be a case of the emperor's clothes, but the money *is* obscenely large and substantial. It is as real and secure and negotiable as the currency of most major European countries and America. One can take a painting to an appropriate gallery, dealer or auction house (auction houses *do* advance immediate money and charge interest for paintings of provable value that are left with them for sale) and walk out with a check in any desired currency, all of which means that art *is* money and appreciably more portable.

Fifty to a hundred million dollars in cash takes up lots of space and weighs a great deal (one million dollars in hundred-dollar bills weighs twenty-two pounds). A painting of like value can be folded into a briefcase. As goes the story, the Wildenstein art fortune (one of the cases later discussed) in America was begun by the elder Wildenstein leaving Europe, one step ahead of the Wehrmacht, with a Velázquez rolled up in his suitcase to be sold for seed money.

* * *

THE BATTLE OF THE SCULLS

Ethel Scull was christened by the press as "the Mom of Pop Art." Tom Wolfe described her and her husband as "The folk heroes of every social climber who ever hit New York." But the day she came into my office, she was an unhappy person. She was in her mid-fifties, her face plain and lined with etchings of a mask of depression.

I had seen eyes like hers before, dulled by defeat and empty as a broken doll's. Her dress was simple and looked like she shared a couturier with the night cleaning women in an office building.

I knew the Scull story in broad strokes. Robert was born on the Lower East Side, in those days, a neighborhood of pushcarts and immigrants. Poverty does different things to different people. Some become stronger because of it and at journey's end have achieved good or even great things. Others flee from it as they would from a pestilence, pretend it never existed and hide it in the attic of their lives. For some, their moral compasses, in their flight from it, becomes askew. Such a man was Robert Scull, rejecting and reinventing his past and along the way, allowed his poverty of origin to become the destroyer of his soul.

Ruby Sokolnikoff became Robert Scull, and in 1944, as an acceptable alternative to membership in the lucky sperm club, he married Ethel. Prior to marriage, he worked in an advertising agency. Ethel's father was a taxi mogul and as a wedding present gave the newlyweds half his fleet of taxis. By virtue of this gift, Robert was now in the taxicab business. In his revisionist version of history, Robert said that the taxi business was started by him and his brother. He soon built up a fleet of 135 cabs, employed 400 drivers and also owned a taxi-insurance business. He named the fleet "Scull's Angels," and soon, its telephone number, Il 7-7777, was on countless Rolodexes throughout the city.

With money generated by the taxi business, the Sculls began to acquire contemporary American art. Robert's first venture in the art world was his purchase of a Utrillo. It turned out to be a fake.

In the nineteen fifties and sixties, New York was the center of the art world. Everything was available for a price, and the price was dirt cheap, and arguably, what people were buying *was* dirt.

Robert would brag about his early purchase of the works of Michael Heizer. What he bought was simply a hole. Years later, I met a collector who bought another hole made by another artist for

$400,000. Obviously, the price of holes had, with time, gone up. Perhaps it was a reflection of the fact that with each hole dug, there was an equivalent less land available to create a similar work of art. The collector told me she asked the artist, after he had placed his hole in the sculpture garden behind her house, what would happen if she moved to another home? He explained that he would come and dig another hole for her.

At one point in my subsequent relationship with Ethel, she advised me to buy a painting by Ellsworth Kelly that was coming up for sale at a Sotheby's auction. When she told me the expected sale price, I declined to bid on it even though she assured me it would greatly rise in value in the coming years. I subsequently had occasion to see the piece on display. It was simply a canvas painted yellow—flat, unvarying, unchanging, pitilessly plain yellow. Lacking, in my unschooled eyes any redeeming social, artistic or intellectual value, and barring an unexpected depletion of civilization's stock of cadmium yellow paint, I had as much interest in it as I would square dancing. However, such is my ignorance of these things that one of the Scull's pieces, *Police Gazette*, sold at Sotheby's in 1973 for $180,000 and then was sold again at Sotheby's in 2006 for $63.5 million.

The Sculls began a divorce case that was to last eleven years. Each claimed to be the one with the eye for art of potentially great future value. Ethel had, indeed, studied art for years, while Robert claimed to have developed *his* eye for it while working at the advertising agency. Robert's bona fides were somewhat put into question when I examined him, and he admitted he was color blind. This is a bit like being a great saxophone player when one is tone deaf.

Ethel mothered and nurtured the artists, and they, in turn, came to care for and respect her. She performed in the mode of Gertrude Stein who offered solace and sustenance to artists and writers in the Paris of the twenties, or today, perhaps like the now-deceased famous restaurateur Elaine Kaufman (whom I also represented) and her similar coterie.

Andy Warhol sent Ethel flowers with a note signed "Andy Pie" and painted an iconic 36 shot silkscreen portrait of her. For a battalion of other now-famous contemporary artists, she was the purchaser of first resort, the purchases being made by her to provide them with funds and dignity more than for profit.

Robert, on the other hand, announced privately and publicly that the art was purchased by him alone with his own money. Putting aside the uncharitable observation that the genesis of Robert's money was Ethel's father's checkbook, Robert managed to have an important exhibit of the couple's painting at the Parke-Bernet Galleries bearing a label stating that the art was from the "Collection of Robert Scull."

When the Scull divorce case went to trial, according to *Forbes* magazine, Robert's position was "Ethel had done little more than order canapés." The judge inexplicably bought Robert's view of the world hook, line and canvas and awarded Ethel a mere seven minor paintings from the collection. The statues of justice atop courthouses all across America portray a lady, modestly robed, but blindfolded. This is meant to convey justice's impartiality. In Ethel's case, she was also deaf and dumb.

Back in my office, Ethel, in a voice redolent with the music of the Bronx, told me she had lost her case. I was vaguely aware from the New York lawyers' jungle telegraph that there was a divorce case going on between the Sculls and that she had lost the case. But, I was unaware that she had lost the case to such an extraordinary degree.

Thus began the long journey for Ethel.

Eleven years: In the aging of a rock, it is as a second in time; in the observation of the stars, their trajectory, their moments of births and fiery deaths, eleven years is imperceptible, but in man, it could be the measure of the transition from childhood to adulthood or from adulthood to senility. In the life of a divorce, it is an impossibly long period of time. The formalized dance required to obtain a divorce is a sluggish brutalization of the judicial process. When it lasts for eleven years, events are submerged in the sludge of time. However, some like twinkling stars on a cloudy night, do stand out.

In the Scull case, Robert claimed he did not have possession of certain paintings, and yet we had eyewitness evidence that these very paintings were hung on the wall of his apartment. Because of this discrepancy in testimony, I obtained a court order that allowed us to inspect his apartment and see whether the paintings were, in fact, there. The court set down a particular date for the inspection. Several days later, when we arrived at the appointed time, there were no paintings to be found, but there were clearly the outlines on the walls of paintings that had been removed. We took pictures of the walls with the outlines of the missing paintings and presented them to the court.

This experience taught me a lesson about having prearranged appointments that gave people an opportunity to manipulate reality. Several years later when I was representing actor Anthony Quinn's wife, Iolanda, there also arose a question of "missing" paintings. This time I obtained a court order to *immediately* inspect Mister Quinn's apartment, and I was able to have the judge instruct us to leave court and go directly to the apartment to inspect for the paintings. I had a driver standing by in a sports car. Mister Quinn and his lawyer, however, were relegated to the usual hired-by-the-hour black car. We raced to his uptown apartment, dodging in and out of traffic, and arrived fifteen minutes prior to Quinn and his lawyer's arrival. This time, we actually saw the crates of paintings awaiting pickup and clearly labeled to be shipped to a home he had purchased in Rhode Island. The game was up.

* * *

There was a direct correlation between Mister Scull's health and his success in the case. Once we got involved, Scull lost virtually every issue as it arose in the courts. With each of our successes, his health further deteriorated. At one point, he sought to avoid a deposition, claiming ill health. His lawyer produced a doctor's certificate that indicated Robert was in Lenox Hill Hospital and could not be deposed. Possessed of lawyer's paranoia, I visited the hospital to see things for myself and make sure he was really a patient. I went to his room, stood just outside the door and peeked in. He was, indeed, in the bed and looked terrible. He seemed to be asleep or comatose. I walked over to the nurses' station and in an authoritative manner, took his chart from its allotted space on the wall. It is remarkable what can be accomplished just by the way one presents oneself. I looked at the chart, and he was, indeed, in bad shape. There was a notation on the chart that he was delusional and saw "Lilliputian men." My suggestion the next day to hire several midgets to walk around his room was shot down.

Scull, having lost each successive appeal, must certainly, as would any sensible person, have realized that he was going to lose the ultimate appeal in New York's highest court, the Court of Appeals. Three days before the final appeal was to be argued, he died. It was a case of "death before defeat." Any reasonable person would have, if given a choice, preferred the reverse. His death only served to delay the inevitable, and shortly thereafter, we won this last final appeal. Now the fun started.

Ethel had the right to acquire 35 percent of the value of the art. To avoid another round of disputes as to how much each piece of art was worth, we agreed to use a Sotheby's appraisal done several years earlier. The appraisal consisted of multiple sheets of paper with the name of the particular work of art and the value Sotheby's assigned to that particular piece. The process would be that we'd flip coins, and Robert's representatives and Ethel would each pick a work of art, doing so by virtue of the value assigned to that work, so that at the end of the day, Ethel would have 35 percent of the paintings. There was, however, one multimillion-dollar problem. A Jasper Johns titled *Out the Window* was valued at a modest figure. Since the time the appraisal was made, Jasper Johns' work had appreciably gone up in value, and at a recent auction, one of his works was sold for millions and millions of dollars. Whoever won the flip of the coin would undoubtedly choose *Out the Window* first since immediately, he or she would pick up at least several millions of dollars because of it being undervalued in the appraisal.

It was decided I would flip the coin and my adversary would make the first call. The night before the coin flip, I studied mathematical texts dealing with the issue of probability. Although theoretically, a coin in each flip would have an equal chance of ending up heads or tails, I first believed that one side of the coin may have had slightly more metal on it because of a larger raised figure being embossed as opposed to the figure on the "other" side of the coin and therefore, would have been more likely to end with the "other" side ending facing up. That theory, in practice, didn't seem to pan out. Then thinking about things, I came to the conclusion, after telephoning fourteen people that most people would say "heads" if they were asked to call a coin flip. That was what happened with twelve of the fourteen I called.

Now came the hard part. Since I was flipping the coin, I could chose whichever side would be facing upward at the beginning of the toss. I kept flipping the coin during the night until I became so attuned to the act that virtually every time I made the flip, if I began with the head uppermost, it would end up tails. The act of flipping so it would land on tails was indeliby etched on the neurological pathways of my arm and hand. The only problem now was to hope that my adversary would say "heads" when I flipped the coin.

The paintings were all kept in an art warehouse. They were held in cavernous rooms divided into large fenced partitions. Each partition had a padlocked door.

When we arrived, the lawyer for Mister Scull was accompanied by two gentlemen, one a neatly packaged compact, rather swarthy individual whom I would have assumed to be a Levanter. He came over and shook my hand. This would be a handshake whose ghost returned to me sixteen years later. These two gentlemen were obviously there to assist Robert's lawyer in choosing paintings. We were now ready for the toss. I flipped the coin, and sure enough, my adversary said "heads." However, I became so nervous that instead of catching it in my hand, it hit the floor and rolled away. I then flipped the coin again, and he again said "heads." This time my practice paid off, and the coin came up tails. On that flip of the coin, Ethel Scull picked up an extra several million dollars.

After all the art was removed to separate locked "his and hers" spaces, I was leaving the now virtually empty room that previously held both parties' paintings. I caught my foot on a piece of something that appeared to be a piece of driftwood with rope around it. I picked it up in my hands, and one of the employees of the warehouse asked me what I was doing. I said I was going to throw it away. He said to me, "You can't do that." I answered "I'm a lawyer and trust me, that's a lawsuit waiting to happen. Somebody is going to trip and fall over this junk." He then advised me that it, in fact, what I held in my hands was a piece of art worth several hundred thousand dollars.

* * *

THE BRIDE OF WILDENSTEIN
AND BILLIONS OF DOLLARS

"... the juiciest divorce in years ..."

New York magazine, (September 12, 1998)

"I feel good because I look good."

Frankenstein's monster, *Young Frankenstein*

Nancy, my assistant, led the prospective client into my office. Preceding her, she opened the door and rolled her eyes skyward in a "wait till you see *this*" look.

Jocelyn Wildenstein was a bizarre arrangement of human proto-plasm—a face I dared not meet in nightmares. When she entered my office, nothing Nancy could have indicated to me would have pre-pared me for this visual assault to my senses. My first impression was that I was looking at a man, dressed as a woman, in a state of mental or physical derangement. Each feature on her face was pumped up or dis-torted; her cheekbones enlarged, shiny and bulbous; her lips fattened and fleshy spread upon the space above her upper lip and lower lip below and toward her chin; her eyes artificially widened to make the outer corners of her eyelids curl upwards to give them a feline aspect. She had a hairdo arrangement in which her scalp line was set back on her forehead, creating hair that jutted straight out like wheatgrass, sur-rounding her head like a halo. The thought of Arcimboldo's vegetable heads came immediately to mind—and there is a respectable body of criticism suggesting they were borne of the painter's lunacy.

She was the stuff of a bad hangover, and it was not without justi-fication that the press ran amok in describing her. It culminated in a *New York Post*, now-iconic, full front-page headline together with her photograph and in the large print usually reserved for national disasters, named her, "*The Bride of Wildenstein.*"

It is a paradox that in a radically altered face, a deeper flesh is revealed and rather than obscuring or changing an imagined infir-mity, sometimes a more profound malady is exposed for all the world to see.

There are people who are mesmerized by deformity or ugliness and even some who find in such unfortunate conditions an exotic physi-cal attraction. Ruskin said that beauty exists in the imperfection as does wabi-sabi, the quintessential Japanese aesthetic. I have never seen beauty in scars and hair lips, but blessed be those who do. Benjamin Franklin was wrong when he said, "In the dark, all cats are gray." In Mrs. Wildenstein's case, the room would have to be pitch black.

Mrs. Wildenstein arrived at my office in the company of a man I assumed was her assistant. I remember nothing of him other than the fact that he, like Mrs. Wildenstein, had a French accent. Frankly, her appearance obscured everything else in my memory. Like the violin placed next to sounding brass in an orchestra, he was merely background noise. I listened to her, though it was difficult for me to look at her face. It was not simply my inability to gaze at something so bizarre, but rather to look at her would make me somehow complicit or at least connected to what I perceived to be, her malady. I willed myself to focus my gaze on a stack of papers her assistant had placed on my desk and tried my best to listen to her, although I had trouble understanding what she said. The result was that my inability to look at her coupled with my difficulty in understanding her reduced the conversation to my uttering polite babble and responsive grunts—not unlike inane conversation at a cocktail party. Finally, I gave up and suggested that she leave the papers with me and told her when I had reviewed them I would get back to her. The papers sat on my desk unread, and indeed, I avoided even touching them, distancing myself from a bizarre and unpleasant memory. Ultimately, I had a messenger return the unread documents to her.

Some years earlier, I had represented Alec Wildenstein, Jocelyn's husband, in a personal matter that was litigated, but ultimately resolved in a manner quite satisfactory to him. A short time after Mrs. Wildenstein came to see me, Alec unexpectedly appeared at my office to ask me to represent him in his disintegrating marriage. I explained to him that I could not oblige him because his wife had already consulted me. Alec was quite annoyed by what I told him. He said that this was "nonsense" and that I had been his lawyer in the past and there was no reason why I could not continue as his lawyer. The problem was, as I explained to him, that even if I had no knowledge of his wife's complaint or even a recollection of anything she might have told me, because she had come to see me, I had no choice but to turn him down as a matter of legal protocol. Actually, it is an old and perfectly legal scam for clients in prospective divorce cases to have consultations with a series of lawyers. By doing this,

World champion Mike Tyson and Robin Givens in happier times. This was the divorce of the year, and I represented Robin.

An Historic Moment
Robin Givins, Raoul Felder, Marvin Mitchelson;
Oct. 1988

New York Times *cartoon memorializing the changing of the guard. At that time, Marvin Mitchelson was the most famous divorce lawyer in America. Robin Givens fired him and hired me.*

Claude Picasso is Pablo's son. The jury returned a verdict within fifteen minutes that totally supported Claude's position.

My client, David Gest, married Liza Minnelli in a media-frenzied wedding. He got a rough deal (all totally undeserved) from the same media in his divorce.

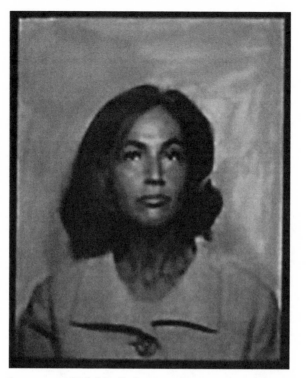

The divorce case of Ethel Scull, the Mom of Pop-Art, lasted eleven years.

Sadly, Jocelyn Wildenstein's altered face was the stuff of nightmares—a bizarre arrangement of human protoplasm. The New York Post's *iconic front-page headline was "The Bride of Wildenstein." I represented her husband, Alec.*

Judge Marylin Diamond was under assault by the press because she claimed she was being poisoned by anthrax. She was not the judge of my dreams.

Elizabeth Taylor's final unhappy marriage. I represented the groom, Larry Fortensky.

David Merrick, who was featured on the cover of Time *magazine, was the undisputed King of Broadway. I represented his wife against him, and then he hired me to represent him against his next wife.*

My client Riddick Bowe, former undefeated heavyweight champion of the world, was in a battle with his wife. Johnnie Cochrane and I represented him. Previously, I had represented Johnnie Cochrane's paramour, but nevertheless, he recommended Riddick Bowe to me.

Anthony Quinn was a great actor, but a poor litigant. He arrived at his apartment too late for me not to spot boxes of valuable paintings he was about to ship to Rhode Island.

Stephanie Seymour was the real deal. Socrates wrote about the "tyranny of beauty." If there is such a thing, every man's choice would be to be tyrannized by Stephanie. She was not only beautiful, but also intelligent, sensitive, and deeply concerned about family and children.

Bess Myerson, a former Miss America, Judge Hortense Gabel, and her daughter, Sukhreet, were involved in a widely reported federal criminal trial that arose from a divorce.

they can effectively prevent their warring spouses from ever hiring any lawyer they had already consulted. Though that ploy was not the case with Mrs. Wildenstein, the result was the same.

I was not a stranger to this game. I had represented a movie star whose legal home was in one of the Caribbean islands, but he did not want to litigate on the island. He felt that because he was so visible and well known, his personal life would be unduly intruded upon. He explained to me that all the lawyers in the community were located on one particular main street. The actor had gone to each lawyer except for one—that one was off fishing—obtained a consultation, told them his side of the story and paid them for the visit. The result was that none of these lawyers would be available for hire by his wife. He knew that the "missing" lawyer was off fishing because while he was consulting another lawyer, that lawyer received a call from his daughter. He overheard the daughter say that she was about to get on a fishing boat with her fiancé. It turned out that the fiancé was the lawyer who was not available that day.

Early in my career, after I left the government, I had offices at 342 Madison Avenue on the eleventh floor, suite 1101. Irving Erdheim, another divorce lawyer and who was very popular, had his offices in the same building in suite 2002. Erdheim was extremely aggressive and routinely pushed the ethical envelope. Perhaps there is no connection at all with the two events, but his lawyer-son ended up in jail, and his partner was forced to resign from the bar. Clients used to go to Irving first and then to me or vice versa to prevent one or the other of us from representing a spouse.

I thought I effectively made it clear that I could not involve myself in the Wildenstein matter after having explained to Alec that because his wife had come in to see me, I didn't feel comfortable even signing on as an "adviser" to his lawyer of record. Shortly thereafter, however, I received a very friendly call from lawyer "X." Mister X told me that Jocelyn Wildenstein had come in to see him, hired him and had given him a $50,000 check as a retainer. Obviously, this was a very large retainer, particularly back then in 1997. He asked me whether the check was good. I told him I had no idea one way or the other. He then wanted me to ask Alec whether the check was good. I explained to him that since I was not Alec's lawyer, it would be inappropriate for me to call Alec on his behalf. He then asked me that if his client waived any conflict, basically waiving any right to oppose my representing Alec, could I make the call. I told him that if this were the case, I would ask Alec the question. (Actually, in any event, if I *were* Alec's lawyer, it would have been my duty to make such inquiries of him.) He told me he was quite sure that Jocelyn would waive any conflict. I said if this were the case, I wanted to have it clearly stated in writing. Shortly thereafter, I received the waiver in writing and called Alec, who took the position that, of course, the check was good, and his wife was entitled to any lawyer she saw fit to hire. This was entirely consistent with the way Alec approached life.

* * *

It was late in the evening on September 3, 1997, and I was doing what any middle-aged man should be doing at that hour: I was in bed reading a book when I received a call from Richard Bernstein, who was Alec's family-business lawyer, an expert in art and a consummate gentleman. In that late-night telephone conversation, he told me Alec had been arrested and was being held in the Tombs—the central city jail. His knowledge of the details was somewhat sketchy. I dressed and rushed down to night court.

Night court is a dumping ground for the human debris of the evening that the shovel of justice has scooped up from the sidewalks of New York. The people who had been arrested were put into holding pens, the equivalent of the Black Hole of Calcutta, until their appearance before a judge. A bored, overworked and tired judge usually presides, but is only able to arraign the people arrested *after* the defendants have been booked and their fingerprints run through the computers in the state capital, Albany. Until then, the persons arrested are simply "in the system." The only problem was that the computers were (and are) invariably "down," and therefore, the guilty as well as the innocent remain in the holding pens, sometimes for a day and a night, and sometimes, they simply get lost in the "process." Any inquiries are met with the answer "Sorry, but he's in the system." Translation: Somewhere in the universe of thousands of prisoners, the person you are concerned about is floating in a netherworld waiting to be pigeonholed. Theoretically, habeas corpus is available, but since the time one evening when a politician was able to get a friendly judge to sign a writ to get his son out of jail and the newspapers found out about it, the judges have instructions not to sign writs of habeas corpus.

I am familiar with the state system of criminal justice, but not because of any general hands-on experience in those local courts. In fact, as a result of my stint at the Department of Justice, my professional experience in depth in the area of criminal law is really limited to federal crimes and the government's related facilities that, incidentally, are much superior and humane than those that the city provides for the unhappy people the police have taken into custody. However, I have had many clients who had been arrested for domestic violence, and so I have extensive experience with this initial step in the process. Only a wall separates the courtroom from the holding pens: a wall where on one side is civilization and on the other is society's surrender to expediency.

Not long ago, a female client of mine was arrested. When I visited her in the women's holding pen, I was appalled at the conditions: women in a cage, stripped of their dignity and humanity. I was particularly puzzled by the sight of a very muscular inmate with a long mustache and a goatee, arms covered with tattoos, who was in the large cell along with the women arrested during the night. When I queried one of the guards as to why he was there, she explained to me that this bearded person with the bulging muscles and tattoos was, in fact, a woman.

When I arrived at the criminal court building to see Alec, I sat in a segregated row of seats with a sheet of paper taped to it indicating it was reserved for lawyers. It is without any particular pride that I suggest that at that moment, I was the only normal-looking person in this room. In fact, I was one of the few who was awake and the even fewer who had bathed in recent memory. The judge, upon seeing me in the audience, immediately called me to the bench and explained to me there was nothing he could do to speed up the process and, "Why wait around? Go home, and come back in the morning." I felt that I could not do this to Alec and leave him abandoned. I used the opportunity that allows a lawyer to speak to his client in a small private room that resembles a confessional. Even though our consultation was brief, he was out of that horrible environment.

I stayed in the courtroom until morning and was able to sit with him a couple of times during the night discussing his case. Surprisingly, he did not look any worse for wear. In the meantime, I was also able to examine the police officer's affidavit together with the accompanying papers in the file. The claim was that when Alec found his wife and two private detectives in his residence, he threatened them with a gun. Of course, there was a lot more to the story.

The next morning, Alec's case was finally called. He was arraigned and released on his own recognizance. *Vanity Fair* described his face as being "haggard after a night in prison." Nothing could be further from the truth. Alec met me, albeit looking slightly in need of a shave, but nevertheless, he appeared unfazed, debonair, his stylish jacket unwrinkled—he had recently lost weight and had purchased a new Armani wardrobe, a not unusual occurrence when an older man takes up with a younger woman. I asked him how he was treated in the jail, and he said "Fine." He observed my surprise and told me, "When they [his fellow prisoners] asked what I was 'in for,' I told them 'I murdered my wife.' After that, they left me alone and in fact, offered to share their cigarettes with me." Apparently, even criminals have unfilled fantasies about murdering their own wives.

The criminal case was never tried; therefore we don't have any testimony under oath, correct or incorrect, truthful or untruthful, but much is known and has been publicized about the incident.

On the night of September 3, 1997, Alec was doing what any healthy, libidinous unhappily married man would do if he had the opportunity. He found himself in bed with (as described in a blog) "a nineteen year old, long-legged blonde."

Alec's wife was supposed to have been on a visit to Alec's ranch in Kenya. Instead, she showed up late at night at his townhouse accompanied by two private detectives and found him in bed with the girl. Alec quickly wrapped himself in a towel, picked up his Smith & Wesson 9-mm automatic and pointed it at his wife and the two bodyguards, informing them of the obvious, "I wasn't expecting anyone." He then told them, "You're trespassing and don't belong here." The bodyguards called the police, Alec was arrested and charged with three counts of second-degree menacing—nothing more serious than that since he possessed a New York City license for the handgun, but still, if found guilty, punishable by a year in jail.

I knew of another similar experience—but with a milder outcome. A famous entertainer, who sought my advice on an unrelated matter, was appearing in Tokyo and was sharing his bed with a young lady, secure in the knowledge that his wife remained in New York. He was at the Imperial Hotel, a Frank Lloyd Wright-designed, earthquake-proof structure, but, unfortunately, the hotel was not designed to be wife proof. In the early morning hours, his wife burst into the suite. The surprised entertainer was a lot more cool than Alec. He spoke only one sentence to her. It replays in my mind when I have an out-of-control client in the office. "Baby, why can't we just be civilized?"

Many people said Alec was set up, but actually all's fair in love and its disintegration. What I believe happened was that the "setup," if one wants to use that word, was perfectly legal. His wife basically led him to believe she was out of town, thousands of miles away in Africa, and then, she correctly operated under the assumption "While the cat's away…"

There was a difference of opinion as to what occurred after the moment of confrontation, but it seemed to me that it was perfectly sensible for Alec to have a handgun next to his bed, being more or less alone in a townhouse with millions of dollars of art on the walls.

We were prepared, basically, to demonstrate that many of the specifics of the allegations were not correct or certainly improbable and that the events did not happen *exactly* as alleged. One never knows if we would have been successful, but with the added factor of the jury viewing a person who had a reasonable expectation of privacy being confronted by strange men in his own house in the middle of the night, not to mention accompanied by a stranger-looking wife, I thought the odds were with us. Indeed, I believed that a jury would find that he acted reasonably for a person in this situation and that his wife contributed to his response by her and her detectives' orchestrated arrival. I have found that many of these protracted, hard-fought marital situations could have been resolved in a rapid, dignified fashion but for one or the other of the spouses firing an opening salvo by initiating police intervention.

Alec never appeared before the criminal court again in connection with this case until a deal was worked out three years later in which he pleaded guilty to "menacing." At the sentencing, the punishment was the judge signing an order barring him from contacting his former wife—I believe Alec would had *paid* a substantial sum of money *not* to have to contact his former wife, having so little interest in her—and he was placed on probation for a year, facing neither jail nor a fine if he was not arrested during that time. The only casualties were that his New York City pistol license was lifted and legal fees incurred.

The Wildenstein family was the most famous art-dealer family in the world. Putting aside their inventory, which included thousands of paintings by artists such as Renoir, Van Gogh, Cezanne, Gauguin, Rembrandt, Picasso and El Greco. Additionally, Alec's family owned the 66,000-acre (four-and-a-half times the size of Manhattan Island) Ol Jogi Ranch in Kenya. The ranch included hundreds of buildings, 400 employees, a hospital, schools, animals, etc. The Wildensteins were acquirers: owning a castle, the largest private residence in metropolitan Paris, a compound in the Virgin Islands, an apartment in Switzerland and three adjacent townhouses located on East Sixty-fourth Street between Madison and Fifth avenues. In New York, one of the buildings was the actual gallery, its interior copied from the Wildenstein Gallery in Paris. Another building was for living purposes, with Alec and his family living on the third, fifth and sixth floors.

I had occasion to visit his home. In the basement, there was an aquarium, swimming pool, with the area around the pool decorated with tables and chairs in a replica of a French café. Outside the door leading into the pool room sat a guard in a business suit. It reminded me of the White House where Secret Service agents in somber business suits are seated in chairs or standing outside various rooms of the family's living quarters.

The third-floor master bedroom of the townhouse was most unusual. In addition to all the sumptuous furnishings one would expect, part of the bedroom was divided by a Plexiglas-enclosed space that was decorated with tree branches, bushes, flowers, etc.—the kind of thing one would expect to see in a natural history museum as a setting for stuffed animals or depictions of wildlife in their natural habitat. However here, it was the home of the Wildenstein's rare pet monkey.

Alec, as soon as he got out of jail, acted rapidly—canceling credit cards, cutting off his wife's telephone lines, locking the rooms in the townhouse, except for his wife's bedroom and sitting room, shutting off access to bank accounts, directing the chauffeurs not to drive her around, discharging her accountant and in a final act of retribution, instructing the household staff to stop cooking for her.

The next move was totally predictable, and we were ready for it. Jocelyn moved for exclusive occupancy and temporary support. She said (according to England's *Sunday Mail*), "The truth is, we spend a million dollars a month." She pointed to the various homes; legions of servants; annual expenses in Manhattan including monthly telephone bills as high as $60,000; $547,000 per year for food and wine; $36,000 for laundry and dry cleaning; $60,000 for flowers; $42,000 for massages and pedicures; $82,000 to insure her jewelry and furs; $60,000 for veterinarian bills, pet food; $24,000 for a dermatologist; $36,000 for pharmaceuticals; and her American Express and Visa bills, which in one year totaled $494,000. Jocelyn's payroll for the townhouse consisted of: $48,000 a year for a chambermaid; $48,000 for a maid to attend to the dogs; $60,000 each for two butlers; $60,000 for a chauffeur; $84,000 each for two chefs; $102,000 for an assistant; and $102,000 for a secretary. Wherever she went, she said she flew in a private jet accompanied by the pet monkey and five Italian greyhounds. Since Alec and his family were not in a "cash" business, all the amounts expended were aboveboard and subject to verification.

All of this was breathlessly reported particularly in the American, but also worldwide press.

Alec had said he had "less than $75,000 in bank accounts." His only earnings were approximately $175,000 a year (supported by multiple affidavits), and his occupation was "unpaid personal assistant to father Daniel Wildenstein." Alec also pointed out that he continued to pay Jocelyn $50,000 a month. In addition, he offered to divide on the spot one-half of part of a portion of the marital property, i.e., $10 million, the worth of her personal jewelry.

In the Wildenstein family, Alec's bills were basically covered by his father. The bills were paid from "... other bank accounts in New York, Paris and Switzerland," others were paid by "The Wildenstein & Company account, The Wildenstein & Company Special Account and family businesses." Alec was not a citizen of the United States, nor was his money earned here, nor did he even have a green card. He was legally a tourist.

Jocelyn demanded through the court, a $200,000-monthly living allowance, payment of her personal staff's salary and expenses and a $50-million security deposit pending distribution of the marital property.

The jewelry became the subject of an overheard conversation much later—long after the case was history. Jocelyn had accumulated jewelry valued at $10 million, which she acknowledged was marital property and therefore subject to division by the court.

Under the general subject heading "Only in New York," years after the Wildenstein case was over, I was as some event or gallery opening or cocktail reception, and the cluster of people directly behind me were chatting with each other. I do not recall if Jocelyn was present. I heard the name Wildenstein mentioned, and it naturally caught my attention.

Under New York law, it is only "*marital*" property that is equitably divided, not "*separate*" property. Separate property is defined as anything one of the parties has acquired before marriage, together with any form into which it has been transmuted. Therefore, if one of the parties had a yacht before marriage and then after marriage sold the yacht and with the proceeds bought a farm, that farm would still be "separate" property and would not be divided in the parties' divorce case.

From what I heard, the people were talking about a well-known jewel robbery that took place years earlier in which Jocelyn was a victim. It occurred in France, perhaps Paris. The speaker indicated the jewels were a gift from a former boyfriend or admirer (obviously *before* her marriage to Alec). I believe the person might have said the donor was an Arab or of other exotic lineage.

In a divorce case, both parties have to submit a net-worth statement as to their assets. From memory, Jocelyn submitted a statement listing as an asset of the marriage the $10 million in jewelry. Alec looked through Jocelyn's net-worth statement and basically agreed that the jewelry was, indeed, purchased during the marriage, and there it rested as far as both parties and their lawyers were concerned. But what I overheard that evening was that the people seemed to be saying that Jocelyn bought the $10 million worth of jewelry with insurance proceeds from the theft of the jewelry she had received *prior* to marriage. When I looked around to see who was speaking, the people had already melded into the general crowd. I never did see who was doing the talking, and the conversation simply passed out of my mind as merely some cocktail chitchat. The potential significance of what I heard did not occur to me until months, or it could have been years later. The entire story may be a fable and simply more New York cocktail gossip, and since the Wildensteins were something long off my radar screen, it went completely out of my mind and memory until now. But if true, it would mean that Jocelyn may have made a serious mistake if, computed in her thinking for arriving at the ultimate settlement was $10 million in *marital* jewelry, when in fact, it was her *separate* property. Frankly though, I have no recollection if the issue was ever addressed in any negotiation.

The judge awarded temporary support of $140,000 a month and denied Jocelyn's application for expert's fees, i.e. accountants, valuation experts, a security deposit and separate payments to her personal staff, etc. When Jocelyn complained that she did not know how to operate a stove, the judge suggested she invest in a microwave oven. The judge, in her decision, wrote that "The Wildenstein family is fabled to be the richest and most powerful art dealers in the world and the family's wealth by some accounts exceeds $5 billion" (in today's dollars it would be appreciably more).

In spite of cutting down Jocelyn's demand, the judge seemed partial—perhaps unfairly partial—to my adversary, but lawyers are sometimes paranoid when unhappy with results, and she *was* affirmed on appeal. So I wrote the judge's actions off to our disappointment and general lawyer's paranoia. But Doctor Kissinger once said, "Sometimes even paranoids have something to be paranoid about." Nevertheless, in the fullness of time, I believed that what the judge did was probably correct. But the tale of the judge does not stop there and is another story or at least, another chapter.

The interesting side issue: The lifestyle portrayed of the family was accurate, which is usually not the case. Exaggeration is endemic in partisan court papers. The point was that it was not Alec's money that supported his wife and children, it was his father's. When the case went up on appeal, the Appellate Court acknowledged that the money flowed basically from "imputed" income and was a result of gifts from his father and from payments made through various companies owned by his father, and determined that "…the extraordinarily lavish marital lifestyle provided a basis for the court to conclude that the husband's actual income and financial resources were substantially greater than he reported." This decision had broad-reaching consequences in other cases, particularly to fathers who had been underwriting their children's lifestyle. It demonstrated that a temporary support award could be made based on a father's largesse.

The next problem was Jocelyn's right to remain in the townhouse (not owned by her husband) while the case was ongoing. This is a situation that arises many times. Parents allow their children to live in a home that they (the parents) own or provide. The judge indicated that "During their marriage the parties and their children shared a townhouse…" and "…the law is clear—when a matrimonial action is pending, regardless of whether the husband or wife is the owner of the marital premises, the other may not be evicted …" Admittedly, Alec did not own the house. In fact, the ownership traveled through a number of other entities and never landed with Alec. But, Alec nevertheless, because of alleged violence, lost the right to remain in the house while the case went on.

Years later when I represented Mayor Giuliani, the Appellate Court, in a case of first impression, denied him the right to bring his future wife even to the *public* parts of Gracie Mansion. Even though he was battling cancer at the time, Gracie Mansion was owned by the city, and nobody elected the mayor's wife to anything. Obviously, it seemed to me to be an unfair and shaky-on-the-law decision. Some lawyers just plain out said it was "bad law." However, on the positive side, the facts probably would never be repeated in any other case. There would be no future mayor finding him or herself in the same circumstances surrounded by the same drama as Giuliani.

The Wildensteins were and are a very private international family. They are the kind of people who would hire public-relations experts to keep their name *out* of the paper. I believe, perhaps unfairly so, that Jocelyn knew this and not surprisingly believed that cooperating with the press would be the best way to get what she wanted. A friend of the family said, "It's her way of taking revenge on people who never, never have their names in the paper." *Vanity Fair* reported "…she has a powerful trump card, the story no one had ever heard."

As was reflected in court papers, Alec still had feelings for her and was concerned that the press, both here and abroad, were painting Jocelyn as a freak and that, worse yet, she didn't seem to realize it and just kept feeding the media frenzy. He instructed me to move for a "gag" order.

To obtain a gag order in America is difficult. There are decisions that go up to the United States Supreme Court protecting the media's "right to know." The law seems to create a moral equivalency between the revelation of government misconduct and marital dalliances.

It is somewhat easier to obtain a change in the title of a case to "*Anonymous* v. *Anonymous.*" But in short order, identities of the parties become obvious to the media. In this particular case even had Jocelyn been cooperative in merely changing the caption of the case (which she was not), it would have been meaningless in protecting the parties.

I have encountered the problem of gag orders many times. Virtually all such attempts are unsuccessful, and even when I was able to change the title of a case to "*Anonymous*"—as with Rudy Giuliani— the time before the press found out who the parties were lasted as long as it took to boil a three-minute egg.

One of the first things I tell young lawyers in a case that has any media potential is not to give the story "legs." The quickest way to limit the damages is not to give any statement. I usually pursue this path and did so in the Wildenstein matter. We made the best we could out of the situation in requesting a gag order, but the judge decided otherwise.

"In a divorce action, defendant husband [Alec] moved to bar the press from the proceedings, 'gag' the lawyers and proceed anonymously. His attorney's supporting affirmation cited concern about ridicule of the wife in the newspapers. It also stated that the family disliked publicity and worried about its deleterious effect on the family fortune and safety. Wife opposed. The court found no compelling reasons to grant the motion."

Question: Can one think of any more compelling reason for a gag order other than those set forth in her opinion?

The particular judge in Giuliani's case acted, in my opinion, from good motives, but simply arrived at the wrong result. Judges, even well-meaning, conscientious appellate judges, *do* make mistakes. The disease is the human frailties of man.

After the whirl of activity, privately, in the courts and in the press, after almost two years, the case limped its tortuous path to a negotiated conclusion. We considered the final resolution extremely favorable to Alec. I always believed the test is whether after the resolution, my client's life (if I am representing a husband) is going to be any worse than it was before the settlement. Clearly, Alec's life did not change one whit, and I suppose that the settlement did not in any appreciable way really affect his or his family's fortunes. Sadly, I don't believe the same could have been said for Jocelyn.

There are some men, who if they had to choose between having a woman and nobody knowing, as opposed to *not* having her and everyone *believing* they did, would rather have the latter over the former. Similarly, I have also observed this is true for some women and their divorce settlements. I believe that to be the case with Mayor Giuliani's former wife and Christie Brinkley in her interviews about her highly publicized divorce settlement. For the men involved in such situations, allowing the lady to boast, particularly when there was really little to boast about, is usually a modest price to pay for a soon-to-be-former spouse's momentary happiness . . . and certainly so if they do it while counting the money that they did not have to pay her.

Jocelyn Wildenstein was declared by the press to be "jubilant" over her settlement. She said she planned to start her own line of perfume and jewelry and write her autobiography, and ". . . is looking to attach her surgically altered likeness to promising ventures in film, publishing, fashion and fine art." This was in April of 1999. If she did any of those things, she will die with her secret. She never remarried and apparently still lives in New York, having purchased and lived in three different residences in a relatively short period of time.

When Jocelyn finally left the family's Sixty-fourth Street residence, the press reported that her staff walked out on her en masse and were snatched up by Edgar Bronfman Jr., who owned the next-door mansion.

People who dwell on such things assume that the one-time settlement to Jocelyn equated to the value of one painting in the family vault. But it was never about money. Be that as it may, there is obviously more to happiness than the money received in a divorce settlement. In this case, even considering the financial rewards for Jocelyn, I doubt that her life after the settlement was any less troubled, nor was she able to maintain the same standard of living as when she was married.

As far as the bugles and drums are concerned, Jocelyn's legal journey seemed not to end in a crescendo of drumbeats, but rather in whimpering violins.

Alec went off to relative anonymity, remarrying, devoting his time to the art business, the breeding and running of racehorses in Europe, dividing his time between his various estates, until his death in 2008.

Jocelyn was, and may still be, in the last analysis, one of those unhappy, perhaps pathetic people who look into a mirror and see a reflection that is not reality. The trajectory of the reflection that travels from the mirror to their brains becomes a great deceiver. To some degree, we all look into the mirror and try to ignore a double chin or count hairs that are not quite there on an otherwise bald head or look this way or that covering or dismissing some perceived flaw in our appearance. And then there are the Jocelyn Wildensteins of the world who have themselves cut, scraped, stitched, pumped, suctioned and altered in pursuit of an ever-changing, nonexistent ideal. They look, but alas, they do not see.

A caveat: A woman called and made an appointment to see me. The attractive woman sitting across the desk handed me a photograph and said "This is my husband." Usually, nothing said or done in these initial interviews ever shocks me, but here, I was taken aback. I was viewing a photograph of a male version of Jocelyn Wildenstein. The story became even stranger, and shortly it would become public property. Her husband, a lawyer, had met Jocelyn, and they shortly became a public "item." The relationship eventually made its way to the popular press and resulted in yet another headline in the *New York Post*. The paper now published a picture of the husband of the woman who consulted and ultimately hired me under the heading "Her Mane Man," obviously a reference to Mrs. Wildenstein and her new beau's hairdo. Jocelyn's new companion was one Kenneth Godt, and as was noted in the press, there were "... several mysteries about Godt." Reporters tried to track him down, and "... calls to a phone number listed on Kenneth Godt's business card were not answered and no home number was listed."

The ever-vigilant media, on February 22, 1999, reported "The couple shared a subtle smooch Friday night at the Soho restaurant Cipriani Downtown ... and they were led to a back table where they kissed, their towering manes mingling." Still representing Alec, I thought the less said about this the better. My comment to the press was "[I] did not know anything about the new romance and as far as I know, he is a lawyer who is vigorously representing Mrs. Wildenstein." Since a settlement was in the works, the last thing I wanted to do was to undermine her confidence in her lawyer. When the final steps to the settlement were made, the press reported "Also in court was Jocelyn's pompadoured paramour and personal advisor Ken Godt."

Paradise lasted a little longer than it did in the Garden of Eden, and on November 10, 1999, the headline read "Jocelyn Gives Bankrupt Beau the Brush Off." The smaller print read "Long Island divorce lawyer Kenneth Godt, who has filed for personal professional bankruptcy, is no longer wealthy divorce [sic] Jocelyne Wildenstein's mane man."

The only other loose end was Judge Marylin Diamond, the judge in Alec's case and my subsequent personal dealings with her that resulted in her being deposed in my office accompanied by bodyguards and later, a visit to me from agents of the FBI.

* * *

STEPHANIE SEYMOUR

You are too beautiful
My dear to be true
And I am a fool for beauty . . .

Lorenz Hart, Richard Rodgers

There is a doomed quality about love, even the best of it, since nothing is forever, even if "forever" ends in the big sleep in the lilac-scented sod of a country churchyard. Hart could have written these lines about Stephanie Seymour.

The Seymour case was the largest in Connecticut's history. Sadly, money and "things" are the yardsticks of measuring most aspects of life. Particularly this is true when talking about divorce cases and taking note of their readings on life's Richter scale. At the very center, divorce cases, give or take some custody battles, are usually not about principles: the struggle between good and evil, right or wrong, the eternal questions of being or nothingness, the existence of God or the chaos of the universe or really even about children. It is about *Things*: buildings, works of art, boats, bank accounts, money slumbering in Swiss banks or under a mattress, jewels, stocks and bonds, real estate and all the other toys and objects that are suddenly meaningless when the game of doctors, hospitals and life being more about sleep than wakening begins. Divorce lawyers, that breed of man that trembles between humanity and barbarity, like to observe that when the money is worked out, everything else invariably falls into place.

The Stephanie Seymour case, because of its complexity and breadth, was beyond the capabilities of any single lawyer. Stephanie had employed two law firms and one accounting firm to represent her. But it was, Stephanie decided, time to change horses. This happens often in divorce cases, that are in the last analysis themselves about changing horses, or at least about jumping off one of them while waiting for the next to come by. Lawyers are dumped because they get burned out, clients lose confidence in them. Because there are disputes about monies, approaches, tactics, attitude, divergent astrological signs, failure to produce results or simply for no good reason other than ennui. Hitler, Churchill and Lincoln changed generals more often than the bed sheets in a second-rate brothel. Law is a business where the customer is always right, and I have found, mostly they, in fact, are.

* * *

Stephanie Seymour has a bump on the bridge of her nose. She could have had the best, most expensive and brightest of plastic surgeons crawl up, into and around her nose until it would have been as perfect as that of a Polish chambermaid. But she chose to keep the bump. She was *that* secure in her beauty. Maybe, Havelock Ellis, who admittedly was no expert on beauty nor considering where his field of endeavor took his nose, also not on noses, nevertheless may have had it right when he said, "The absence of flaw in beauty is itself a flaw."

Stephanie started her professional life at the age of fourteen as a model. Being a model by itself would have been enough to turn a young person's life into a shipwreck. A model is measured by that most superficial of all things human: the gaudy wrapping of flesh and the arrangement of features. The lack of interest in anything under that winding pendant of skin usually insults and degrades the mind and soul that lies beneath.

Stephanie was "discovered" ("condemned" one might better say) as a supermodel when she was barely past adolescence. The story of her life is now public property. At sixteen, she lived with John Casablancas, the much-older married head of Elite Model Management. She then had a one year marriage (1989-1990) to guitarist Tommy Andrews. There was one child, Dylan, born of the union. This was followed by a relationship with actor Warren Beatty. In mid-1991, she became involved with Axl Rose, the lead singer of Guns 'N Roses. By 1993, she and Rose had sued each other for assault. After her breakup with him, she dated and then married much older Peter Brant, described by the press as a publisher, real-estate developer and art collector. There were three children born of the union. In 2009, they became locked in a divorce death struggle.

Often, you never really know why a client has hired you. It could be your track record or the convergence of astrological signs or an unexpected meeting in a restaurant. This question was dealt with when the court-appointed psychiatrist testified at deposition. The following questions and answers ensued:

Q: Are you familiar with the attorney from New York, Raoul Lionel Felder?

A: I haven't met him in person. I know his reputation and his name.

Q: Are you aware that Stephanie has sought to have him come into this case?

A: Yes.

Q: What relevance, if any, do you make of that?

A: I talked with her briefly about the arrangement. She said that he is a great comfort to her ...

Q: ... does it surprise you that she feels comfort with a gentleman with a reputation such as his?

A: No. I think it probably makes her feel safer in some way.

Q: Why safer?

A: A senior family law attorney and an older man who is reputed to be famous and such, I would think that would appeal to her.

I had known Stephanie for some time before the divorce case and was impressed by her intelligence and sensitivity. But, my first assignment when she hired me was, since this was in Connecticut, to choose, or at least recommend to her, Connecticut counsel who would work along with me. There is no shortage of fine lawyers anywhere in the United States, but New York lawyers sometimes have more experience in certain kinds of high net-worth cases with certain kinds of litigants. The perception—right or wrong—is that they are better suited to playing hardball and dealing with big-money cases than lawyers in other communities who are used to more bucolic litigation.

My initial task involved interviewing prospective Connecticut lawyers. Lawyers do not like to be auditioned and often resent this sort of beauty contest. Usually, their reaction is everything from an outraged refusal to partake of the interview to, on the other hand, a quiet murmur that they would prefer to take a pass. It always seemed to me that lawyers secure in their positions and reputation generally have no problem with being interviewed provided it involved a case of significant magnitude and complexity. Stephanie's was such a case.

We finally ended up with two superb lawyers, Anne Dranginis, former chief appellate judge in the Family Part in Connecticut, and Austin McGuigan, former chief prosecutor for Connecticut. Anne was charming yet stern, with a fine knowledge of the players. Her grasp of the law in this area and the dynamics of the courtroom was unique since she was able to view things through the eyes of both lawyer and judge. Austin was a crusty and tough litigator who maintained and juggled numbers, calculations and events in the computer of his memory bank. He knew what he wanted and how to get it and if necessary, take few prisoners in the process. Most important, Austin and Anne had sufficient backup facilities consisting of expert and dedicated lawyers.

Now something arose that should have been dealt with in an absolutely routine manner: my admission to the Connecticut bar for the purposes of this one case. America is virtually the only country in the Western world where lawyers are licensed on a state-by-state basis. A lawyer in the south of Germany is also a lawyer in the north of Germany. But, a lawyer in New York is not a lawyer and therefore not permitted to practice fifteen minutes away in New Jersey nor an hour away in Connecticut.

Some states have reasons to be restrictive in permitting outside lawyers to appear in their courts. Florida and California understandably do not want to be used as retirement homes for lawyers who simply have decided that they would like to simultaneously carry on a practice of law and at the same time, live in semiretirement in a place with more salubrious weather. Having made this point, I have tried cases and had no difficulty in a temporary admission to both the Florida and California bar for individual cases—usually a one-shot deal. Other states, like New Jersey, have a local bar that, with some justification, may feel threatened at one end of the state by Philadelphia lawyers taking their business and at the other end of the state, by New York lawyers. Lawyers from New York have a tough and earthy reputation and dance to the lyrics of the old blues song, "Save your money and railroad fare/When you leave New York you ain't going nowhere."

There is, however, a well-utilized procedure for a lawyer from one state to obtain admission to the bar of another state for an individual case.

In the last analysis, trials are generally all pretty much the same whether in state or federal courts. Differences in state law as it may involve a particular case are usually circumscribed and for an experienced lawyer, simple to master. The admission for a particular case is done by a motion to the court for admission *pro hac vice*. A local lawyer has to propose the out-of-state lawyer for limited admission to the bar and in effect, be responsible for that lawyer's actions during the case. Lawyers do cooperate with one another in this regard since there is a general recognition that a client has a right to have a lawyer with whom he or she is comfortable as part of the team.

In the Seymour case, up until the point I came on board, there had already been a lawyer for the children appointed, Mister S. I was surprised that after I was retained, a lawyer I knew who apparently knew the attorney for the children, told me that the lawyer for the children told him that there was an antagonism between us (Mister S and me) as a result of a motion he argued against me years earlier. This was also repeated to me by one of our Connecticut lawyers. For the life of me, I could not recall who this lawyer was, but he had said it involved a motion in the Liza Minnelli case in which I represented her husband, David Gest. I gather Mister S was an associate of the lawyer who represented Ms. Minnelli. I recollected that there was, indeed, a motion in that case, recalled nothing about its substance nor who argued it for the other side. It was merely one motion out of hundreds that I had been involved with in the intervening years. I was sure that if I had seen this person, I would not have recognized him.

My immediate reaction was that Mister S must have been one of those pygmies of the law who sometimes argue motions, do the routine almost ministerial work necessary to move cases along the conveyor belt of justice. I came—right or wrong—to this conclusion. Unique to the legal profession, an experienced lawyer can usually arrive at a judgment about an adversary after he or she speaks for a moment or so. You can tell little about the ability of a surgeon when the initial incision is made. One would have to observe his or her technique as the operation progresses and see the final result achieved, which could take days or weeks. Not so, in law.

Of course, in law, in many cases, the lawyer has no control over results. A drug dealer who sells narcotics to a law-enforcement agent will invariably be convicted. Famed trial lawyer Edward Bennett Williams said that in a case, a lawyer can only make a 10-percent difference.

To be fair, judging lawyers are subjective events, and one person's pygmy may be another's giant. It should be noted that without pygmies, we could not have giants.

I told the person who relayed the information about my alleged antagonistic relationship with Mister S that I had no recollection of him, at all. As I said this, I knew I had made a mistake. The worst thing you can do to a person with perhaps a fragile ego is to say you do not remember him or her. People can accept the fact that you have fought with them or argued against them, do not like them or hold them in less than high repute. But, *not* to dignify a person by not even *remembering* them is perhaps the ultimate insult. I thought and thought, but I could not remember what the motion was about, and I had only a vague sense recollection of some large person who argued on the other side who did not particularly impress me, but I could recollect nothing further. As a matter of fact, my memory was still not jogged even when I eventually shook hands with Mister S at an evening meeting while I was coming and he was going. I simply shook hands with the person who smiled at me, as one does in such a situation. If his name was given to me or he mentioned it when shaking hands, it went right by me. It was only after the handshake, when Mister S rapidly left and I asked who the person was with whom I had shaken hands, was he identified to me. I then realized that, in addition to whatever traits or deficits I may have ascribed to him based on reports from others, his smiling countenance and eager handshake allowed me to now add that of intellectual cowardice.

Generally speaking, lawyers, as a matter of course and practice, do not oppose an out-of-state lawyer coming into a case. I have not opposed—as a matter of fact, *proposed*—Marvin Mitchelson, when at the height of fame and notoriety, he wanted to come into a hotly contested major case *pro hac vice*.

However, in Connecticut, when it came time for my admission *pro hac vice*, Mister S opposed my admission.

I could only suppose that my failure to even *remember* him inflamed him to the degree that he must have overlooked the personal embarrassment of the situation. He objected to my admission for petty and admittedly technical reasons, even questioning the judge's right to allow my admission and said in part, "... but I do question whether Your Honor, in all due respect, has the jurisdiction and authority to even address the application." He was clearly grasping at technical straws seeking reasons for me not to be admitted. I was not present at the proceeding, but Ms. Dranginis pointed out to the judge the obvious. "I believe our client has the constitutional right to counsel of her choice." Nevertheless, Mister S kept right on going, now claiming that there were procedural defects in the papers submitted, saying, "... Ms. Brant is being represented by very fine lawyers who know Connecticut law, who are more than capable of protecting her interests ..." Apparently, his new tack was that *he* could or should decide who should represent Stephanie. Obviously, it was not for him to decide who would be capable of protecting Stephanie's interests. He then told the court, "It's a little late to be bringing in Mister Felder. We have a trial next month, and they're bringing him in, and you talk about a Monday morning quarterback, it's a little bit late."

Obviously none of this was his affair. Whether I came into the case late or early or hovered above it, he should have nothing to do with that decision. At that point, I believe he drowned with the remnants of the straw clutched. The court said, "... with certain limitations, that every person has the right to chose the counsel that they want to represent them, and that is a basic protected right ..." He went on, in substance, to say that whether we like a person or not, "that is not the criteria we use. She has an absolute choice to do that ..."

It is hard to understand what thoughts could have engendered the silly arguments of the lawyer for the children. Was it fear? Was it ego? Insecurity? Like many people who act out of personal passion, he just went down a foolish path, and once embarked, there was no turning back. I will never know, and perhaps neither will he, but certainly the impulses that compelled him to proceed down his chosen path did not do him credit.

Although Stephanie was a battleground over which men fought, she was basically untouched and innocent. Innocence, like splendor, cannot be faked, and Stephanie was the genuine article.

At one point in the case, I was at her home to prepare for the litigation. She just returned with the children from Morocco. I had arrived a bit early for our meeting, and we were waiting for Ms. Dranginis to show up. Stephanie told me she wanted me to come upstairs to show me something. Apparently, in Morocco she had bought some rugs that she had now piled against the wall. She then proceeded to pull out rug after rug, spreading them out on the floor, showing them to me with all the innocence, glee and enthusiasm of a child opening presents on Christmas morning. She was as untouched as the morning's first butterfly.

Things do come around full circle. As I arrived at the office where a settlement conference was being held, I saw Mister Brant, Stephanie's husband. I recognized him from newspaper photographs. Later, when we bumped into each other in one of the rooms with his lawyer sitting at the table, he came over to me and said, "Don't you remember when we shook hands sixteen years ago?" I had absolutely no idea what he was talking about, but I tried to be polite and

I told him I did not and made a weak joke about not remembering what I had for breakfast that morning. He then told me that he was at the warehouse the day I flipped the coins in the Scull matter. He was there at the behest of Mister Scull's people to give expert advice as to which of the paintings should be chosen by them.

The Seymour case was building to a crescendo. My team from New York and I had reserved hotel rooms at the Hyatt in Greenwich, Connecticut, for the following three weeks. Three weeks would be a major discombobulation of my personal and professional life. The trial was set for Monday, September 20. There are things that one never really thinks about while preparing for a trial. For instance, the place of the trial was in Middletown, Connecticut, a distance too far for commuting back and forth from New York. This meant that I would have to bring with me five suits, shirts, ties, etc., to last me until I could exchange them for another five suits, shirts, ties, etc. for the following week. It also meant that since I am the lead lawyer in my office, I would still have to tend to office business after hours by telephone, etc. This sort of thing would have to go on for three weeks, not to mention preparation and time for the trial itself.

I learned, starting Saturday, that the parties, Stephanie Seymour and Peter Brant, were talking. Talking is good! Talking indicates communication. Many wars are fought because of lack of communication. So it was all to the good that they were speaking with each other. In a poll taken after two years of fighting in World War I, the majority of soldiers could not explain what the war was about.

By Sunday night, I learned that the divorce had been called off. The *Daily News* the next day echoed other papers' reports, and the headline was "Model Stephanie Seymour calls off bitter divorce from Peter Brandt, announces reconciliation."

The ways of love and its flip side hate are strange and unpredictable. The case died suddenly, inexplicably and with a smothered whimper.

PABLO DIEGO JOSÉ FRANCISCO DE PAULA JUAN NEPOMUCENO MARIA DE LOS REMEDIOS CIPRIANO DE LA SANTÍSIMA TRINIDAD RUIZ Y PICASSO

A rose by any other name . . .

Pablo Picasso towered over the art of the twentieth century. Indeed, his artistic expressions shifted from one medium to another, one period or style to another. Be it Cubism, Classicism, Surrealism, a Blue, Rose and African Period, as soon as he mastered one particular form or style, he defined them and carried them to their last outermost parameter. He then stopped, closed his books on the particular period or form and turned his attention to the next artistic mountain that had to be climbed. I always felt an affinity to him because he was, as I, among other things, a collector of junk in enormous quantities. When one house was filled up, he simply locked it and moved on to another home. He refused to let housekeepers dust his rooms, his rationale being "Nobody dusts the earth, and nobody says it's dirty, so why should I have the rooms dusted?"

Well on into an age when for most men there is more dreaming than waking, he began a live-in relationship with Françoise Gilot, an art student forty years younger than he. She later became an extraordinary artist in her own right. From that union was born a son, Claude, and a daughter, Paloma. As with other women, she became his muse, and as with his other women, she was the subject of paintings whose fame would long outlive both painter and subject. There were those portraits where her features were fragmented and then rearranged. There were line drawings that with a paucity of line and form, her gentleness of spirit was captured. Indeed, the Picasso family, if not as celebrated by those of sitcoms, seemed to be close-knit and happy. There is a famous photograph that has now been made into a greeting card showing Françoise in a long cotton dress walking across a beach. Picasso following her, holding a parasol over her head. Behind him smiling, Claude, then a little boy. The joy of these people was casual and unfeigned. They were sprinkled with magic dust.

Their relationship lasted ten years until 1953 when Françoise left him. Because of his abuse and infidelity, she moved out with the children. In 1964, she wrote a book, *Life with Picasso*. This book was to Picasso a declaration of war, and rapidly, he cut ties with both his children.

In 1970, Françoise married Dr. Jonas Salk, developer of the polio vaccine.

In connection with my representation of Claude, I met Françoise when she was in her seventies. I had been anxious to meet this extraordinary woman who had captured the hearts of two of the best-known men of our time. These two men—Picasso and Salk—could not have been further apart in their respective fields of endeavor. Indeed, the only similarity between them was the fact that they stood above all other contemporaries, at the absolute pinnacle of all other people in the world doing similar work.

Françoise was a dark-complexioned woman, her facial features strong, but not craggy or sharp. She had cut short the hair that Picasso memorialized in portraits, luxuriant, wild and flowing. She was not cute or pretty in any conventional way, but rather was handsome in the way that intelligence blesses some women and is submerged in others. Her eyes were dark and luminous and had none of the dullness that comes with age. They were the eyes of a young woman.

She had an extraordinary quality. As I observed, when you spoke to her, she looked at you intensely as if you were saying the most profound, extraordinary of things, even though what you were talking about was trivial or banal or just talk for its own sake, meant merely to fill a void in time. When I offered her my arm to cross a street, she took it as if I was guiding her as she stepped on rocks to ford a stream.

I first met Claude when he was in his twenties and seeking to divorce his wife, Sarah. Claude was a darkly handsome young man, much in the mold of his father, but his features were of much finer line and better chiseled. I represented him, and the divorce took place in due course.

Sometime afterward, Sarah again appeared and refused to return two items of personal property to Claude. Claude, who would eventually be the recipient of great wealth, was, at that stage, a photographer, living a modest existence as a borderline bohemian in the best sense of the word. I still have on my wall a photograph he took of a speeding subway train that captured in the split second of being memorialized on film the blurring bundled energy of a passing train. His interests were more artistic than monetary.

I was surprised that Claude seemed prepared to do battle over these items. He just did not seem to be that kind of person. One of the items was a sort of get-well card, and the other seemed to be a lump of gold that might have been a piece of jewelry. But then he explained, and his passion to recover them made sense. When a small boy, he was ill. An ordinary father might send his son a get-well card purchased at a gift shop. Claude's father was no ordinary father. His father drew one for his son. It was drawn with colored crayon and depicted a bullfight scene with, center ring, a diminutive bullfighter. Inscribed in French, the father handwrote, "Claude, in the costume of a boy of Aragon."

The lump of gold had a sort of engraving of a face. Claude explained to me when he was a little boy, his father took him to a dentist in the south of France for some procedure. The boy was understandably upset at the prospect of dental work, so his father tried to amuse him. He asked the dentist if he could use his electric drill. With some of the dentist's gold and using the drill, which certainly was as an unknown instrument of art to Picasso or for that matter anybody else in the world, he carved in the gold a drawing of a face.

I understood immediately that these sorts of pieces are intensely personal to a child. Particularly precious to a child who, through no fault of his own, had been rejected by his father. These would be the *last* things that he would toss to a former wife as a parting gift in a divorce case.

The case ensued for their return, and the battle lines were soon drawn. There were, as is usual, oral depositions before trial. Claude's native language is French. Having seen him recently interviewed on a talk show, today his command of English is virtually perfect. Back then, at the time of his divorce, his English was problematic. In the deposition, he was asked by Sarah's lawyer whether he made a promise to Sarah to give her the two items now in contention. His answer was "No, not that I could recollect." What Claude meant to say was simply "No." Somehow, when Claude translated his thought in French to words in English, the translation was transmuted to a politer turn of phrase than a simple "No." Such was the slender thread on which Sarah's claim hung. Sarah and her tears would have the jury believe that the import of this answer was simply he did not remember whether he promised the items to Sarah. The significance of this juxtaposing recollections is that if one party says he does not remember and the other party says she *does* remember, usually the latter carries the day. I believe Sarah's lawyer's game plan was to put enough of a case on so that it could survive all the usual legal motions to dismiss and get to a jury, suggesting that Claude really did not remember whether he made the promise. In this atmosphere of confusion, then, the monies or fame would bedazzle the juror's and produce a decision based on charity, with the thought that Claude is or would be a very wealthy young man.

Initially, we had a choice. We could have the case heard by a jury or a judge.

We opted for a jury trial. I prefer a judge when there is pure issue of law involved. The judge examines the law on both sides of the issue and makes his or her best call, knowing it will often be reviewed or second-guessed by an appellate panel. On issues of fact, or fact mixed law and fact, judges, however, are, after all, human beings, and often it is hard to define their cross-currents of sympathy, personal feelings or proclivities, outlook on life, even religion, etc., that may unconsciously go into making a decision. Whereas with a jury, in the deliberation room when each of the jurors is involved in the ping-ponging back and forth of their feelings and ideas, an individual juror may not be prepared to defend his position and explain to his colleagues that he was prepared to make a decision based on sympathy.

Sometimes the most crucial part of a jury trial is choosing the jury. There is a lucrative cottage industry that has arisen to assist lawyers in this task. Enter the jury consultants. The trade of jury consulting requires no license or state testing, Typically, jury consultants have entered this occupation possessed of a large variety of skills, but some have none at all.

Years ago, I tried an important criminal case, and the client wanted us to hire jury consultants. The consultants came at a fancy price and gave us a list of questions to ask each specific juror. Each question had a number assigned to it, and each possible answer had another number assigned to it. The idea was, once finished questioning a prospective juror, when the numbers assigned to the questions and answers reached a certain total, we did not want that person to serve on the jury. One of the questions was "What daily newspaper do you read?" Every one of the prospective jurors immediately said they read *The New York Times*. When we impaneled the finally selected jury, as the trial went on day by day, I observed that every juror either read one of two papers, the *New York Post* or the *Daily News*, both tabloids. The point is that people lie or perhaps tell you something that they believe would impress you.

My co-counsel in that criminal case was a well-known criminal lawyer. Before we used the jury consultants, we each made our individual notes as to whom we thought from the panel should be on the jury, neither of us telling the other our conclusions. When we compared notes on each juror, we were surprised to see that we picked the identical ones, and in the end, we basically ignored the jury consultants. Incidentally, in that case, the jury was out less than an hour, and our client was found not guilty.

My big problem in selecting a jury in the Picasso case was that the jurors might be hypnotized by the name, fame, wealth or supposed wealth of my client and engage in a court-approved method of redistribution of wealth. It seemed to me that the more modest as far as wealth was concerned, the juror might be more prone to give away someone else's money.

There was one particular juror that disturbed me because reading down next to the word "occupation," he listed "doorman" at a particular Park Avenue building with which I was familiar. He also was, by name and obvious appearance, Hispanic, which created another problem. Since Picasso was Spanish, I had no idea if and whether that would create a cross-current that may bounce our way or the other side's way. My mind was put mostly at ease when I asked the prospective doorman/juror the question whether his decision would be affected by virtue of the fact that he would hear the name Pablo Picasso as an integral part of the litigation, he answered "no." I took him at his word, but I was still uneasy. My mind was put completely at rest when I overheard him ask a fellow juror as we were picking the panel, "Who is Picasso?"

Claude took the stand and explained the intense emotional meanings to him of the two items his former wife sought to retain. I debated whether to put Françoise Gilot on the stand and/or her husband, Dr. Jonas Salk. In the last analysis, I did not do so because I felt they were both such powerful people that they would deflect from our message, which was basically: A greedy attempt is being made to take a beloved piece of memorabilia from a son who had been estranged from his father.

We made our summations. The jury was out, and no sooner had we left the building than we were called back, and the decision was in our favor. After the jury was discharged, the judge said to me, "Well, you can't blame a girl for trying." My response to him was "Yes, you can."

35

THE JEWISH JUDGE

Funny how bigots see things through the prisms of their own sickness. A bastard is not just a bastard, but he is a *black* bastard. The doctors that ministered to the dying tyrant Stalin were not just doctors, they were somehow transmuted by the Russian press into "the *Jewish* doctors who killed Stalin," and of course, President Roosevelt's real name was Rosenfeld, and Hitler's proof that the American press was controlled by Jews was his asking, at one of his all-night diatribes, the question "What is *Times* spelled backward?" And, to a similar twisted mind, a judge who does something bad, is a *Jewish* judge, and if it is real bad, he is a *Jew* judge.

The Christian Party (and don't feel neglected if you are not invited to the party) had an article about New York State Acting Supreme Court Justice Marylin Diamond.

The crawl at the top of the page read "Looney Tune jew [sic] judges." But aside from learning about Judge Diamond, you would have learned that "Jews knew about 9/11 9 years before it happened," and that, "AIDS, 1. Kills MOSTLY jews [sic], 2. Kills mostly jew [sic] 'DOCTORS' who needless to say are killing US by the hundreds of thousands, ANNUALLY," and in a spirit of egalitarianism, paradoxically informs the reader than "...[it is] mostly if not exclusively blacks who carry AIDS."

The awful part is that, as far as Judge Diamond, the article itself is pretty much accurate in describing some of the judge's problems. All of this should suggest that people of privilege who also enjoy minority status should realize that they have a responsibility or at least should have an awareness of the fodder they can provide to mission-bent lunatics that have larger targets.

The first time I saw Diamond was when the Wildenstein case appeared on the court calendar. Her face was a celebration of the plastic surgeon's art, as opposed to Mrs. Wildenstein's that was in the "I want my money back together with damages" category. Save for the fact that the surgeon made her nose a bit too narrow for the width of her face, her features were symmetrical, uninteresting and perfect and looked exactly like all the other women that have money—and smell like it—that come, go and air-kiss in all the smart East Side restaurants that serve little portions on big plates. The fact that they all look like each other never bothered me much. If Caravaggio painted two pictures of a woman and hung them side by side, they would each be equally beautiful, and he could charge the same price for both.

Having served as a member of the New York State Commission on Judicial Conduct and then as its vice chairman and ultimately its chairman, I was in a position to observe a great deal of and about judges. In each pre-meeting package I received from the commission, in addition to the confidential material involving the state judges who were the subject of my attention, there was a summary of public reports about misbehaving judges from around the country.

For years, I had lingered over the good and bad, the knaves and fools, judges who masturbate behind the bench or watch pornography on court computers and those who simply fall asleep at the bench and maybe some who probably fall asleep while masturbating or watching pornography because they had passed across the border into the queasy embrace of senility. Therefore, I have credentials in judge judging, but it should not go unsaid that as a class of people, they are among the most overworked and underpaid of public servants. Overwhelmingly, they are effectively self-policing, dedicated, intelligent and fair minded, but alas, one would undoubtedly find some few that should have been discarded before being marketed to the public.

Judge Diamond, although I have never had a personal (as opposed to a professional) conversation with her, has intersected in several different areas of my professional life—from the Wildenstein case and her alleged involvement concerning Mrs. Wildenstein's lawyer, to the affair of the Gelman billions and her personal connection with it—in which the judge acquired a seven-figure fortune—to an FBI investigation, to a questionable anthrax attack upon her and two years of state paid-for bodyguards and even to the Giuliani administration.

It will be apparent from various public documents and references that there was a perception that the commission I headed conducted one or more investigations of the judge. It would be inappropriate for me to reveal any of that or even acknowledge if there were any matters concerning her before the commission. But, if there were, I would have recused myself from such proceedings, and my custom would be, although not required to do so, even to leave the room while it was discussed in such a circumstance.

* * *

THE FBI COMES TO CALL

The two FBI agents who looked like they bought their suits and haircuts at the same place showed me their identification. They also made me feel very old. When I was with the Department of Justice years ago, I frequently dealt with agents and supervisors who, at the time, were at least a few years older than I was, and since we were working together, our relationship was a collegial one—lunches, perhaps a drink at the end of the day, lots of small talk. *These* young men, who now sat across from me at the other side of my desk, were young enough to be my sons.

I knew that it must be a serious matter that brought them to my office. Today with all the demands on the agency, non-agents do a great deal of the work. Agents used to conduct the background checks, and now clerks making telephone calls often do this. Non-agents will often do personal interviews and use language to introduce themselves, saying something ambiguous like, "I'm with the FBI." Every bank robbery used to be investigated by agents who responded to the scene of the crime, and now, this is left to the city police, unless there was a gun involved.

The two young men explained that they were from the FBI's Public Integrity Section. I think they felt a bit more at ease after glancing over at a table that held, among other things, a going-away plaque from my former colleagues embossed with the Justice Department's seal.

They were here to question me about Judge Diamond. Their questions covered the landscape of her *alleged* activities—things both great and small—and it was clear to me that they had done their homework. Much of what they asked me about were things I had read in the papers and other things I had heard about, but were basically the stuff of gossip. Some of the areas, of course, I knew about to my own sure knowledge.

Since so much has appeared in the press about the judge's activities, I am uncertain at what point in time juxtaposed against her various problems, our interview took place, so it is difficult for me to remember the grounds and subject matter discussed. The judge had retained, at different time, a series of high-priced lawyers to represent her in her many troubles. At one point, she hired retired federal Judge Harold Tyler, and it is logical to assume this was at a coincidence in time with my FBI interview. Tyler, referring to Judge Diamond, was quoted in the *New York Post* as making the insightful comment, "What she did, she did." And they say that lawyers are not smart!

The Wildenstein case was the most important matrimonial case presided over by Judge Diamond—at least it was if you believe what you read in the papers. Many of the stories appearing in the press about the judge usually include in their opening paragraph something like, "Judge Diamond, who presided over the Wildenstein billion-dollar art case." In point of fact, it was not an "art case" nor was there a "billion dollars" in value or dollars involved in the divorce case. She did, however, preside over it, and there was, indeed, the gentility and otherworldliness that billions of dollars provides to members of the luck sperm club.

I had occasion to see her a few times prior to the Wildenstein case, and my first impression—which, historically, are usually 95 percent accurate about 40 percent of the time—was that she was an extremely insecure person with all the paraphernalia of insecurity: the plastic surgery, discomfort with men she believed powerful and as "powerful" represented a threat to her, like any threatened person, she reacted with a hostility proportionate to the perceived threat. Her choice of two husbands—both nice men, but certainly both nonassertive types—supported my conclusion. Putting aside the validity or invalidity of my judgment, one thing I did get right: I should have as little to do with her as possible, and she should be left to have her power struggles with those who have testosterone to spare—or waste.

* * *

THE CASE IS CALLED

Clients resent that when their case appears on the court calendar often the first thing that happens is that the lawyers and the judge go into the back room, called in the trade "The Robing Room."

Historically, it is the room immediately in back of the wall behind the judge's throne where the judge puts on his or her black robe before appearing in the courtroom. The room is usually small with space for a battered desk, a few chairs and a private bathroom for the judge's use. There was an elderly judge in Brooklyn who would continue his conversations with lawyers while he urinated—which, because of the unfortunate state of his prostate, was often—with the door open. Thankfully—at least on the occasions I was there— female lawyers were spared the spectacle, including the accompanying sound effects.

The Robing Room is also the place where deals are made to settle cases, lawyers practice their puffery, laugh at a judge's unfunny jokes; where judges tell lawyers what they think of their cases, discuss last night's football game; and where barnyard language is frequently used and business is an almost afterthought. One rule is inviolable. Judges do not meet with a lawyer for only one of the parties unless both lawyers agree to allow this to happen. This sometimes does happen as the negotiations are in crucial stages. A judge might ask if he or she may speak to one of the lawyers separately. Then, alone with the lawyers for a litigant, he will lean across the desk and in a sympathetic tone tell the lawyer he should settle the case since he probably is not going to do as well if the case is tried. Having done that, the lawyer leaves, and then the judge sees the *other* lawyer alone and tells him precisely the same thing and in precisely the same sympathetic tone in which he spoke to the lawyer who just left the room.

This is the way cases are settled. It is an unfortunate reality of our judicial system that it would soon be flat-lined if more than 10 percent of cases actually go to completed trials. There simply is not enough time, money, plant facilities or work force for it to be otherwise. So, for the sake of expediency, if not bare functioning, it is a good thing for judges to attempt to settle cases in the back room. However, an obvious caveat is that judges must never, never meet in the Robing Room with only one of the lawyers unless it is with the prior agreement of the other. Any law student would know this before he or she buys the first textbook.

The court clerk announced, *Wildenstein* v. *Wildenstein*, and when the lawyers stood up to signify their respective presences, the clerk indicated that the case would be heard on the second call. Second call, as the name suggests, means that the clerk would run through the entire list of cases—really motions—appearing on the day's calendar. At the end of the calendar call, he or she can determine which of the cases are ready to be dealt with by the judge, which had been withdrawn or resolved or whether both lawyers have even shown up in court. If a matter is extremely vexatious, or is the subject of much publicity, the judge may hold it to the end of all calendars, either to allow the courtroom to empty or to give it the extra time it might require.

I sat on one side of the crowded room and Mr. X, Mrs. Wildenstein's lawyer, on the other side, near the window. Sometimes it is an hour or more between the first and second calendar call, and lawyers usually go out into the hall to make phone calls, talk with their client, gossip with other lawyers, etc. I remained seated, but Mr. X caught my eye as he moved to the front of the room toward the judge's Robing Room.

When I saw that Mr. X had gone into the Robing Room, I thought that perhaps he had a prior case and I simply had not heard it called, or perhaps he was going in the back room to drop off some papers. But I kept my eye on the door. He did not come out immediately, and I looked at my watch, and I fidgeted as three minutes were ticked off, then five minutes, and ultimately he came out about eight minutes later. It could have actually been longer because I may not have started looking at my watch immediately upon his entering the room. Finally, sometime much later, the judge came out.

When the Wildenstein case was called, I walked up to the bench, and I told Judge Diamond quietly, with Mr. X beside me, that I felt it was inappropriate for him to be alone in the Robing Room while I, an adversary, was left sitting in the courtroom. She was taken aback and said to me, I suppose without thinking, "Why didn't you object?" I stared at her in disbelief. "Are you serious? *I* have the burden of telling *you* when you do something you know is not right?" She seemed angry and just brushed it off. She must have realized what she said to me was absurd, and no judge should have to be told that she cannot meet alone with only one of the lawyers in a case and that somehow it is the *lawyer's* responsibility to tell the *judge* that this is not permissible or acceptable. Inferentially, it would mean that it is quite OK for a judge to do something improper unless somebody objects. This was not a felicitous beginning to our dealings with the judge.

* * *

INSENSITIVITY

Some people are threatened by words—and they are usually people whom you would not want to bring home for a bonding session. Dictators, for instance, are threatened so greatly by oppositional speech that they call out the secret service, and Churchill noted tyrants are threatened by "words spoken abroad."

Insecure people race to the battlements when threatened by often innocuous words: "What did he mean by that?" "Is he talking about me?" "Are they making fun of me?" And when this happens, they often utter the most stupid, insipid, inane things, shooting from their verbal hips.

When I hire a lawyer, I never ask about their personal life for two reasons: One, it's none of my business, and two, by making inquiry, you frequently find yourself sucked into the mess—every twist and turn—that is central to many people's lives.

I once hired a female lawyer who tried to tell me on several occasions about personal problems she had with a previous employer. I always changed the subject when this occurred. However, she told everyone else in the office about the situation, so it filtered back to me in some sort of diluted form that she had a nightmarish experience with a prior employer, almost being held like a sexual servant for a protracted period of time. Maybe I should have listened better. Ultimately, I was shocked to read it noted in the *New York Post* column, *Page Six*.

"John Jones" (not, of course, his real name) was a lawyer I hired. As usual at the initial interview, I neither asked nor did he offer to tell me about his marital status. Most people do not bring up the subject unless it is in connection with money ("I have two children in college, and I need a salary of . . ."). One day, after returning to the office, he seemed very disturbed. I asked him what the matter was. He told me that he appeared before Judge Diamond, and as it happened, she had presided over his *own* divorce. She mentioned this fact in conference with the other lawyer in a case when my employee appealed on behalf of one of my firm's clients. He was obviously embarrassed, and of course, it was inappropriate for the judge to do that, certainly in front of the other lawyer. Mister Jones was concerned that her conduct in this regard would go on and asked me what to do. I told him the best thing to do was talk to her frankly and tell her that what she did was inappropriate, and he would appreciate it if she did not do this again. When he followed my advice, he reported to me his version of her response was "What's the difference, everybody gets divorced." It seems the Queen of Conflicts (as she was dubbed by the press) might also be the Queen of Sensitivity.

* * *

THE JUDGE GETS A MILLION-PLUS

The underlying facts are not in dispute. Jacques and Natasha Gelman were very, very rich. Jacques was in the movie business and discovered Cantinflas, a Mexican comedian who became world famous and in the process made lots of money for Jacques. Jacques and Natasha lived in Mexico and acquired one of the foremost art collections in the world. Ultimately, it was given as the largest single bequest ever made to the Metropolitan Museum in New York. Jacques died and along the way, Natasha used the services of a New York law firm. A member of that firm was none other than Marylin Diamond. Diamond not only worked on Natasha's legal matters, but also became quite friendly on a social basis with her, even sharing a bedroom when they traveled.

At some point in time, a friend was concerned that Natasha might have been suffering from Alzheimer's disease and took her to the world-famous neurologist Fred Plum. Doctor Plum was the physician who treated President Reagan when he suffered from Alzheimer's. The doctor found that, indeed, Natasha had the disease and apparently for some time. Doctor Plum, in his report of March 30, 1995, wrote:

> *"When asked directly whether she knows of any recent changes in the economy of Mexico, where she normally lives, she was unable to think of any. When I asked her to comment on any changes in the recent presidents of Mexico and scandals surrounding those appointments, she was unable to remember any ... She was unable to identify the present director of the Metropolitan Museum of Art despite the fact that she recently had given a considerably valuable collection of paintings to that institution ... She thought today was a Friday or a Saturday (it is Monday), she doesn't recall the month ... Her close companion ... verifies that her memory has steadily deteriorated over the past ten years ... Impression: Mrs. Gelman appears to have progressive Alzheimer's disease ... Furthermore, the results of the present examination indicate that she lacks testamentary mental capacity."*

In her capacity as a lawyer before she went on the bench, Judge Diamond, acting as a member of the firm, drew several wills. Obviously, after she became a judge, she could no longer do legal work or prepare wills or trusts for Natasha.

There is only one other fact that must be explained to fill out the picture. A judge is not allowed, as a general proposition, to act as a trustee without permission of the chief administrative judge. This rule is designed to allow for a personal situation where a judge is asked to be a trustee for a relative or close friend. It is not intended for a judge to do this to generate large sums of money for him or herself. Most people acting as trustees or executors for a relative or friend's estate obtain very little or no remuneration for their services. It is done more as a courtesy or an act of friendship than anything else.

Here, the facts are not in dispute. From that point on, different folks, in good faith, could come to different conclusions.

Judge Diamond, it turns out, was a co-trustee under Natasha's will. She, of course, because of the rule prohibiting a judge from being a trustee, had to receive authorization to do this from the administrative judge since, in the ordinary course, she would be prohibited from acting in this role.

I was retained by the lawyer for relatives of Natasha. I believed, cynic that I am, without seeing the documents, that Judge Diamond probably did not reveal to the administrative judge that she would be receiving immense sums of money as a result of the approval allowing her to be a trustee.

There was legal infighting to keep me from obtaining copies of the representations made by Judge Diamond to induce her superior to allow her to serve as a trustee. I finally obtained her representations through a tortuous route.

My original query to the administrative judge was dealt with by what appeared to be a form letter enclosing only a copy of the letter from him *to* Judge Diamond giving her permission. It stated merely:

"Based on the longstanding personal relationship of trust And confidence described in your letter, permission to serve as co-trustee under the Last Will and Testament of Natasha Gelman is granted pursuant to section 100.4(E)(i) of the Rules Governing Judicial Conduct (22 NYCRR 100.4(E)[i]), provided that your service as a fiduciary will in no way interfere with the performance of your judicial duties."

This letter still did not address my concern: exactly what did Judge Diamond represent to the judge that convinced him to waive the normal rule. Specifically, I was most concerned whether it was revealed to the administrative judge the amount of money Judge Diamond would make as a result of this situation, and I directly asked in a letter:

"What I now ask of your offices is whether Judge Diamond at any time advised your office of the substantial sums of money involved or the fact that as part and parcel of the same interaction with the deceased she would receive outright an amount that we understand to be $1,100,000, in addition to what we believe could be a six figure sum each year for acting as Trustee (Judge Diamond is co-trustee)."

The administrative judge answered back that his permission was based solely on the judge's prior letter. I *finally* received a copy of Judge Diamond's original request letter, and it, of course, nicely omitted the fact that she was to receive an immense sum of money as a result of serving as trustee. Her reason for asking for the rule to be waived:

"During the many years in which I represented Mrs. Gelman, I was a close personal friend and confidant. She was a feminist and delighted in having a female attorney. She relied upon me

for advice in every area of her personal life and frequently sought
my views with respect to her charitable trusts ... My services as
co-trustee can easily be performed on weekends and evenings
and will not interfere with my judicial duties in anyway."

Charitably, the way she couched her request, was deceptive. The battle lines were now drawn.

I finally had an opportunity to depose Judge Diamond. She appeared in my office with a state-paid bodyguard (more on this later). The most dangerous weapon in my hand when I deposed her was a pencil, but perhaps, it was the questions I posed to her that caused her to feel threatened. In any event, she did not need an armed bodyguard, sitting in the waiting room in my office. When I tried to pin her down and asked to see her old diaries, her answer was "To the best of my knowledge they no longer exist." I asked, "Why is that? They're destroyed periodically, to your knowledge?"

Her answer—"They are no longer anything that I need, so they are disposed of."

Of course, she could have been absolutely accurate in describing what she did with her old diaries. However, my personal experience has been that lawyers save old diaries for a number of reasons. Lawyers frequently are called to testify about past events or clients, or there might be billing questions, etc., and they retain their old diaries. But, on the other hand, maybe she did simply throw away these records.

Of course, once the judge assumed the bench, she could no longer work at her former law firm or on any other legal project or have any business relationships with the people at the firm, but obviously, her personal friendships with her colleagues could continue.

Her former friend and law firm drew the documents that made Judge Diamond a rich person (or at least richer by a million dollars or more). Judge Diamond's position was that she knew she was going to receive some money under the terms of the trust, but her former partners, friends, etc., at the law firm never told her how much was involved. She was not surprised to receive a letter after Natasha's death that she would be getting $1.1 million (tax-free incidentally), but she never previously knew the amount. This all made no sense to me, but if it were me, I would build an altar around that life-altering letter, not to mention lighting some candles for Natasha.

I questioned her about the letter.

This letter basically says that you're going to get $1,100,000?

That's what it says.

You were surprised of this?

No.

Well, why were you not surprised?

Because I knew earlier that she had talked about leaving money.

Well there is a world of difference between talking and doing. This is the first time you knew that this person actually left you money?

This is the first time that I knew she had left me money and that she had passed—left me money and that she has passed away. That's correct ... No, it was the first time that I knew I was the beneficiary ...

You indicated you knew about this entity abroad, you knew that she told you that she wanted to leave you money and, eventually according to the letter, that is the last exhibit, that you were left over a million dollars.

Did you make any inquiry to determine any more specifics of this entity when she told you she wanted to leave you money and you knew at that point or a later point there was an entity?

I didn't ask any specifics.

And you never inquired with your former law partners or anybody else, any of the background or any of the fact surrounding this entity?

Not prior to her death, no.

At this point I must admit I had the unworthy thought that her testimony was absurd. I further queried her in a series of almost nonsensical exchanges:

> "Q.   *So that you left that meeting or during the meeting you had a sense that you were going to get a million dollars, give or take?*
>
> *No, I had a sense that she wanted to leave me 3 percent of her will.*
>
> *MR. RUBEINSTEIN (her attorney): Of her will?*
>
> *Excuse me. Of Switzerland. I am sorry. I misspoke. And that from her calculation there, it might be roughly a million dollars, but I didn't know I was going to get a million dollars.*
>
> *No, but I believe you said that she made it clear by translating francs into dollars, whatever it is, what the amounts were, and I think it's fair to say that at the meeting you felt that she would do it, you would end up getting about a million dollars?*
>
> *There was a possibility...*

I believed her lack of any curiosity as to how much her prospective commissions would be transports her answers from the realm of disbelief to that of the ridiculous:

"Have you made any inquiries to see what your prospective commissions would be?

I have not.

As we sit here today you have no idea what your commissions might be?

No.

MR. RUBEINSTEIN: You mean yes."

The reader must draw his or her own conclusions as to whether I have been unfair to the judge.

* * *

THE TRANSCRIPTS

Later on in the Wildenstein case, there was a motion dealing with some interim question. A motion is a method that lawyers have of bringing something before the court during the months while the case works its way through the system, seeking a favorable decision on some problem or impasse. Usually this is done by each side submitting papers and making oral arguments. Then the judge makes an oral decision on the motion from the bench or makes a later written decision. Since I was not happy with the result, I wanted to obtain the stenographic minutes of the exchange of views and her oral decision in order to determine whether an appeal was in order.

In courts of record all across the country, a governmental employee—a stenotypist—makes a physical transcript of what occurs in the courtroom. When I started practicing law, this was taken down by stenographers (called official court reporters) in either Gregg or Pitman shorthand—that is, pen to paper. Then the method of transcribing improved, and stenotype machines were used—machines that imprint their own shorthand symbols on a tape, later to be transcribed by a typist as a permanent record. Today, they even have machines that actually not only are able to print out in short-hand what the parties and the judge say, but can type the transcript in, one hopes, intelligible English as it goes forward. Rarely, a lawyer doesn't trust a court reporter to make an accurate record—and this is not done because of any suspected motive of the stenotypist, but usually it is a question of a lack of faith in their skills. So the lawyer will hire a private stenographer to sit in the courtroom to make his or her own record that can later be compared with the "official" transcript.

Several days after I argued the motion and received an adverse decision from Judge Diamond, I called the court reporter and said I would like to come by to pick up and pay for the transcript. Transcripts are for sale at a certain officially set price per page. The court reporter seemed to me to be evasive and said he didn't have it ready yet. The more I pressed him, the more evasive he became. Indeed, the evasiveness morphed into embarrassment. I called him again the next day with no better result. Finally, I said to him there had to be some problem because the excuses he gave me did not make sense. Unfairly, he had been placed in an impossible position. He hesitatingly told me that the judge wanted to see the transcript before he could give me a copy. To me, this would give the judge an opportunity to "correct" the transcript, and it would be patently unfair. For instance, if the judge had changed the transcript and it ended up different than what she actually said in court, I might have responded differently and a different result might have ensued. It is for this reason that the court reporters do not work for the judge or the lawyers. They work for the state and are part of the court system.

I believed it would have been pointless for me to contact the judge herself, so I telephoned the state chief administrative judge for matrimonial matters, Jacqueline Silbermann, and explained the situation. After listening to me, she said "It was wrong," but went no further than that. However, the next day I was informed my transcript was ready to be picked up.

It is not without note that often lawyers, and indeed judges, circle the wagons when there are problems. Indeed, Judge Silbermann, when questioned about Judge Diamond and her then-mounting problems by a *New York Daily News* reporter in September 2002 said, "She is a terrific judge." Frankly, in the balance between loyalty to subordinates and objectivity, many say it is probably more morally commendable to choose loyalty. I am not a member of that school of thought.

If I were the only one that had happened to, the matter might rightfully have died an ignominious death since my particular problem was remedied in short order. However, the *New York Post* in May of 2006 revealed:

> *The state court watchdog is investigating charges of Manhattan Supreme Court Judge Marilyn [Marylin] Diamond changed official transcripts, allegedly to help cover up favorable rulings she made for pals.*

> *The Commission on Judicial Conduct interviewed court reporter Maurice Schwartzberg two weeks ago — and he admitted making 'substantial revisions' to transcripts at the judge's request in one case.*

> *Diamond is the central figure in an FBI probe into whether judges hid personal and professional ties to litigants then ruled in their favor.*

> *The case involving Schwartzberg pitted a co-op owner against his building at 40 5th Ave ...*

I cannot comment on anything the commission has investigated in any fashion, and as I indicated, if such even had occurred, I would certainly recuse myself in the matter.

* * *

QUEEN OF CONFLICTS

In *The History of the World: Part I*, Mel Brooks plays Louis the Some-thing, and after inappropriately fondling women he says, "It's good to be the king." It's also good to be the queen. There was apparently a queen in the State Supreme Court, the coronation taking place on February 11, 2004, on the pages of the *Daily News*, when it dubbed Marylin Diamond the "Queen of Conflicts." Bob Port, the *News'* reporter, summed it up: "A clean slate with a fair referee—that is what most citizens' want when they go to civil court." This is not only true in civil courts, it is true in criminal courts, in hockey games, football games, tennis matches and in the boxing ring. The point is that the referee or judge should not have a dog in the hunt. Impartiality is the centerpiece of any adversarial system. One or the other combatants is supposed to win . . . but not the judge.

It was revealed in the *Daily News* that Judge Diamond since 2000 heard "19 civil cases . . . without disclosing that she or her husband owned stock in one of the parties before her."

You don't have to be Oliver Wendell Holmes to be sensitive to the fact that, as a general proposition, if a judge holds stock in a company that is one of the litigants before her, she shouldn't be sitting on the case. In fact, the federal courts—one of them ten minutes away from her courthouse—have upgraded their computer system to prevent this from happening. In the federal court, a computer compares the judge's financial holdings and interests with the name of the com-pany involved in any case before the judge.

The Chase Manhattan Mortgage Corp., a subsidiary of JPMorgan Chase, attempted to foreclose on a mortgage and dispossess Anthony DeRosa. Judge Diamond owned stock in JPMorgan Chase without telling anyone—at least none of the litigants. DeRosa lost the case, and his apartment was sold at auction. The case went up on appeal, and the appellate court agreed with him and voided her ruling and then, as reported in the *New York Post* on December 13:

> *". . . instead of sending DeRosa's foreclosure case to another judge, the court did something that hadn't been done since 1928: ruled on the case itself and came to the same result as Judge Diamond."*

In March 2004, the Appellate Court *also* said that Diamond should have disclosed that she and her husband owned stock in JPMorgan Chase & Company and disqualified herself. That was in March. On August 26, 2004, the appellate court reviewed the issue again and reversed themselves and said she did *not* have to disqualify herself because the lawsuit named Chase Manhattan Mortgage Corp. as a defendant and not JPMorgan Chase. In arriving at that conclusion, the appellate court relied on an advisory ethics opinion from April 2004. In a six-page dissent, well-regarded Appellate Judge Richard Andrias said, "There is no doubt that Chase, in whatever guise, has a financial interest in this litigation."

For more than a century, New York has required judges to disqualify themselves if a judge or his family has an "economic interest" in a party to a case—"however small" that interest might be. The administrative judge changed the rules, and on September 9, 2004, handed down new rules that basically ". . . puts the burden on the judges to comply." The administrative judge (now the chief judge of the state), Lippman, said "The judge is trusted to interpret what is 'insignificant.'" I would point out to Judge Lippman, an otherwise reasonable man, that there is an obvious problem with this new rule. If the judge decides that his or her interest as far as a stock is concerned is too small and therefore, he or she is not required to reveal it, how would the litigants ever know that it even existed in the first place?

Again, Judge Andrias dissented and said that "Justice Diamond's undisputed ownership of JPMorgan Chase stock (however small), of which we may take judicial notice, disqualified her pursuant to judiciary law, §§14 ..." He pointed out that the rules of the chief administrator, as opposed to the judiciary law, was nonbinding. He also noted that the majority relied on the advisory ethics opinion, which was written almost two years *after* Judge Diamond made her initial decision and five months after the appeals were argued.

* * *

Jacoby & Meyers became a household name by virtue of aggressive television advertising. It was a law firm offering its services to the public at usually a better than competitive rate. Gail Koff was the co-founder of Jacoby & Meyers and was married to Ralph Brill. They had an unusual prenuptial agreement providing for "particular sex acts" and even "specifying their frequency." The agreement went on to be specific about children, residences, anniversary trips, etc., and, of course, indicated what would happen in the event of a divorce: the assets would be split 50/50. Trouble, as it has a way of doing, arose in paradise—or at least the Koff-Brill version of it, and the couple ended up in divorce court. The judge, Diamond, awarded 65 percent of the couple's assets to Koff. When it was appealed, by a vote of 3-2, the appellate court upheld Judge Diamond and said, "The evidence unquestionably establishes that the wife undertook the Herculean combined roles of full-time lawyer, primary homemaker and primary parent of the three children, all with, at best, marginal help and support of the father."

But there was more to the story, not to mention that Brill denied any cruelty to his wife, saying he encouraged her to take a year off from work and move in with him. The appellate court also agreed with Judge Diamond when she found that Jacoby & Meyers at that point had a valuation of zero with debt of $8 million.

There was a vigorous twenty-five-page dissent by two highly respected judges pointing out that "[The] husband received 35% of the marital assets while being saddled with half the wife's enormous debt liability." The court should have taken into account, rather than rejecting out of hand, the established fact that the parties agreed to an unconventional marriage in which the spouses would reside apart, even in the event they had children, and it should not have so severely punished the defendant for a form of conduct that both parties had decided as the foundation of the marriage. Additionally, they found no ethical violation by Judge Diamond in that in her re-election campaign she received a $777 contribution from Ms. Koff's attorney, Mr. X. Mister X had also hired the judge's former legal clerk *while arguing the case.* The court found "[T]he judge violated no controlling ethics opinion or rule."

Now, just picture yourself as a litigant appearing in a case coming to court and finding your opponent's lawyer has donated money to a judge's campaign *and* hired the judge's former law secretary while the case was ongoing.

* * *

ANTHRAX

It comes as a powder, either fine and white or coarse, gray and granular. It can attack a victim by it being inhaled, touching the skin or by ingestion. If inhaled, the victim may believe that it is the onset of a common cold. After several days, severe breathing problems begin and then ultimately an awful death: gasping, trying to capture a next elusive breath of air, straining for something that is no longer there and yet is everywhere, bathing the people around the victim who casually accept the gift of inhaled air as they do the blood that flows through their veins. Inhaled anthrax is often fatal. There are remedies, but they require early treatment and delay lessens the chances of survival. Anthrax is nasty, deadly stuff, and the only people who traffic in it are the ones in governments preparing for the next war.

In 2001, letters containing anthrax spores were mailed to several news-media offices and two Democratic U.S. senators. Five people died, and fifteen others were infected. The senators received a fine white powder, the other recipients, a coarse brown material. All the mailed poison was derived from the same bacterial strain—the Ames—developed by the U.S. army. The search for the culprit led the FBI to six different continents, interviews of more than 9,000 people, 67 searches and the issuance of 6,000 subpoenas.

Joining the senators and media people, Judge Diamond claimed to be the recipient of threatening letters containing a white power.

One of the first letters (there were forty-eight in all) to arrive in 1999 contained baby powder and read, "You bitch. I see you every day on the train. I'm going to … crucify you. Maybe I'll see you in hell." In some of the letters, the writer called her a "pig." Others were anti-Semitic, and some featured a roughly scrawled heart with a dagger through it. All of this was revealed through "sources" to the *Daily News.*

The case was immediately assigned to the Threat Assessment Unit of NYPD's elite Intelligence Division.

As a former prosecutor, I learned from firsthand experience that when it is a matter of importance, there is no police force in the world as capable as the NYPD. Scotland Yard, the Royal Canadian Mounted Police and even many of our own federal agencies, compared to New York's finest are like children playing cops and robbers.

Notwithstanding any doubts the police had, the authorities supplied Diamond with round-the-clock protection because, for not the least of reasons, no law-enforcement agencies want to see a judge murdered on their watch. The police—and court officers—guarded the judge at hairdressing appointments, lunch dates, social functions and escorted her from her Upper East Side home to the courthouse and to a weekend home in Westport, Connecticut. They did, however, maintain their doubts, which caused them to go into high gear.

The detectives continued to do the thing they do best—detecting. One posed as a waiter at her favorite neighborhood bistro to obtain her fingerprints. Undercover police followed her through Saks Fifth Avenue. A camera was set up outside her home, and handwriting analysts compared her signatures on court documents with the notes she received. They went through her garbage, and at one point, the judge gave the investigators another letter containing a white powder. The substance was found to be Bisquick Mix. Lo and behold, as the *Daily News* reported, the same week the letter arrived, investigators found an "empty Bisquick Mix box in the garbage at Diamond's East Side townhouse." The *News* attributed the information to "sources."

Things proceeded on both these fronts—protection and investigation—until the police decided to call in a profiler. The *News,* on September 16, 2002, reported, "When NYPD investigators were unable to find the culprits or even possible motives, they asked Ray Pierce, a retired detective and founder of the department's Criminal Assessment and Profiling Unit, for help, sources said. Pierce reviewed 48 letters and told investigators he had 'no doubt' Diamond wrote them herself, sources said."

The *News* in their story of September 14, 2002, reported, "She needed to justify her security detail, so she was writing the letters to herself, one law enforcement source told the *News.* It's a crazy case. Detectives were trying to determine who was sending her the letters, and everything was coming back to her." The article continued

"Pierce...also found the letters were written by an insecure woman, according to sources."

In the first week of September 2002, the *Daily News* contacted the NYPD and the State Office of Court Administration about the case. That same day, her armed security detail was removed.

They said Pierce reached that conclusion by considering a combination of factors: A barrage of letters would come when there was talk of her security detail ending or during times of terror alerts. After one September 11, for example, Diamond received a letter containing baby powder during the anthrax scare.

"She has a serious problem. She thrives on attention. She had a security escort to her daughter's wedding, she's very impressed with that," Pierce told investigators, according to one source familiar with his findings.

"There was a vicious theme in all of the letters, but an obvious failure on the part of the person sending them to act. It became obvious after a while it was just a farce," Pierce concluded, according to the source. Pierce himself, declined to comment on the case.

Diamond, according to the press, turned over a list of about twenty men to investigators shortly after the letters began arriving in 1999, saying the litigants were potential suspects with possible motives to write menacing phrases such as "Die bitch ..." Among these names was Alec Wildenstein. When he was in New York, Alec, as a result of being on the list, was shadowed by undercover operatives. I was also called in relation to Alec. Back in the real world, Diamond was as much in his thinking as—or perhaps less than—the archbishop of Canterbury. But if he had known about it, undoubtedly, it would have been the source of a chuckle.

Diamond has denied the charges and as well has her protectors. Her immediate supervisor, Justice Jacqueline Silbermann, said the criminal profiler's contention that Diamond made up the threats was "preposterous" and "she is as mature and balanced as any person I've ever met." This, of course, depends on the people she has met. And, of course, there was Mr. X who said, "There are a lot of cowardly husbands out there who are not used to a woman who stands up to them publicly and without hesitation. Any one of those idiots could be writing those notes."

36

THE MAN WHO RULED BROADWAY

On April 27, 2000, former *New York Times* critic, Frank Rich, whom I have known for many years, and an admirer of David Merrick, wrote an elegant *Times* obituary for him titled "David Merrick, 88, Showman Who Ruled Broadway, Dies." The second paragraph read:

"For a quarter-century that ended with his last blockbuster, the musical '42nd Street,' in 1980, Mister Merrick was the dominant showman in the Broadway theater. When *Time* magazine put him on its cover in 1966, it estimated that 20 percent of Broadway's work force was in his employment."

Rich referred to Merrick as a "Study in darkness—with his tailored suits, sleek black hair, moustache, sardonic wit and low insinuating voice, he went out of his way to resemble a villain out of a Victorian melodrama."

For Merrick, time was a villain. The suit became wrinkled, its shoulders sprinkled with dandruff, the "sleek black hair" was store bought from a toupee maker in California, who also supplied Burt Reynolds with his toupee and for whom I signed a large check to fly him to New York to service David's hairpieces; the moustache dyed, and the insinuating voice, stilled by a stroke that ravaged the part of his brain that governed speech so that he spoke, if at all, in monosyllabic, barely understandable words. However, in response to my asking him how he felt having been thus stricken, he did manage to croak the word "angry." Merrick's philosophy of life that he shared with associates was summed up in, perhaps his favorite expression, "Disaster lurks behind every corner."

Merrick's life, if not a wilderness of mirrors, was composed of secrets within secrets, enigmas within enigmas and much fantasy wrapped around an abiding and all-encompassing anger.

Merrick was born on November 27, 1911, in St. Louis, but said of his birth, "I was born on November 4, 1954, the night my first big show 'Fanny' opened on Broadway." He hated St. Louis—the place where he was David Margulois—with such ferocity that he would not take airplane trips that had a flight plan over St. Louis because he feared they might be forced to land in the city. He became a lawyer, having graduated the Jesuit-run St. Louis University School of Law, and while he did not have much of a legal career, it affected—one might better say "infected"—his future career as a theatrical producer.

In the sixties, Merrick, typically in one season, produced a half-dozen or more plays and musicals and, as Rich noted, "...on occasion as many as four in a single month. His parallel record of productivity and profitability has been unmatched by any single impresario before or since in the history of New York's commercial theater."

The first time I ever saw him in person was by accident when he sat in a vacant space next to me on a lipstick-red leather banquette. It was at a cast party for *I Can Get It for You Wholesale*. Barbra Streisand was sitting further down the bench to my right, and Merrick wanted to talk to her. They engaged in what passed for a conversation in New

York. I was struck by the coarseness of her voice, manner and content of the conversation and the fact that he seemed to tolerate what appeared to be at least, mild verbal abuse. He and she completely ignored both me and the fact that I could obviously overhear them.

The club was the breeding ground of gossip columnists and overcrowded with girls sporting exposed and silken flesh; the air was overhung with smoke and expensive perfume. The next time I had contact with him was as an adversary representing his then-wife Etan, and after that case was over, I represented him against a subsequent wife.

Given my then age and lack of sophistication, the supper-club event was indelibly impressed on my memory. However, in subsequent years, each time I mentioned it to him, he denied such an event ever took place.

Merrick created his own reality, entered and dwelt within it, expecting everyone else to join him in the journey.

Late one morning, Merrick attended a rehearsal of one of his shows. He stopped the rehearsal complaining of a ringing sound coming over the speaker system. He directed one of the crew to tend to getting rid of the ringing. After the person duly reported to him that the sound system was now OK, Merrick ordered the rehearsal to begin again. No sooner had it started than Merrick again stopped it because of the ringing he heard. He became more annoyed and again dispatched someone to fix the problem. The individual came back and assured Merrick that everything was now fine in the sound system. Merrick again ordered the rehearsal to resume. No sooner had it started when Merrick stood up, furious, screaming that they were all incompetent, and the ringing was still there. He announced he was leaving the theater and would not return until the situation was remedied.

He went home, sat down for lunch, and suddenly he stood, shouting that he would not tolerate the situation a moment longer. There was the same "Damn ringing" somewhere in his home, and somebody had to be called in "immediately" to fix it. He threw his napkin down on the table and stormed out of his apartment.

Etan Merrick was, when I first met her, in her early thirties. She was tall, slim, athletically built and very Scandinavian—at least, in her facial features. She had high cheekbones, clear, almost-translucent pale skin stretched tight to the bone, deep-set sad eyes that looked as if they had seen and were marked by the burden of some great tragedy. She had light-brown, fine hair, sparse to the point of being thin, cut boyishly short with the remnants of bangs falling across her high forehead. When she spoke, she had a way of tossing her head to the side as do women whose hair is long and full. When something she found distasteful was said, she looked down and to her left, cupping her right hand over her right eyebrow as if the offensive words would thus be deflected and pass over her. Her voice, I thought her most attractive feature, was low and musical. Her English was caressed by a slight Swedish accent, in fact so slight that it was difficult to identify it as such. In any event, it was the modulated voice of an educated woman used to walking on her own thick carpets and softly giving instructions to servants. But in fact, her last employment before becoming Mrs. David Merrick was that of an airline stewardess.

Women, at least some women, found her to be extraordinarily beautiful in the mode of Greta Garbo. I thought, at the time, that she *was* attractive—in an unorchestrated. scrubbed kind of way—but for me, on this issue, the jury would be out for another twenty years when the artifacts of beauty would have long fled and the remains, in their varying states of decay, would repose awaiting the decision of time and the withheld judgment of admirers. For some women, time is a gentle companion; for others, a thief.

I did have occasion to see a published photo of her attending an April 2007 reception for a Chinese artist. I would not have recognized her except for the caption beneath the photograph. She was at once matronly and elegant, but no one looking at her image would imagine her gaudy past and that she was the stuff of headlines ... at least those in certain newspapers.

Most cases begin with a phone call taken first by a receptionist and then transferred to my assistant who sets up an appointment. If it involves a person of note or notoriety, my assistant will jot down mention of it in my daily schedule, particularly if it involves a sports figure since my knowledge of sports equates with that of early Etruscan pottery. Because the name "Merrick" is not that uncommon, I looked at the handsome well-dressed woman across the desk from me expecting to hear a mundane, if not banal tale of the disintegration of love in the valley of the hedge funds. The lyrics are usually a bit different, but woefully, the music is always the same ... especially when they begin by telling you, "I'm sure you never heard anything like this before ..."

David Merrick's soon-to-be-former wife, as he would introduce Etan Aronson before he married her, was an airline stewardess whose boyfriend was reputedly a medical partner of Robert Atkins of diet book fame (Jackie Mason said, the only person to ever die from the Atkins diet was Doctor Atkins). Atkins, in New York's socially, politically and professionally incestuous society, also became my client years later. Atkins invited both Merrick and Aronson to a party. Once there, Merrick was instantaneous victim to something akin to what is described in the Oscar Hammerstein lyric:

You may see a stranger
Across a crowded room

Merrick, blinded or blind-sided by love or whatever passes for that hormone-infused madness, tumbled into the abyss in the special and foolish way of older men in pursuit of younger women— all in the quest of recapturing a memory of something that usually never was. But, Merrick had two additional qualities. The first was a derangement of whatever cranial molecules that determine sanity—a condition that Wilhelm Stekel daintily referred to as "tainted blood" (Merrick's mother and his first child being thus afflicted). The second: The capacity to be vicious. The latter being enhanced or even driven by the first condition.

By the time I was consulted by the then-Mrs. Merrick, Merrick had circulated a vicious and untrue story about her, namely that when she came to Bob Atkins' party, she asked who were the two richest men in the room and then promptly began an affair with both of them before finally choosing David.

Their marriage took place in September 1969, but gentle insanity trumped love. Three weeks after the marriage, Merrick insisted on a Mexican divorce while at the same time continuing to hold Etan out to the world as his wife. In fact, he even moved with Etan into the same building that Cecilia Ann, his child by his second wife, lived with her governess. Merrick's logic: The only way he could remain happily married to Etan was to be immediately divorced from her. This would, of course, make perfect sense to any of the citizens of our local lunatic asylums.

Under these bizarre terms, the "marriage" to Etan survived and was viable to the degree that there was a daughter, Marguerita, born in 1972. As could be reasonably expected, there was trouble in paradise, and by 1976, things finally fell apart. My mission from Etan was to secure an American divorce. Of course, the initial issue was "How do you divorce a person you already divorced seven years ago?" However, as academic as that proposition might be, there were still open questions of the custody of Marguerita, child support, alimony, etc. We ultimately settled these, and each side was reasonably unhappy—the hallmark of a fair settlement under the law as it then existed.

Unfortunately, all of this took place before July 19, 1980, a watershed date in New York divorce law when an equitable distribution law was enacted and women received not only support, i.e. periodic payments of alimony, but now, they were also entitled to a part of the pie, i.e. a portion of the assets accumulated during the marriage. Additionally, this new law had specific provisions designed to protect people in Etan's divorced-but-still married position. If it had been in effect at the time of her divorce, she would have fared much better financially than when she finally split from David.

The case was briefly resurrected after we all thought it was over. There remained, according to Merrick, an open, overlooked item after the divorce had been finalized. Merrick suddenly took the position that a few pieces of jewelry—I seem to recollect earrings and a necklace—he had given to Etan were actually his own and that his intention at purchase was that they should be his and not Etan's. He hired Burton Monash, a very bright New York lawyer to press his claim. Before the case was to be heard, I released a statement that we would consider his claim, but before we would do this, since Merrick's position was that the jewelry was purchased for himself, he would have to wear the pieces to court. After the press release and some fussing, Merrick dropped the case, and the jewelry remained with Etan.

Monash and I were friendly and shared cases in the sense that he was on one side and I, the other. Some weeks later, in a telephone call with him on another matter, he told me he no longer represented Merrick. He explained that Merrick owed him a great deal of money for legal services rendered, but ignored his repeated bills. Finally, Monash called him and asked politely, when he could expect payment of his bill. Merrick's response: Go f_ _ _ yourself. Monash thereupon slammed the phone down on the receiver and directed that a lawsuit be commenced against Merrick for payment of his bill.

A few days later, after Merrick was served with a summons, he called Monash. As described to me by Monash, the conversation consisted of the following brief exchange:

"Buddy [Monash's nickname], why did you sue me?"

"I politely asked when we could expect payment of our bill and, in answer, you told me to go f_ _ _ myself."

Merrick replied, "Is that any reason to sue somebody?"

Based on my own experience with Merrick and what I learned about him from speaking with others, that brief exchange encapsulated Merrick's business model.

* * *

Nineteen eighty-three—4680 on the Chinese calendar, 5744 on the Hebrew and 4619 on the Buddhist—drifted into existence for this still young country as a year of ominous portent, dangerous journeys begun and bitter memories stirred. In January, the infamous Sing Sing riot broke out; Nazi war criminal Klaus Barbie was arrested in Bolivia and red rain fell on the UK. In February, Iran invaded Iraq, and in March, President Reagan labeled the Soviet Union an "evil empire" and embarked on a "Strategic Defense Initiative" (dubbed by the media as "Star Wars").

February 13, 1983, was, arguably, the most important day in David Merrick's life and one that marked the beginning of a grotesque journey for him and me. I hopped off the train after many unexpected and odd twists in the road. The debris of lives lost, damaged or forever changed were left scattered along the side of the road. And, at journey's end, Merrick died a miserable, mumbling and probably clinically insane old man.

* * *

"Have you heard the one about the old Jew that goes into a noodle factory? Well, it seems this old Jew ..."

* * *

A person who gets a divorce is like a person who goes to a doctor to have his hemorrhoids fixed. After being treated, he prefers not to think of it again and banishes the doctor who cured him from his memory, unless, of course, he gets another case of hemorrhoids. In the eight years after the divorce, I had not heard from anyone connected with the Merrick situation, but I did follow his career in a casual fashion as it was chronicled in gossip-column items and occasional stories in the drama sections of the newspapers.

If you are the spawn of the streets of New York, looking over the tenement tops, the chimneys, the wash hung out on roofs to dry, the tracks of the elevated trains, your eyes fixed over the horizon of decaying buildings, toward the setting sun, the land stretching west to the Pacific Ocean is a vast American plain: an undifferentiated wasteland, alien and uninteresting. Of course, as you get older, you appreciate its diversity and power; its distinctions of culture and class and for some, its ability to attract and beckon. Looking at girls, hormone-infused judgments were quickly made and usually based on chest measurements and the prospect of supplication. However, if you are Jewish or nonathletic, as you get older, the protoplasm between a girl's ears trumps that between her limbs. If you are lucky (or perhaps unlucky) in adulthood, these latter, mature perceptions dominate the naïve former ones, but, they do not obliterate them, and for those happy few, the child's mindset remains embedded as an instinctive, alterative primitive prism to view life, and in the blink of an eye, a judgment is made by the hibernating child's mind.

When I first saw Karen Prunczik, my gut-propelled childhood sense of the world caused me to make an instant, and I am sure, inaccurate, judgment: a rather sweet, but plain-of-face shiksa from somewhere "out there"—a farm town without sidewalks, who probably was popular in high school, had won local talent contests and after drinking too much punch spiked by boys with pimples, had her first sex experience, vertical rather than horizontal, behind the school, shielded by darkness and foliage to the music from a distant phonograph while the senior-class party in the gym was in progress.

Such is the arrogance of casual bigotry because she was none of those things.

David Merrick was not as gentle as I about Karen; in fact, he was outright vicious. In Howard Kissel's fine biography of Merrick, he relates that after Prunczik was hired by director Gower Champion to be in *42nd Street*, in the first day of rehearsal, Merrick spotted her and told him, "That girl is pockmarked, and she's ugly. I want her fired." Champion refused. Later, when she appeared in a scene wearing a lavish gown, Merrick told Champion, "She's too ugly to wear those clothes." Champion still refused to fire her and in fact, made her understudy to one of the show's stars, Wanda Richert (Champion's then mistress and my future witness).

The years 1970-1980 were not particularly happy ones for Merrick or, indeed, for the Broadway that Merrick knew. The emphasis now was on lavish imported shows without well-known stars, brought prepackaged to Broadway directly from London. Merrick went west and occupied himself in Hollywood—it might be better said that he *entertained* himself there since nobody else seemed to be particularly entertained by his products. In 1977 and 1980, he produced two Burt Reynolds movies—*Semi-Tough* and *Rough Cut*—that were forgettable, and a large big-budget movie, *The Great Gatsby*, that was *expensively* forgettable. In 1980, however, he struck gold again on Broadway with *42nd Street*. Happily for him, Gower Champion, the show's director and Merrick's on-again, off-again nemesis, had the good taste to die the day of opening night. Merrick was able to transform disaster into profitability. In what must have been an apogee of bad taste, Merrick stepped in front of the curtains during intermission and announced Champion's death and told the cast, now in tears, basically to "Win one for the Gipper" (albeit, the Gipper, in this case was now critic proof, if not dwelling in the place where Merrick often told him to go to). Tasteless as his show-must-go-on performance (has anyone ever questioned exactly *why* the show must go on?), it did box-office wonders for the musical. My own life experience has been that no bettor ever lost money by underrating the taste of the American public on any particular thing—and that also includes their taste in politicians.

On July 1, 1982, Merrick, in an Alexandria, Virginia, courthouse, married the object of his insults, Karen Prunczik. Shortly after the marriage, he placed her in the Chicago company of *42nd Street*, promptly became fed up with her and according to Kissel, told the company manager to "Fire her from the show and fire her as my wife." To add insult to injury, he left it to her to pay their hotel bill. Shortly thereafter, I received a call from Etan Merrick telling me she wanted to meet with me. I had learned prior to that call that she had had a rapprochement with Merrick, and they had been seen around town as a couple.

She arrived at my office with Mort Mitosky, looking about the same as when I had last seen her a half-dozen years earlier. Mitosky was an elderly man and as I remember, a nonpracticing lawyer. He had a full head of white hair, a booming voice, a banged-up nose that appeared to be a monument to a long-ago lost fistfight, a strong and craggy face and the kind of profile one might find on the side of an ancient Roman coin. He was probably closer to Merrick than any other man and probably any other female (including any of Merrick's wives). Mitosky's girlfriend—and later wife—Joy Klein, was the guardian of Merrick's child, Cecilia Ann, whose custody Merrick won in an ugly court contest based on the questionable proposition that he could afford to pay for better care for the child than her troubled mother. Apparently, unexplored was the proposition that if he gave her sufficient funds, she could afford the same kind of household help.

Mitosky was highly thought of in the theatrical community and was, at the same time, respected by Merrick, insulted by Merrick, dependent upon Merrick, abused by Merrick and needed by Merrick. It was a friendship of love-hate, each one having something the other possessed; each of them being something the other envied. They were inextricably interwoven in each other's existence; their sometimes-mutual hatred being the adhesive, but clearly, Mort was the flower that could only blossom in the shade of Merrick. Similarly, I recalled that Mickey Rudin, who was Frank Sinatra's lawyer for many years, told me that when he died, his tombstone would read "Here lies Frank Sinatra's lawyer." The Merrick/Mitosky was of a similar nature.

Among other things, Merrick used Mitosky to raise money for his shows. When I met Mitosky, we became instant friends and also had a nexus in that my Uncle Sam was one of his Broadway investors. Additionally, Merrick used Mitosky to get out of self-created problems.

There was a time when the theater workers in a successful Merrick musical attempted to negotiate an increase in salary. Merrick, in his usual fashion, told them that if they did not accept his terms, they should all get out of the theater. They did as he suggested, and all went out on strike. Merrick was then left with a hit play and none of the people possessed of the myriad of skills necessary for a play to be presented on Broadway. He then turned to Mitosky and asked him to go to the workers and make peace. In much the same way, in his deteriorating marital situation with Prunczik, Merrick dispatched Etan together with Mitosky to speak to me on his behalf.

Soon the roles in the Merrick-Mitosky symbiotic relationship would be reversed.

I represented Merrick, and a divorce case began. While it crept forward, as divorce cases tend to do, on the day before Valentine's Day 1983, Merrick had a luncheon date with Etan. On that day, a typical massive, preglobal warming snowstorm descended upon New York. Moving cars disappeared from silent streets; offices closed; department stores were empty, manned by a faithful few to serve nonexistent customers. The city's blood pressure throbbed to a barely discernible beat; its citizens sequestered in apartments squalid and grand, rich or poor, powerful and powerless, near-helpless victims of a quixotic natural force.

Merrick did not show up for the luncheon, nor did he respond to any of Etan's calls. Merrick was use to dealing with snowstorms.

Snowstorms were to him a personal insult designed to hurt the box-office receipts. Etan called the building staff at his home, The Galleria—a fancy condominium building on 57th Street just east of Park Avenue—but they were unable to get him to come to the door of his apartment in response to their calls and bell ringing.

She became increasingly worried and wanted to check on him herself. As a Scandinavian, drifts of fallen snow and snow-laden winds blowing through the city's canyons offered no impediment to her. She must get to David. However, ex-wives do not have any standing to break into former husband's apartments. In fact, when they do, they usually end up in jail. The police take the reasonable position that an ex-wife is usually the last person they should listen to if a door is requested to be broken down. In fact, when a man is found murdered, the first suspect is usually an ex-wife, after, quite sensibly, his present wife.

She called Mort Mitosky, and together, best friend and concerned former wife, they persuaded the police to break in. They found Merrick lying on the bathroom floor, the victim of a stroke, weak, partially paralyzed and unable to speak.

Merrick was taken to the hospital. Karen Prunczik now, notwithstanding her disintegrating marriage, flew back to New York and took Merrick to her home. She quickly realized she could not adequately care for him and sought out the best facility to treat a person in his condition. She was able to place him in the Rusk Institute, a world-renowned facility devoted to the rehabilitation of stroke victims and patients with similar infirmities—and one that ordinarily had a long waiting list of potential patients seeking admission.

Merrick was there for one day before deciding that the disciplined routine of treatments, exercises and the necessity that a patient be compliant was not for him. The next day, there was a driving rainstorm in New York City. In a hard-to-imagine feat of will, given his physical infirmities, he propelled his wheelchair down the corridors, out of the hospital into the heavy rain, onto First Avenue, over to

Second Avenue and sought refuge four blocks away in a Korean noodle factory. The Koreans called the cops. Merrick could not speak, but was able to hand the police a piece of paper containing Mitosky's name. Still not realizing the identity of this odd, speechless, partially paralyzed, rain-soaked individual surrounded by noodles in varying stages of completion and Koreans in varying stages of comprehensibility, they called Mitosky who initially was as confounded as the police, not to mention the Koreans. Mitosky showed up and identified Merrick, who was promptly returned to the Rusk Institute. As a side note, one of the police officers who rescued Merrick was subsequently put on Merrick's payroll as, I suppose, an aide-de-camp cum driver and was, as Mitosky once told me, probably the only New York City police officer who made enough on his off-hours job to drive around in a Porsche.

Prunczik then took him back into her apartment and together with nurses, tried to tend to him. One day when he was alone, he again managed to contact Mitosky. Message: I want to get out of here. As soon as the opportunity presented itself, Mitosky was able to get him away from the apartment, take him to California and check him into a Los Angeles hospital.

It was now not just a divorcing husband fighting his wife, but worse yet, it was ex-wife fighting soon-to-be ex-wife. If not a battle of the monumental proportions of the Devil and Daniel Webster fighting for the soul of Jabez Stone, it was at least the stuff of headlines in the popular press.

Prunczik hired attorney Lester Wallman, a placid-enough fellow with tousled hair, who always seemed to be wearing the same wrinkled corduroy jacket and baggy trousers. Wallman brought on a writ of habeas corpus—named at the Constitutional Convention, "The Great Writ." Jefferson, if he were alive, would probably take the next horse back to Monticello if he saw that the writ was used as a weapon in a catfight between two women battling over a half-mad rich man. The writ claimed that Merrick had been kidnapped and was being held against his will. The court appointed former New York State Attorney General Louis Lefkowitz to be Merrick's legal guardian. He was the first of two ex-politicians to be foisted on Merrick, the second, being former New York City Mayor Robert Wagner.

Guardianship appointments by the New York State Supreme Court were extremely lucrative to the recipient. Merrick's was among the most appealing of all since it not only represented lots of potential money for the guardian with little legal work involved (and the same judge who made the appointment decided how much he was going to be paid), but it was also a way for an aged politician to remain in the headlines.

Lefkowitz was a slim, spry and feisty little guy and had been a popular state attorney general in the Rockefeller years and beyond. He was attorney general longer than anyone else in New York State history (twenty-two years). He was in his late seventies or early eighties when he was appointed Merrick's guardian. I felt this was good for us since he could identify with Merrick who was somewhat younger, but certainly closer to his age and sensibilities than was Prunczik. He lived on Park Avenue, as did I and walked to work each day as much for the exercise, I suspect, as for the greeting of "Hiya, Louie" he would receive from doormen and passersby. Prior to his appointment as guardian, on, at least half a dozen occasions when our schedules coincided, I walked downtown with him for a while, and we chatted about that morning's news or legal gossip. While not friends, we were on a first-name basis. So when he became guardian, I had the advantage of having casual access to him, ensuring at least that my telephone calls would not go unanswered.

Lefkowitz' only prior connection with the theater was when as attorney general, he conducted an investigation of "Ice"—the illegal selling of tickets to Broadway shows. I had also learned that he had tried to establish a position of czar to the theater industry, in the same manner that there was a czar in the movie business. His first recommendation for the post was himself, at a ridiculous salary. The producers turned him down flat. This was yet another current, or at least an eddy, that might have an impact on the impartiality of his judgment. I urged on him the obvious—that it could hardly be expected that a wife in the throes of a divorce case would have her husband's best interests at heart.

Lefkowitz' report to the court was that Merrick was happy under the Etan and Mitosky regime and was being well cared for. Mitosky was appointed Merrick's conservator. In those days, the appointment of a conservator, as opposed to a "committee," was necessary when a person couldn't do the mechanical things that were required in the daily conduct of life. A *committee* is appointed when a person lacks the underlying mental capacity to protect himself or is under so great a mental handicap that he cannot process the life that swirls about him. Merrick's problem was that he could not do the physical act—basically talking—necessary for the conduct of his day-to-day activities, such as ordering food, giving instructions to employees, hiring and firing household staff, having business meetings, transacting banking business, etc.

One of the judges involved in the case insisted that Merrick undergo a psychiatric examination to make sure he still had mental capacity. At that point, it was clear to me that Merrick's only impediment was that he was unable to talk. He appeared a bit weaker than when I first met him, and his mental peculiarities were the same as prior to his stroke, but otherwise, his only problem was not having the ability to speak coherently. I felt that I should accompany Merrick to the psychiatric evaluation since if it did not turn out well, I would be in a better position to cross-examine the psychiatrist.

The examination was to take place at Bellevue Hospital's psychiatric facility. The building—dark, Gothic and foreboding with barred windows—looked like something out of a low budget horror film. We waited in an anteroom and were able to look through a glass window into a sort of community room. There were about a dozen inmates in the room, some wearing hospital gowns, seemingly drifting, aimless and silent, constantly in motion in weaving trajectories, avoiding contact with each other. I thought this sight would upset Merrick. However, he merely turned to me and pointed his forefinger to his head and made circles with it: the universal sign for "crazy."

While waiting, I had an interesting discussion with him in the slow and difficult way that it was to talk with him because of his speech impairment. However, it was clear to me, that while, understandably saying little, he perceived much and with an acuity of perception that I little suspected.

The psychiatrist came out, greeted us and then led us to a bare room with a table and chairs and bars on the one window. It looked like the visitor's room in a second-rate jail. The doctor occupied some exalted position at the institution, but in any event, he clearly never went to charm school. Considering the money he was going to be paid for his brief services, he was remarkably cold—even unfriendly. Perhaps this was because I insisted upon being present at the interview, and like other criminal types, generally, psychiatrists do not like witnesses to observe them at their work. The principal test, as I recollect, was that he placed a quarter, a nickel, a dime and a penny in a row on the table and asked Merrick that if he had to choose a coin, which would it be. Merrick looked at him as if *he* should be in the room with the other mental cases. All his other "tests" seemed to break down because of Merrick's difficulty speaking. The doctor appeared to run out of time, bid us "Good day" and asked where his bill should be sent. I was concerned that Merrick, using again his finger, would tell him where it should go or, at least again point his finger to his forehead and make circles. We were both happy to step out into the air and into Merrick's limousine. As an institution, the place we had just left ranked just ahead of slavery. Merrick, of course, received a clean bill of mental health, as well as one for the doctor's services.

The divorce case with Prunczik now came up for trial. Deciding to put her money on another knight, she dumped Lester Wallman and hired the flavor of the day, America's most famous divorce lawyer, Marvin Mitchelson.

The matter came on to be heard by a cantankerous old judge, Hilda Schwartz. Mitchelson came into court clearly expecting to be treated as a visiting celebrity. I believe the judge had been offended by his casual, offhand manner and gave him no slack and indeed, was only barely courteous to him. Mitchelson's performance in court reflected his inability to adjust to this unexpected, if not hostile, environment. His case should have been a divorce lawyer's dream (although "scheming," rather than "dreaming" is often thought by the public to be the divorce lawyer's province). Imagine, trying a case against a man who could not speak in his own behalf! But, it turned out to be his nightmare.

In the divorce case, Prunczik tried to present Merrick as having drug and mental problems. Her problems: there was no proof of Merrick having any drug problems and if he did, still less of a showing that it resulted in her being subjected to any mistreatment because of it. As a matter of incidental observation, if he *had* such problems, (and I never saw him in any such situation,) in the area of drugs, he would have been in bush leagues compared to Mitchelson. As far as having mental problems, Merrick's unusual behavior was no better or worse than it was *before* he had his stroke. Prunczik also had a general underlying difficulty in her case: Her presentation of being a loving, caring wife was undercut by the very nature of her accusations against her husband. Triers of fact, whether judges or juries, to put it crudely, are like dogs, in that a desired result can usually only be achieved by reinforcing a simple theme: innocent or guilty; loving or hateful; victim or victimizer. In fact, I use that same unpleasant analogy in my client's relations with me. I get their attention very quickly when I tell them I am like a dog. I must have simple instructions about what the client wants to achieve as the desired ends—the wish list—in his or her case. Lawyers drown in crosscurrents. The trial system does not usually allow for the construction of nuances or subtleties. That is for the novelists, not courtroom lawyers. The goal of the trial lawyer is to convince the judge or jury of the underlying validity of his or her position and then guide them through the supporting evidence.

After a day of trial, that included our producing Prunczik's former best friend and roommate, star of *42nd Street*, Wanda Richert to testify against her (with best friends like that, who needs enemies?) and getting ping-ponged between the judge and me, I sensed Mitchelson was *hors de combat*. The case was quickly settled—practically, a mercy killing. The divorce itself, in the ordinary course, could take up to a few months to be processed. Since I was concerned that Merrick could have another stroke in the interim, I was able to accomplish it in about an hour's time.

Merrick was taken by Etan on restful trips to South America and the south of France. He returned to New York chafing under the conservatorship of Mitosky. Merrick, I believed, was as much bothered by the expense involved in the conservatorship as by the ignominy of the situation. Merrick wanted Mitosky removed and Etan appointed conservator. However, only a judge can remove and then appoint a substitute conservator.

One evening, I spoke to Mitosky as a friend, not as a lawyer. "Mort, what do you need this for? You accomplished a lot as a conservator and to now be mixed up in the kind of row that's embedded in David's DNA—and maybe that he actually enjoys—can only damage your fine reputation on Broadway." Mort felt that to resign would be insulting to him. I opined that there comes a time when our own dignity demands that we leave the party. He finally, after a long while, agreed, but little did I think that there would shortly come a time when I heeded my own advice to Mort.

My own unspoken thought, which I shared with no one, was that the best way to secure Etan as a conservator was for her to be married to David. Actually, most conservators are the spouses of their wards.

Additionally, by this time, their relationship had weathered so many storms, I believed that they would have gotten married anyway, conservatorship or not. Given the realities of the situation, it was generally known that the couple did not share the same household, but that was a relatively minor matter compared to the ties that by now, bound them to each other.

By the end of 1983, Etan was appointed conservator along with former New York mayor Robert Wagner. I do not recollect how Wagner got into the act, but I doubt that it was a result of any of our efforts. It was probably just a case, as with former Attorney General Lefkowitz, of the court delivering high-paying patronage to a former political heavyweight. Ironically, Lefkowitz and Wagner, although one was a Republican, the other a Democrat, shared a political communality. They ran against each other, both candidates for the job of mayor of New York with Wagner's race ending successfully. Working with Wagner on the case, I found him to be bright and resourceful, but his acuity seemed to diminish after lunchtime, which made me believe, from past similar experience with other lawyers, that there were liquid components to his lunch. I did enjoy watching his popularity when we went to court and thought it remarkable, until I represented Giuliani years later when popularity turned to adulation.

A new player came upon the stage. Bill Goodstein, the same Bill Goodstein who had an interesting adventure in the State Supreme Court when he represented Reggie Jackson and brought me into the matter, was a lawyer who had been on the other side of a minor case I handled. He was fat and sloppy-tall with unkempt red-blond hair, a bulbous nose, tiny store-bought teeth, a large stomach bulging over his belt, a small thin mouth usually pursed in a half-smile and possessed of an utterly beguiling personality.

Goodstein had been extremely popular in college and law school and was a college athlete as well as being successfully active in school politics. He propelled himself by shambling from place to place. Looking at him, I searched without success for the coordination of muscle or balletic grace of an athlete in his walk or his movements, somehow buried in all that flesh. Beneath his benign exterior, the carcass of a soul flailed by disappointments dwelt in a world of it-might-have-beens. He was a very angry person.

A revealing episode: Because he was so well thought of at Columbia Law School, he was placed on a committee of alumni whose purpose was to contact other graduates with the hope of raising funds for some projects at the school. Each member of the committee was assigned to make calls from a list of other classmates.

One day, I walked into his room and found him cursing aloud to himself, staring at the telephone. Asking him what the trouble was, he told me that he called on one of his former classmates who agreed to contribute a sum of money to the school. I said, "Then you did great in raising money." "But that jerk was a 'nothing' in law school and now is able to give away this kind of money." His face darkened, and in a low, even tone, he said, "I hate him."

I originally met Goodstein when I represented the wife, he represented the husband. At the end of the matter, he told me a law firm that allowed him to rent space was either moving or reorganizing or something of that nature, and they would not have any further room for him. It sounded like they just did not want him as a tenant any longer. I told him that he was welcome to set up shop in an empty back room in my office and the rent would be considerably less than market rate. The room was windowless, but of a good size, and I had wooden paneling put up and sliding doors behind, which was ample file space. Overall, it was quite presentable.

He moved in, sometimes paying rent, sometimes not, but soon the room became a wreck: files and papers everywhere, piled on the desk and floor, and a nightly ritual of a frantic search for the documents and papers that might be buried in the mess. He kept unusual hours, hanging out until extremely late in the office, sometimes into the early morning hours and always insisted upon taking one or two heavy briefcases home with him in spite of the fact, as I repeatedly pointed out to him, that there was absolutely no likelihood he would open the briefcase between the time he left the office and when he arrived the next day.

When he was in the office, he would spend hours on the phone, sometimes working with a gadget that was on the instrument. He would speak into the receiver and then immediately put the speakerphone on when the other party responded, the person on the other end of the line not knowing that he was being broadcast all over the office. This often had embarrassing results. Goodstein was indifferent to how awkward this was to whomever was in or about his room. Sometimes there were calls to other lawyers, clients, judges and calls of a casual or personal nature. Most of the time, I or whoever else was in the office usually tried to find a reason to leave the room when this occurred.

Goodstein, after he was admitted to the bar, became the law secretary for Judge Sol Streit. Streit apparently was not related to the matzo family, but Goodstein told me he liked people to believe that to be the case. However, he *was* the administrative judge and as such, wielded a great deal of power since it was, as Goodstein told me, the judge who assigned judges to preside in the various parts of the court. Depending upon the administrative judge's appointments, judges could end up doing legal work that they found interesting or pleasant, or doing the judicial gutter work that judges, quite reasonably, would want to avoid. As a result of the power of his boss, Goodstein enjoyed good relationships with most of the sitting judges in the state supreme court. Because the presiding judge of the appellate court was also his friend, Goodstein was appointed by him to the disciplinary body that hears complaints against lawyers.

Goodstein was also, through his connections, able to obtain some sort of guardianship appointment from judges. In connection with the appointments, he would have to write reports on persons in varying degrees of incapacity. His reports were invariably late, and at least on several occasions, one of these unfortunate people showed up in the office pleading with him to complete his report. On another occasion, there was actually a person who passed away during this period of delay.

We had an arrangement where one of my secretaries would do his work, and he would reimburse me for their time spent on an hourly basis. I basically worked on an "honor" system. He would simply tell me the amount of time he used a secretary and would pay accordingly. The particular secretary in question, Allison, would make fun of the hourly bills he would give me. The bill would indicate, for example, a half-hour's secretarial time used when, in reality, it clearly involved hours and hours. In fact, the next morning, she would bring the wastebasket into my office showing me the paper volume of drafts and rewrites she did for Goodstein that obviously indicated many hours of secretarial work. I simply ignored this issue since I felt he was driven by economic necessity. In short, he was broke or close to it.

Somewhere along the way, Goodstein had a heart attack, and I managed as best as possible to keep his practice—or what there was of it—afloat. After he got out of the hospital, he was soon back to his old ways of erratic hours, overeating, hanging out at night until the daylight hours, etc.

At some point in time, Goodstein decided to become a sports agent. He would drive around New York in the early morning hours looking, I believe, for people to talk to, probably also for girls. On one of these nocturnal journeys, he ran into Reggie Jackson, who was at that time a Yankee superstar, and struck up a friendship. He was then able to sign up some Yankees. They were usually Dominican. That business soon crashed in a mountain of lost papers, neglect and angry arguments with accusations flowing back and forth between him and his athlete clients. During this episode in his professional life, I remember he went to the airport and ended up carrying the bags of one of the ballplayers. I shared with him my thoughts that it was absolutely crazy for a man who was recuperating from a heart attack to carry the bags of a professional athlete.

When the whole story is told, one might consider him as some sort of absolute villain, a person to be shunned. Quite the contrary, he was charming and fun to be with. He had the ability to both manipulate and entertain. Because he was in the office, he had frequent contact with the Merrick crew, particularly Etan, and we would frequently chat with him about the various proclivities of the judges involved in the case, tactics, etc.

Enter into this semi-madness a supreme court judge, Arthur Blyn. Blyn was one of those pygmies of the law who found a particular delight in using statutes and rules, parsing out phrases, nuances, etc., all in an effort to "catch" lawyers. I believe he was a nasty man who was basically a Dickensian celebration of legal minutia.

Somehow Blyn, as a judge, inherited the Merrick matters, and I found myself at frequent loggerheads with him. At one point, Blyn barred Merrick from investing $1.5 million dollars in the London production of *42nd Street* and indicated that it was too speculative. This seemed ridiculous to me since investing in plays was the one thing Merrick really knew about, and Blyn's knowledge of the subject was probably relegated to buying a ticket. In fact, I pointed out to Blyn an article in *Variety* that had come out that same week that reported Merrick was making half-a-million dollars a week for his efforts (probably today the equivalent of $1.5 million), which represented the greatest weekly profit for any producer in the history of Broadway.

I began to think that my very presence made a problem for my clients because they were forced to bring their matters before Judge Blyn. Goodstein had been Blyn's campaign manager, as I recollect, therefore, I made a simple arrangement with Goodstein: We would be partners on the case. Since Goodstein had a problem producing paperwork—any paperwork—good or even bad, I would do all the legal paperwork, research, drafting of documents, editing, etc., and Goodstein would make the oral arguments in the case. At least, he should be able to receive a fair shot from Blyn, and I would no longer be the problem. We certainly anticipated that Blyn, given his miserable character, would give no special preference to Goodstein or help him in any way, but he would at least be cordial, and Goodstein would be able to get a fair hearing. The fees received would be divided as per the division of labors. Economically, I received the short end, but it was the right thing to do for this client. We informed the client of the arrangement, and this seemed to work out well for a while.

I usually sort the mail when it is received in the office. Going through the incoming mail affords me an opportunity to stay on top of the lawyers working for me and make sure they deal with things in a timely fashion. Nonpersonal correspondence to any member of my firm is opened. If I open a letter addressed to one of the lawyers and I see something that sounds like "I've been trying to call you for two days ...," I am in a position to quickly remedy the situation. Of course, since Goodstein was not my employee, I did not open his mail.

After Goodstein had the heart attack, out of concern for his health, I directed that my secretaries do his banking for him. In other words, if he received a check, they would run it down to the bank, along with our deposits, to put it into his account to save him the trip. One day, we received our mail amid a howling snowstorm. When I put a snow-damp, unopened letter on Goodstein's pile, I vaguely recognized the handwriting, but I could not quite place it. I handed it to Goodstein, and shortly thereafter, I saw him preparing to go out in to the snowstorm. I asked him, "Where in the world are you going in this weather?"

"I'm going to the bank. I have to make a deposit."

"I have somebody going to the bank. Why go out in the snowstorm?"

"No, no, I want to go to the bank."

I thought this rather odd, and it was bouncing around in my thoughts for the next several days. Suddenly, I realized where I had seen the handwriting before—it belonged to Mort Mitosky. Mitosky was still involved in the matter in some sort of—perhaps advisory, perhaps transitional—position. I had kept up a friendship with him during the period particularly since I was still writing all the papers and doing the legal work and had to stay abreast with what was going on and sometimes needing information for papers I prepared. I called Mitosky and asked him if he sent a letter to Goodstein. He told me that he had, but said it was simply payment for a bill rendered in the Merrick proceeding—indeed, a sizable check for legal services. Of course, under my arrangement with Goodstein, we were to share legal fees in an equitable fashion. This required our sitting down and deciding who did what, and what would be a fair division of the fees received.

I said nothing to Goodstein and let day after day go by with the thought that he would notify me of the receipt of the check and sit down with me to decide how to fairly divide it. Each passing day, I was more disturbed and confused. There came a point where I got angrier and angrier. Finally after two weeks or so, I confronted him. He did not even bother to offer any kind of sensible excuse, although at first denying it happened. Then I told him I talked to Mitosky, and in fact, he had given me the check number, date and the amount. I told Goodstein, who at this point sometimes paid rent and sometimes did not, that he could no longer continue in the office after a betrayal of someone who trusted him. He had to leave. He refused, and I actually had to begin a legal proceeding to get him out, but he stayed months and months after that. Litigation to evict a tenant is a slow and drawn-out process. Since he had not paid or only partially paid rent for so long and sporadically at that, I was only able to collect a portion of the rent actually owed because of the lack or informality of records. At any rate, I finally got him out of the office.

I never collected or even sought the payment due me for the legal services I had rendered, happy just to get rid of him.

The last time I saw Merrick was in Etan's apartment with some people from my office. While I cannot relate the events, Merrick's conduct was such that I felt that I no longer wanted to continue representing him. I did not tell him so then, but I made up my mind it was the last time I would have anything to do with him, and in fact, I never saw or spoke to him or Etan again.

In the meantime, Mitosky would call me at least once a week, and we had dinner several times. When he called me, he would bring me up to date and volunteer certain information. I have no idea if it was accurate or not, but published reports seem to support what Mitosky told me. Goodstein, who always had financial problems acquiring, keeping or maintaining an office, was able to get Merrick to pay the rent (directly or indirectly) for one. Merrick would show up, and Goodstein would basically put him in a chair in one of the rooms to watch television. During this time, Goodstein developed a close relationship with Etan.

Goodstein, also around this time, was involved in a memorable and very revealing situation that involved the celebrated columnist, Liz Smith, who was gracious enough to share it with me. She knew Merrick slightly, and Goodstein used this connection to begin a business and quasi-social relationship with her. He handled several contracts for her, and she consistently gave him 10 percent, ostensibly against his will, for every deal he consummated for her. In addition to contract work, he was to handle her taxes. Consistent with the way he handled most things, she eventually learned that he had not been filing any taxes for her. As she puts it, "He just lied and lied from beginning to end." On a more bizarre note, he was constantly proposing marriage to her and, ultimately, "I [she] was pretty surprised to find he had a wife."

As a result of this relationship with the columnist, she was able to get him invited to extremely desirable social events (including Frank Sinatra's seventieth birthday party at the Waldorf), but, she noted

"…he was a social embarrassment, not very attractive and later I discovered, quite a fantasist." Even more succinctly described him to me as "…a master bullshit artist." She "…regretted so much having him in my professional life." She also believed that "…he took advantage of Merrick because of Merrick's stroke and inability to be understood."

Mitosky told me that Goodstein had hired a temporary secretary, an Asian woman, Natalie Lloyd. She saw how Merrick was treated, and Mitosky told me, he believed, she genuinely cared about David and also felt he was being taken advantage of. Lloyd eventually became a producer of Merrick's shows and ended up marrying him. Merrick, according to Mitosky, on a Jewish holiday arrived with moving men and instructed them to take back the furniture and art in the Goodstein office (that Merrick had paid for) and to remove all the files pertaining to his case.

There were other lawyers subsequently involved in the many Merrick matters, almost each player suing another and some new lawsuits, some begun and some continued even after Merrick's death. One day, I noted the following item in the *Boston Globe* (and I saw a similar squib in a New York paper):

> *Merrick's melodrama in new court papers added to a juicy, two-year-old legal battle. David Merrick has accused his estranged wife, Etan, of sleeping with her lawyer, Mr. Y*, who wasn't available for comment. Mr. Y's law partner called the accusation a "very sleazy" move by the producer. David Merrick's lawyer said that Etan Merrick was under "surveillance" when she entertained Mr. Y at her Upper East Side Manhattan digs on May 28 and that he didn't leave until the next day. The law partner said that Mr. Y split from his wife more than a year ago.*

---

* I have omitted the lawyer's name since he is still a fine, active practitioner and happily married.

* * *

The characters in this drama—or farce—are mostly dead or old, and what happened seems part of someone else's long-ago dream. They were all desperate people, part of a dance macabre choreographed by a half-mad megalomaniac, a lion who lived past his winter, clutching to his last vestige of power like a man clinging to a raft of reeds in a roiling sea.

Goodstein was desperate for money and validation of a life that failed its potential.

Mort Mitosky was desperate to prove his love for Merrick, receive payment for past indignities visited upon him, put his heel upon Merrick's neck and at last, be the thing he never was, David Merrick.

But, I believe, the most desperate of all was Etan because she was the brightest of them all. Her insecurity betrayed her natural gifts, caused her to play one against the other, to use and control.

37

RIDDICK BOWE
WORLD'S HEAVYWEIGHT CHAMPION,
THE GENTLE GIANT

It wasn't the airplanes. It was beauty killed the beast.

From the film, King Kong

* * *

What if you can no longer measure up, no longer be involved,
if you have used up all your fantasies? A champion cannot
retire like anyone else ... When a man loses the center of his
being, he loses his being. Retire? It's the filthiest word in the
English language. It's backing up into the grave.

Ernest Hemingway

* * *

Newspapers mostly traffic in disaster—or at least, unhappiness—and when I picked up the November 27, 2008, paper, I was not disappointed. It reported that Riddick Bowe, former World Heavyweight Champion, now aged forty-one and close to 300 pounds, was going to fight in Germany on December 13. Apparently, he had traveled along the same sad trajectory as other great fighters, whose time had come and passed, whose fame outran the man. I remembered him well.

* * *

Duke Ellington composed and Billy Strayhorn did the arrangement of (some say he actually wrote) the Ellington theme song, "Take the A Train." Nobody ever wrote a song suggesting a trip on the L train.

The L train lands you in Brownsville, located in eastern Brooklyn, the end of the line in anyone's life. Its mostly empty streets resemble the wake of a passing rampaging army: tired wrecks of eviscerated buildings long ago abandoned and demolished, its byways littered with the carcasses of burnt-out automobiles, its citizens indifferent to the garbage in the streets, stepping over and around it as one might a stone or puddle of yesterday's rain.

More than half its 65,000 residents live below the poverty level, supported by a myriad of agencies and alphabets—AFDC, SSI, Medicaid, Home Relief, Workfare and various religious groups—all designed to palliate the consciousness of luckier folks and at the same time perpetuate the poverty to which the poor have become so well accustomed.

It was originally a Jewish neighborhood; the ghosts of its pushcarts and street chatter of a dozen Eastern European languages have long ago fled. Then in the sixties, it became predominantly African-American. Its most notable citizens from its Jewish period were Louis "Lepke" Buchalter, chairman of the board of that uniquely American organization of mayhem, Murder Incorporated, who ended his days in the electric chair at Sing Sing and Abe "Kid Twist" Reles, his chief enforcer who became a police informer. This change of profession resulted in his death by defenestration, i.e. being thrown out of a sixth-floor window of the Half Moon Hotel in Coney Island, thereby becoming known as "The canary who sang, but couldn't fly." Brownsville also spawned gentler, but at that time, lesser-known souls: George Gershwin, Danny Kaye and Aaron Copland.

Brownsville, in its African-American period, was the home of Stephanie Mills, Agallah, Masta Ace, Willie Randolph, Saigon, Heltah Skeltah, James "Fly" Williams, Mike Tyson and Riddick Bowe.

Riddick Bowe, nicknamed "Big Daddy" and "Sugar Man," held the title of undisputed heavyweight champion of the world. His record was forty-two wins out of forty-four fights, thirty-three by KOs and one declared to be "No contest."

Odd things would happen to Riddick. In 1992, he fought the first of three fights with then-champion Evander Holyfield, defeated him, thereby becoming world champion. On the rematch, Riddick, overweight (because of his proclivities for Big Macs) at 246 lbs, lost a split decision to Holyfield. During the fight, however, something happened that has never before or since occurred in the history of the sport. In the seventh round, parachutist James Miller jumped from an airplane into the open-air arena and landed in Bowe's corner. Putting aside the imaginative way Mister Miller avoided paying for a ticket, the fight was stopped while the authorities got hold of the jumper and the necessary things argued about and resolved.

In a comeback fight with smaller and lighter Buster Mathis, Riddick could not get through Mathis' bobs and weaves. He did, however, hit Mathis repeatedly when he was down and lying on the canvas, and while in that supine position, he was able to beat him unconscious. Referee Arthur Mercante declared it a "No Contest," but the rest of the boxing world—press, the attending crowd, radio and TV reporters—all said Bowe should have been disqualified.

Riddick won the WBO title and defended it against Cuban Jorge Luis Gonzalez. The Cuban said that he wanted to do something not on the Marquis of Queensbury's menu: eat Riddick's heart. He said he was like a lion and Riddick like a hyena. In their last pre-fight press conferences, the boxing commission felt the need to separate the two fighters by protective glass.

After the Holyfield rematch, Riddick fought Andrew Golota. In the seventh round, Riddick went down after Golota punched him a number of times in his testicles. Golota was disqualified, and a riot of considerable size ensued. It is unclear whether the genesis of the riot was Golota's lack of sportsmanship or his loss by disqualification. Additional police were summoned; a large number of the spectators were injured as well as many police officers. One of the people in Riddick's corner hit Golota over the head (luckily, perhaps the least vulnerable part of his anatomy) with a radio, causing a wound that required eleven stitches to repair. On the rematch, Golota, once again, repeatedly kept punching Riddick in his testicles (Lord only knows what Doctor Freud would have said about this) and was again disqualified. For his performance in both fights, the press gave him the sobriquet of "The Foul Pole."

Riddick retired after the last Golota fight and immediately joined the Marine Corps. At the end of the first day of boot camp, he talked with his superior officer about leaving the corps and actually did so after eleven days.

Late on a warm spring day in 1997, my secretary walked into my office told me that Riddick Bowe was in the waiting room and wanted to see me.

He was big, almost half a foot taller than I. He wore a short-sleeved tee shirt and casual tan cotton trousers. His skin was the color of café au lait and was unmarked by the scars that often are the fighters substitute for the engraved pocket watch marking retirement from a profession to which the recipient had given exceptional service. His nose and ears were spared the disfigurements usual to prizefighters: scars from too many hard right hands that landed on target. His physique was not muscle-builder hard and defined, like those of most modern prizefighters. His was in the nature of Joe Louis'—smooth and flowing, more like that of a channel-crossing swimmer than that of a man whose calling in life is to beat and be beaten up. His hands were large and strong looking, calloused, like those of a stevedore. He ambled, almost strolled into my office, casually glancing at the pictures that lined the walls. He looked down at his hands as he spoke. His voice was quiet and his speaking unhurried.

Although he seemed at ease, I believe he must have been uncomfortable. For most people visiting a lawyer's office for the first time, telling a stranger something personal, often embarrassing, sometimes something they are ashamed of, something perhaps, they have never admitted to anyone else, is difficult. Some hide it better than others. The Catholic Church worked it out two thousand years ago, but confessional booths usually clash with the interior decorating of a law office.

I tried to put him at ease. We chatted, and I told him I was friendly with the great champion, Jack Dempsey, and showed him a print of the famous George Bellows painting of the Dempsey-Firpo fight depicting Dempsey knocked through the ring ropes in the first round. (Dempsey went on to win the fight with a second-round knockout). Jack had given me the print and inscribed it "I'm the guy at the bottom."

I told Riddick the story of when Jack, after his restaurant (located at Broadway and Fiftieth Street) closed for the evening, went to pick up his car that was parked on Eighth Avenue. Three muggers saw this elderly man going to his car late at night and thought they had an easy score. Jack knocked one out cold, the other lay moaning on the sidewalk, and the third managed to run away.

"The punch is the last thing to go," said Riddick, softly and shaking his head. "The first is your legs."

Riddick explained his problems both criminal and domestic. These would have been already familiar to any reader of the sports pages, but unfortunately, I was not such a person. As an example of my disinterest in the reporting of these things, Mark Gastineau's wife once retained me in her case against her husband, who she said was (at that time) a celebrated athlete. The young lawyers in the office told me later that he was, indeed, "famous" and that his particular field of endeavor was football. At the time I was hired, I had not heard of him and quite logically, assumed he was a hockey player because of his name, which seemed to me to be French-Canadian, a nationality quite common in that sport and not at all in football. I am sure his wife, Lisa, who was charming as well as beautiful, must have assumed I was from another planet. Now, I find the same things happening when I am retained by the wives or significant (sometimes insignificant) others of rap stars.

Johnnie Cochran, who recommended my services to Riddick, was handling Riddick's criminal case. I had represented Johnnie's former paramour, with whom he had a child, in a highly publicized palimony case. It may seem strange that having represented his paramour who had sued him in the past, he would recommend a client to me. But lawyers, particularly successful lawyers, keep their personal lives out of things and make recommendations based on what they believe would be best for the client. In fact, he had, over the years, recommended quite a few matters to me, and we continued to enjoy a cordial relationship, often stopping to chat in the lobby of his building (I had a close friend who lived there and often visited) and on the telephone, until his death at an all-too early age.

Riddick and I talked for a few hours, and we still had lots of ground to cover. It was late, and my support staff had left the office. I said we could continue the next morning. Riddick lived in Maryland, and I suggested that rather than go back home and then return, he would stay overnight at the upscale Palace Hotel, which is directly across the street from my office. I would sometimes chat with the personnel when I walked through the hotel—Giuliani, while he was still mayor, lived there for a period when I represented him in his divorce and would visit him there—so I knew many of the employees.

It had come up in my meeting with Riddick that either he did not own credit cards or at least, he did not have any with him. I was concerned that he might be embarrassed when trying to check into The Palace. It would be hypocritical (or just plain dumb) to not be concerned, in those days, that a six-foot-five-inch black man in a polo shirt, without luggage and without a credit card, would have trouble checking into a hotel.

I did not want him to be subjected to this, all too common, kind of humiliation. I told him that since it was on my way home, I would walk across the street with him, and because I knew many of the people there, perhaps I could speed things along. He readily agreed, and it was my intention that they probably would not have the nerve to be obnoxious in front of me, and if they were, I would simply check in Riddick using my credit card for myself and then turn the room over to him.

We crossed the street, and the first doorman we saw jumped out and held the door open for him with a "Good evening, Mister Bowe."

We entered the building, and the bellman came out from behind his station. "Hi ya, Champ."

When we were at the check-in desk, the manager with his body nudged the room clerk aside and said, "No need for you to bother checking in, Mister Bowe. I'll do that for you." He then went on to say that it was a pleasure to welcome him. That they will put him in a suite (of course, at the price of a single room) in "The Towers" (the ritziest part of the hotel usually reserved for visiting Arabs and rock stars) and that they will immediately set him up with a complimentary membership at their private health club. By the time he finished his speech, we had two bellmen and a guest gathered around Riddick for his autograph.

Such is the attraction of being world heavyweight champion, even a retired one. This should have warned me of what I might expect in another battle I was soon to have against Mike Tyson, who at the time was the *reigning* champion.

A professional fighter—at least one who has not had his brain too often flung about against the inside of his skull—is usually a mild, if not gentle fellow. He knows, to a proven certainty, what his short right hook would do to the morning gym-rat loudmouth taunting him from further down the bar. Or, maybe he is like me. I walk away from arguments. Therefore, we both just smile and walk further down the bar, away from the guy who wants us to make a donation of our stock in trade. But somewhere, in the case of the fighter whose professional calling is to beat and be beaten, there must exist the slumbering presence of something akin to rage: the almost genetic memory of the dull, hollow thud of the leather of a boxing glove striking sweaty flesh; the smell of fresh blood streaming from ruptured skin; the pain of organs smashed against each other a millisecond after the swish of air being rent asunder by a fisted glove traveling at bullet speed. Combine all of this with loneliness and under the proper circumstances, a critical mass can rapidly be reached.

The boxers I have known are usually lonely men, and perhaps, somewhere deep within them, they are also men afraid to be alone. Their loneliness is not the loneness of the performer who needs the validation of an audience who has paid to be entertained by him. The fighter's audience has paid to see him physically destroyed or to watch him pummel another human being; to fulfill some primitive blood lust or be part of, as an observer, a deadly sacrificial ceremony. All that the fighter has as far as people who truly care about him in his profession are the people in his corner, and without them, he is as alone as an astronaut drifting in space.

When I represented Robin Givens and I had to serve Mike Tyson legal papers, I knew that he, at that time at the height of his powers, the single most fearsome man on the planet, would not be at his home on a mountaintop in Bernardsville, New Jersey, because he could not be alone in this isolated house.

Riddick Bowe's loneliness began his undoing.

Riddick was rich—$80 million dollars rich—and this was in 1997. Whenever men sit around the commuter's equivalent of a campfire and tell sad tales about the death of kings and the subject comes around to money, somebody always says, "... and you know how much that would be in *today's* money." Riddick was rich in *today's* as well as *yesterday's* money and had enough to have purchased seven $250,000 homes in a suburban Maryland neighborhood for his sisters, in-laws and mother and not hear a squeal from his wallet. When a man has been poor and then becomes rich, he can do more than simply move out of the old neighborhood. He can take with him whatever part of the old neighborhood that gives him a sense of continuity.

Riddick, his wife, Judy, and their five children lived in a sprawling home with a separate building on the land that was a professionally equipped gym. His extended family lived on adjacent properties in the same Maryland suburb, ensconced in Riddick-supplied housing.

Things that happened inside his home were not as pleasant as its bucolic suburban surroundings would suggest. In August of 1997, the local authorities charged Riddick with assaulting Judy. She promptly gathered up the children and moved to North Carolina. The immediate question that arises in such cases is that posed by Mike Tyson: If I wanted to hurt her [Robin Givens], I certainly know how to do it. Yet, the hypothetical woman who might have been the object of the fighter's attention might appear to be relatively undamaged. The fighter's explanation of his innocence might seem like perfect common sense to a layperson, but an experienced lawyer knows that such a defense is in the category of "Do you think that I would have been so stupid to have done it [the crime charged] this way?" The answer is often "Yes, and you were stupid enough to get caught." However, juries frequently buy such a defense, and in the last analysis, I do not know whether Judy was assaulted, but in any event, Riddick absolutely denied doing it. Invitations to prospective witnesses are not sent out for these sorts of things. Nor does an irreproachable neighborhood clergyman ever happen to have been looking in the window when these things allegedly occur and is then subsequently available as a witness. These assaults, if they take place, occur late at night, in a kitchen or bedroom, when the fangs of the soul are bared and anger overtakes common sense.

It might also be fairly said (and I would say it if I were the prosecutor) that a professional fighter is *precisely* the person who would know how to administer pain in such a way that it would leave no trace on its victim.

A lawyer representing a man charged with domestic violence once called me to persuade me to take over the case. I do not represent men charged with wife beating if I believe there is a reasonable possibility that they have committed the crime. When the facts were described to me, I felt uneasy about the situation and asked to have a meeting set up with the lawyer and his client. I wanted to observe the interplay between them before I made up my mind about the case.

At the meeting, the lawyer told me he believed his client to be innocent because if he wanted to inflict pain on his wife, he could have done so without leaving a trace. Then he proceeded to demonstrate to me his point. Using his client as the "victim," he rolled up a thick telephone directory and with its edge, prodded his client in the solar plexus. The client, his eyes glistening, moist lips hung open, seemed unnaturally interested in the lawyer's description as I bid them a hasty good-bye.

It was difficult to obtain a cohesive description of events from Riddick. When a man lies to you, particularly about a complicated series of events, he has worked out the lies in his head, and he tells them in a logical and chronological way. The story has the feel of something well rehearsed—a twice-told tale accompanied by appropriate hand gestures and facial grimaces. It is as good or bad as the art of its author. But since it is a drafted fairy tale, it virtually always has a beginning, middle and end. The sinews between these guideposts are as colorful and filled with the music of events in direct relation to the skill of its creator.

Riddick, on the other hand, told the story in stops and starts, going a bit forward as events occurred to him, then telling the bits and pieces of other happenings that were triggered by something he had just told me. He was like a traveler who goes forward slowly and deliberately and then retraces his steps, then leaps forward. The unhappy parts were related in a quiet almost strangled voice preceded by his raising his eyebrows and looking down. It was as if some act of will dragged the episode out of him after his face announced what was to come. When he spoke of the good things, his face and expression were the happy contemporaneous companion of his narration. By the end of the first day's session, my yellow legal pad was filled with my scribbled notes, quotes from what he had said and dozens of arrows going every which way in trying to make a schematic of a chronologically accurate narrative. But one thing was clear, Riddick was telling me the truth, but it was a confused and often inexplicable truth.

* * *

Nineteen ninety-seven. It was a year that two women—Mother Teresa and Princess Diana—whose lives were lived at opposite ends of the moral spectrum, died a month apart. They affected the world in its collective grief differently; one whose body entombed in a car-coffin, smashed together in death with that of her Arab lover after being chased by the purveyors of the cheap celebrity that she herself pursued; the other woman died wrapped in her religiosity; the public mourning for the former exceeding that of the latter a thousandfold, testimony to a society drunk on the wine of the whore-God celebrity.

It was a year of four major plane crashes and massive needless destruction in life from the Heaven's Gate cult suicides, to massacres that took place in Bentalha, Algeria. On the bright side, Bobbi McCaughey, in Des Moines, Iowa, as a testimony to modern chemistry, gave birth to septuplets (the second known case where all seven babies were born alive) and in Roslin, Scotland, scientists announced that a sheep named Dolly had been cloned. All in all, it was a better year for sheep than people.

Nineteen ninety-seven was not a good year either for Riddick Bowe nor were the years that followed. After Riddick was charged by the local authorities with assaulting his wife in August, the matter could have ended there—a tawdry little tale, one of probably hundreds each year in this suburban Maryland community; a stern lecture from a judge, a suspended sentence, perhaps community service, required attendance with a domestic-violence counselor, men sitting in a circle in the basement of a local church, looking down at the floor, humiliating themselves, less because of the violence they inflicted than because they were forced to explore their violent impulses that were fathers to the acts, discussing how to avoid or deal with triggering events in a manner other than that which causes a call to be made to the police and some of them thinking of when they will visit retribution upon the women who had violated the secret bond between abuser and victim.

Judy, if she *was* a victim, was different from the usual wife who suffered from domestic violence, huddled in her home, torn between inviting the inflictor back or losing her means of support; a choice between economic survival and the terror, or at least the indignity of physical subjugation. Judy had the financial means to put distance between her and the person she claimed abused her. She packed herself and her five children's things in an SUV and moved with them to North Carolina. If her allegations were the basis for her to do something she wanted to do *regardless* of whether Riddick really did hit her or whether it stemmed from simply a need to get away from a famous man whose reach far exceeded his grasp was something only the sharers of the intimacy of their unhappy home would ever know.

Riddick was left alone in the large house silent of even the ghosts of the laughter and sounds of five children and was lonely as only a man can be, living in a very large and empty, once lived-in home.

Riddick did not have the parish of glamorous women that Joe Louis had surrounding him (Lena Horne was one), nor the exotica of foreign lands and women that Jack Johnson enjoyed, nor the noise and hoopla that surrounded Muhammad Ali, nor the adulation of Jack Dempsey sitting in his restaurant, in front of the window, signing autographs and posing for photographs with customers. Riddick was but a speck on the speck that was a small town on the map of Maryland. He walked down the block and moved into the basement of the house he had bought for his mother.

Even in his mother's basement, he was not immune from trouble. Riddick had a nephew from hell. Horace Bowe, a.k.a. Joey, had outstanding warrants for assault, harassment, menacing, unlawful imprisonment and trespassing. Riddick, if the charge against him was to be believed, set him off on the path to righteousness in the abrupt and meaningful way of a man whose currency in life is controlled violence.

As a result of his efforts directed toward the moral awakening of Joey, Riddick was charged with second-degree assault. Joey, if nothing else but consistent in his philosophy of life, offered to drop the charges if Riddick paid him $1 million. History is silent as to the disposition of this proposed business transaction.

By February of 1998, Riddick had had enough of living in his mother's basement, enough of being alone, separated from his family, enough of spending unplanned days that stretched out aimlessly before him. He did what he always did in his life: He made his own future untroubled by the conventional ways of others. He and his brother drove to the town in North Carolina where Judy had moved and went directly to the local elementary school. It was morning, and the children were just arriving. At the school-bus stop, exiting the bus, he spotted his three older children. He got them into the car, drove to Judy's home, ordered her and the two younger children into his vehicle and headed north. While driving through Virginia, Judy said she needed to use a bathroom. Riddick pulled up at a roadside McDonald's, and Judy went in to use the facilities. Riddick needed to stay inside the car with the children. Once inside, she found a phone that was out of Riddick's line of sight and called her sister who, in turn, called the police.

While waiting for Judy, Riddick amused the children, whom he had not seen for some time, with simple car games parents play with children to keep them occupied in an automobile. But, as the moments went by, he realized something was amiss. Just when he decided to go into the McDonald's to fetch Judy, three police cars pulled up and boxed him in, making it impossible to move his car in any direction. Steel-faced policemen, guns drawn, their moment upon the stage having come, ordered him out of the car.

Judy's sister, after calling the police, also telephoned Riddick's manager, Rock Newman. Newman sent a limousine to the station house where Riddick was being held. The car took him to the psychiatric ward at Howard University where he remained under observation for a week.

Congress had passed a federal domestic-violence law in 1994. This enactment fit comfortably into the category of "fearless" congressional actions. It was about as fearless an action as voting to put Elvis' picture on a ten-cent stamp, but it played well to the folks back home. It was pretty much a case of a very serious and potent medicine for an infrequently occurring illness. Domestic violence *does* take place and in frightening numbers, and all too often the perpetrators are modestly—if, at all—punished. However, the new federal law, complete with its draconian punishments, only dealt with domestic violence on an *interstate* basis (an infrequent occurrence). Superimposed upon this situation was the fact that the penalty for violating the new law was determined by the federal minimum-sentencing guidelines with their built-in inflexibility. They were, at the time, the subject of much criticism and litigation. The United States Supreme Court has since knocked down the law, changing its status from being obligatory for judges to follow to now being only "advisory." Clearly, since the potential charge involved a well-known public figure, the United States Attorney had to proceed cautiously and kick the decision to Washington and ultimately, to the person who wore the pants in the situation, the attorney general herself: Janet Reno, victor of the siege (some say "massacre") at Waco, Texas.

While the attorney general was contemplating what to do, in March, Judy served Riddick with a summons for divorce, which is where I came into the picture. In April, we consented to a child-support order of $8,000 a month. Considering Riddick's great wealth and that there were five children, this was an extremely modest award in a case where our potential financial exposure was much greater. In May, I read an item in the press that was bizarre. Riddick was training to become a school-crossing guard. Perhaps, he had listened to advice from the inevitable camp followers of divorce and believed this would demonstrate him being a good parent. I wrote it off as nothing more, but in retrospect, perhaps it was a demonstration of the chaotic state of his psyche.

In June of 1998, Riddick was indicted by a federal grand jury in Charlotte, North Carolina, for kidnapping and interstate domestic violence. The possible sentence under the guidelines was eighteen to twenty-four months. Johnnie Cochran was now fully aboard and operational. He and I danced what would have to be an orchestrated duet since the domestic and criminal matters were inextricably interwoven with one another. We spoke almost daily coordinating actions in our respective cases.

The kidnapping case was never a serious concern. The federal kidnapping statute, carrying with it a potential death penalty, was enacted as a result of the kidnapping and murder of the baby of Charles Lindbergh who was, at the time, still a national hero. He—christened by the media "The Lone Eagle"—was the first man to fly solo across the Atlantic Ocean, from Roosevelt Field in Long Island to Le Bourget Airport in Paris. His later excursions into politics, his high regard for the Nazis and his anti-Semitism tarnished his earlier reputation. The "Lindbergh Law," as it came to be known, was born out of necessity. The automobile made it possible for kidnappers to easily travel from one state to another, hopelessly fragmenting any investigation. Now, since kidnapping became a federal crime, the FBI could easily make a coordinated multistate effort in these situations. The law was clearly not designed for the situation of a man trying to unite his family. But the federal authorities thought that to add the charge would put additional pressure for a plea-bargain deal. This was a common practice by aggressive prosecutors and in the trade, was called, "overcharging."

When the public reads that a man has been indicted—particularly by a *federal* grand jury—it gives the ominous ring of truth to the accusation. This is anything but so. Sol Wachtler, chief judge of New York's court of appeals (the highest court in the state), had written the highly quoted statement, "A grand jury can indict a ham sandwich." Shortly thereafter, unfortunately, as a result of loving well but not wisely, the judge himself was driven to write threatening letters to a former paramour. He was indicted by a grand jury, convicted and sent to jail.

We had something else going for us. Juries treat celebrities deferentially. To a jury, it is often a case where celebrities can do no wrong. With the advent of television, frequently, the celebrity is the last person you see before you go to sleep, and perhaps you see him or her in your bedroom more often than your spouse. Sometimes, you know more about what goes on in the celebrity's life than you do about your sister-in-law's. Celebrities win lawsuits for no other reason but for the fact they are celebrities. Liberace sued a London newspaper for defamation based on the fact it called him a homosexual, won the case and then promptly died of AIDS. From Rodney Dangerfield and Wayne Newton to Errol Flynn, stars walk out of the courtroom with a smile on their face. Riddick's defense, putting aside his fame—and even adulation—as world heavyweight champion, was one that was filled with great pathos and sympathy. He sought only to repair a broken family. It was, in my book, a winner.

In a difficult telephone conversation, Johnnie told me he intended to plead Riddick guilty with a sentencing arrangement that he felt was favorable. While I do not practice criminal law, I believe I have a good sense of where a jury would go in a case like this.

I had been in Los Angeles for the OJ case (reporting for the BBC) and observed Johnnie doing, what I thought, was a superb job. All craftsmen have egos, and my life experience led me to the conclusion that the finer the craftsman, the larger the ego. I played to Johnnie's ego telling him that he could do a job in the case that no other lawyer could, that his pedestal would be raised to the height of Clarence Darrow's, that after winning Riddick's case, no one would ever be able to say of him that O. J. Simpson's case was only a victory in a tawdry murder case won by appealing to racial bias. I reviewed the evidence and shared with him the thought that a divorce case begun by Judy a month after the arrest could, in his hands, taint the criminal case and could be made to mean to a jury, with Johnnie's skill, that it was all about money. That is all it was ever about.

I told him I believed that the coupling of the kidnapping charge—designed to be aimed at the likes of John Dillinger—with a simple domestic situation was a fatal mistake by the prosecutor. Immediately, from the opening statement on, implanted in the jury's minds would be the thought that this indictment was the result of a prosecutor's zeal and ambition run amok. I marshaled my arguments as a general would his troops. I flattered, cajoled and coaxed . . . all to no avail. Johnnie paused. He was impervious to my arguments. "No, no, I hear you and thank you kindly, but I believe this is the way to go. It's a good deal." I did not know, until I much later read it in the newspapers, that the "good deal" was an agreement that Riddick would serve eighteen months to two years in a federal penitentiary.

I was puzzled. A dirty little secret of the law—and perhaps one reason why the jails of America are so overpopulated—is that because some criminal lawyers believe their clients cannot pay them to try their cases, they take the easy way out and talk their clients into pleading guilty even when they have winning cases; even when they are not guilty beyond a reasonable doubt; even when they are innocent. Innocent people are in jail, I believe, not because of race or crooked police or because they are just unlucky. They are victims of the economics of the legal profession or at least some of its members. But Riddick was rich and never remotely balked at his legal fees as even rich people often do. Some lawyers may say *especially* as rich people often do. Sometimes, lawyers who call themselves criminal lawyers are really specialists in plea bargaining and simply lack the ability or experience to try a serious case. Examples of this phenomenon can be seen on the TV news channels whenever a substantial criminal case arises and some drop-dead blond, make-up-perfectly-in-place legal expert critiques the situation, explaining what the real-life lawyers *should* have done. Shakespeare's commentary is still the best. "He jests at scars that never felt a wound." But Johnnie, whether you approved of his tactics in the O.J. case or not, demonstrated to a second-guessing world watching breathlessly that he was an absolutely first-class lawyer.

To this day, I do not know why he refused to try Riddick's case. Maybe he was tired or getting old or his soul was fat with his success or he felt the sickness that ultimately killed him beginning to clutch at him or that he simply believed this was the best deal to be had for Riddick. In any event, I was supportive of his decision—the last thing Riddick needed was a disagreement between his lawyers—but I felt it would all end badly.

In June, Riddick appeared before United States District Court Judge for the Western District of North Carolina Graham Mullen, and Johnnie pleaded him guilty of interstate domestic violence. Pending sentencing, the judge allowed Riddick to return home until he was formally sentenced. He placed him under house arrest and required him to wear an electronic bracelet. Team Riddick was quite upbeat. I was not. Why put these restrictions on a man who probably could not go anywhere in the world without being recognized unless there was something else up the sleeve of the robe of the lady whose statue holding high the scales of justice appears above the entrance of most courthouses (at least the old fashioned ones)? At that point, I still did not know the terms of the plea bargain.

After a guilty plea is accepted, considerable time may pass before the defendant is formally sentenced. A judge cannot impose sentence until the probation department completes a pre-sentencing report and submits it, together with a recommendation, to the court. The report involves personal interviews (and sometimes re-interviews) with present and former employers, the arresting officers, the prosecutors, the defendant's friends, family and the victim. After the interviews have been conducted, there must also be a complete analysis of the defendant's financial situation, but sometimes the economics are so complex that outside experts must be consulted, and when all this is done, the resulting final report works its way up the chain of command at the probation department for ultimate approval.

The process can easily take months—and in some cases, years— before the defendant is sentenced. Usually the defendant takes the position "the longer the better" as far as the report is concerned, since he is usually out on the street having posted bail, or if there is not a risk of flight, he has been ROR'd (released on his own recognizance). But Riddick would have to wait, a prisoner in the velvet cage of his own home, but a prisoner nevertheless, and there was still the matter of the assault charge involving Judy from back in August of 1997.

In November 1998, Riddick received permission from the federal court in North Carolina to leave his home and appear before the local court in Maryland to be sentenced on charges relating to his alleged assault on Judy. Maryland Judge Hovey Johnson dismissed the August second-degree assault charge still pending on the condition that Riddick have no violent contact with Judy and that he complete a ten-day psychiatric evaluation and undergo any recommended course of treatment. Riddick was faced with the situation that if he obeyed the order of the Maryland court and went for psychiatric evaluation and treatment, he would be in violation of the North Carolina order that directed him not to leave his home. Lawyers—at least some lawyers—love this sort of situation: lots of paperwork, lots of running back and forth between two different courts in two states, lots of time spent and billed by junior associates and an assured results.

By spring of 2000, now loaded and locked, the U.S. Judge Graham Mullen was finally prepared to pronounce sentencing: This would be the final act in the drama whose curtain was raised in August of 1997. Maybe.

Everybody apparently counted on the fact that Judge Mullen would be a rubber stamp to the deal. The judge gave Riddick minimal jail time, much less than agreed to even by Riddick's lawyers. The judge sentenced Riddick to thirty days in jail, followed by six months of house arrest, followed by four years of probation and a ban on boxing.

The part of the sentence that banned Riddick from boxing was inherently illogical. It would make more sense *if* a judge believed he *had* a propensity for violence to give him an acceptable outlet for that violence inside, not outside the ring. Others might reasonably argue that if he *did* assault Judy, whether or not he remained a professional boxer would have little correlation with the possibility that he would in the future assault her. Wise or dumb, the sentencing should have been the end of the matter. It was not. The U.S. Attorney was furious.

The deal was that Riddick would receive real jail time, not a thirty-day slap on the wrist. They should have done their homework on Judge Mullen, who had recently said, "I'm tired of sending young black men to jail." The government appealed. This had not been the deal they agreed to. Riddick was supposed to go to jail for longer than a month.

Putting aside a legitimate concern about large amounts of taxpayers' money that was spent prolonging the process—and admittedly Riddick was neither terrorist nor public enemy—armchair lawyers will immediately raise the question of double jeopardy. The defense of double jeopardy comes into play only after *testimony*—no matter how meager—has been taken, but does not prevent the government appealing a mistake in sentencing. However, it *does* prevent the prosecutors from re-indicting and re-prosecuting a defendant who has begun to give his testimony. Experienced lawyers will sometimes put their clients on the stand, ask a few introductory questions and *then* put the settlement on the record. Sadly, no one on Riddick's criminal team thought to take some testimony from him. But, frankly, I have never even heard of a case in which testimony was not taken, a plea bargain worked out and then the government appealed the sentence except in organized-crime cases.

The government's appeal was based on the fact that Judge Mullen's sentencing violated the sentencing-guideline law. The government's position, which the United States Court of Appeals adopted, was that Judge Mullen must follow the guidelines *precisely*—which he did not—and the matter was remanded to him for re-sentencing.

Finally, in January of 2003, Riddick was sentenced to seventeen months in jail for interstate domestic violence. Riddick ultimately surrendered by agreement to the U.S. Marshals, served his eighteen months and was released in May of 2004.

After the Bowe case was over, Judge Mullen was interviewed and asked why he did not want to send him to jail. He explained, "He's a proud man who was told by his mother-in-law that a real man would go down there and get his wife and family and bring them back."

This sounds like a pretty good argument that could have been made to the jury. It sure convinced the judge.

* * *

By March of 2003, Riddick was divorced from Judy with a negotiated settlement and had married Terri. A week before Riddick was scheduled to begin serving his sentence on the federal charge, he was arrested for domestic violence on four counts of second-degree assault in Fort Washington, Maryland. The charges were dismissed when the case was called for trial in June 2003 since Terri and the three other witnesses failed to appear in court. Prosecutors believed that Terri was trying to protect Riddick.

* * *

When I met Riddick Bowe in 1998, he was worth $80 million. In October of 2005, he filed for bankruptcy.

There must be a moral in there somewhere. Maybe it has to do with women or lawyers, or maybe both.

38

WHERE ARE THE EAGLES
AND THE TRUMPETS?

No! I am not Prince Hamlet, nor was meant to be;
Am an attendant lord . . .

T. S. Eliot

But even an attendant lord has his uses.

Forty-seven years ago, not long in the history of any great or portentous thing but long in the natural life of most men, I walked into the Orpheum Theatre to see a revival of Cole Porter's *Anything Goes*. This simple and inconsequential act set in motion a series of events that made the next forty-seven years scream by as a passing moment.

I had a friend who had a role in the show, and I came to see her performance. At the time, I was a lawyer and had a job full of high purpose and fine sounding, but paying $11,000 a year. I was a federal prosecutor, just about fed up with what I did and seeking to better myself in life. In fact, it was the first real job I ever had and as it would turn out, the last.

My friend introduced me to one of the dancers who had a legal problem. Her stage name was Rawley Bates, the first name being the same as the nickname my family gave me. When people at the show called out to her, there was some confusion since I instinctively thought I was the one they wanted.

Most female performers have an IQ about the same number of their chest size. But this one was different. She was a Phi Beta Kappa graduate of Brown University who could do most anything to which she put her mind. On the other hand, I hated school—all schools—and had and probably still have a problem they now call attention deficit disorder. Today, they can probably treat the condition with drugs, but then, it was anything but a "condition." It was being lazy or just plain dumb or someone who had his head in the clouds: a daydreamer.

To me, it is an exhausting thing. It is like several things going on in my head on parallel tracks, causing me to have to make enormous efforts at concentration in order to master any material. It is like playing several games of chess at once with each one competing for my attention. However, it has its advantages—if you consider a mind going sixty miles an hour, dealing simultaneously with two sets of problems, images or situations at the same time, when everyone else's is cruising along comfortably at the speed limit as being an advantage.

As difficult as learning was for me, it was easy for her. I believed that she would waste her time on the stage. Le Carré wrote that an actor is an empty vessel waiting to be filled. He neglected to note that most of the time the vessel is a bit cracked.

I tried to convince her to abandon her theatrical career and throw in her lot with me. As *Anything Goes*, anything *went*, and I was able to convince her as to the latter, but not the former. We got married and lived happily ever after. But, it was a little more complicated than that.

I gave up my government job, started a law practice, and she continued on the stage, although now she was on Broadway. Eventually, common sense triumphed, and she agreed to go back to school. She wanted to study history and eventually teach in college. I needed help in a growing law practice, and there was more money to be had in law than in teaching.

She went to law school, did very well and was in her ninth month of pregnancy when she took the bar examination. It was a toss-up between whether completing the examination or giving birth would occur first. The examination won, and she went directly to the hospital afterward, giving birth to our first child, Rachel. Four years later, she gave birth to our son, James.

In forty-six years, we have never had an argument. I operate under a simple proposition: since I am paid to argue, why give it away for nothing?

I am a lousy husband, but I hope, a good father.

I cannot go to family affairs, being able to sit still at them for about a maximum of twenty minutes. The last wedding in which I stayed to the end was my own. Actually, I did stay until the end of my daughter's, and that was because Mayor Giuliani performed the ceremony at City Hall in about fifteen minutes.

I am nocturnal by nature, only sleeping for about three hours a night. The three hours are cumulative since I am up and down more times a night than a second-rate club fighter. When my brother was alive, since he also seldom slept during the hours of darkness, I would frequently join him in the lobby of the Hotel Forrest as he held court until dawn. None of this contributed to quiet, restful, sleep-inducing nights at home.

My wife likes to travel. I hate to.

My wife likes to eat out at fancy restaurants. I hate to do so and believe it to be a waste of money to pay excessively for the short voyage the food travels on my alimentary canal. It could have traveled less expensively on a cost-per-mile basis on the Concorde.

If we are alone, she likes to send out for food. I like to make my own.

She likes to spend money. I am indifferent to money. It never was important to me, and perhaps, that is why I was able to accumulate a bit.

I am a lousy husband.

About to celebrate a recent birthday, an improvident God, or whatever else it might be, in some celestial scheme of things, struck down her happiness and visited a stroke upon my wife. Perhaps it was settling up ancient unintended wrongs or balancing some unimaginable ledger—this much pain in payment for that much pleasure.

Her thinking and speech were untouched, but she suffered a deficit—the neurologist's way of describing the imprisonment of one's mind in an unresponsive body—in her left leg and arm. Now her world is inhabited by cadres of physical therapists, doctors and aides. But she soldiers on with dignity and determination into a sunlit but uncertain future.

* * *

River of my dreams,
Storm-tossed, rolling river
Black and pitiless river
Carry me home

Death, that bestower of mercy and misery, the mother of that ancient whore Pain, the mother of all religions, the core center and sum of all terrors, visited me three times in short succession. In its majesty, it allowed the visits to occur in the natural order of things.

First, my father. He, aged eighty-five or so, was in a nursing-home facility (another name for a human warehouse). In an effort to keep him from bothering the staff, he was dosed with the wrong medicine and made half-mad and brain numbed.

I brought in a doctor who recognized this and was in the process of changing the medication and at the same time avoid offending the doctor who was the prescriber. While all of this professional courtesy bubbled back and forth, my father, dazed, fell out of his bed, breaking his hip. The institution's visiting surgeon suggested not doing anything to repair the fracture. However, if I insisted, he would operate on my father. If things went wrong in the operating room, he wanted not to take what he called "heroic measures," but rather "Let nature take its course" (a euphemism for standing by and discussing football scores while the patient dies on the table). I suggested he do this with *his* father and not mine.

My father died on the operating table.

Since my father wanted to be cremated, there was no burial service, but there was a funeral service at the Riverside chapel—a place I got to know quite well in the succeeding months. There was a modest crowd for the services composed of, it seemed to me, elderly people from the center he attended that basically were lonely and did not have a better place to go on a rainy afternoon. The rabbi also came from the center, and it was clear that he had never met my father, and if he did, he did not remember him. We spoke to him in a small room off the chapel, and he spent several minutes with us obtaining the names of the immediate family and my father's pastimes or hobbies. My mother, having injured her leg, was in the hospital at the time, so her absence was not questioned.

The rabbi's little speech at the funeral was as sincere as a bill collector's Christmas card. He devoted a portion of it to the warm and loving relationship shared by my father and mother.

After the ceremony, my father's body was taken to the crematorium. The next day, a messenger arrived carrying a tin coffee can with the label removed. It contained my father's ashes. They rattled in the can like pieces of gravel. Gravel: the distilled essence of a life's experiences: beauty and ugliness, thinking, feeling, love, hate, fear, hurt, passion, anger, pain, rage, humiliation, dreams shattered and hopes dashed, ratiocination and impulse, shame and pride, deception and jealousy, unhappiness and despair. All ground down, battered and beaten, reduced to the sound of gravel rattling in a tin can.

* * *

Several months later, my mother ran an unexplained fever and was admitted to Doctors Hospital on East End Avenue. This was a fancy hospital whose major claim to fame was that Jackie Gleason was a patient at their high-class drunk tank.

I visited her the morning after she was admitted. The hospital was located adjacent to the river and had an obstructed view to the east and over the East River. She told me that the previous night, she remained awake looking at the stars, and she had never seen them so bright. She felt that they were just beyond her window, that she could have reached out and touched them. We spoke of things that perhaps should have been spoken about years earlier. She told me she was not afraid of dying, and I told her that this was foolish talk, and I changed the topic.

She was discharged that afternoon and returned to her apartment. She lived on West Seventy-second Street, west of Central Park. My brother lived on the same street, one block further down, and an unending supply of cooked food traveled west from her apartment to my brothers'.

She lived in an old, but large apartment. There was a center room leading to a terrace. To the right of the living room, she had her bedroom and bath, and to the left, my father had the same arrangement. When my father was alive, and I would visit, I would go into a bedroom, speak to one of them and then walk across the living room to visit with the other. I was the conduit of messages across no man's land. "Tell your mother" or "Tell your father . . ."

My father would wait until I finished the visit with my mother. When I came into his room, he usually had a prepared list of grievances, sometimes a list of things that he had recently done that he considered praiseworthy. I would sit and not interrupt him while he worked his way down the list.

My mother, now in her eighties, had retired as a director of a large home and hospital for the aged. After retirement, she became a paid consultant for the Mayor's Office for the Aging. The morning after returning from the hospital, she insisted upon going to work.

I sent my driver to take her to the office. He usually met her at around seven-thirty in the morning. At eight o'clock, he called to tell me she neither came down nor answered his call.

I knew.

I raced across town and went up to her apartment, letting myself in with the spare key I insisted she give me and that I carried on my key ring.

The apartment was quiet. I walked slowly down the hall to her bedroom calling her name. There was no answer.

I knew.

I looked at her on the floor not daring to focus my eyes. She was dressed for work and lay, as if asleep, on the floor where she had fallen, her life stolen from her.

I called 911, and the police and an ambulance came in a few minutes. The police seemed large and hulking and out of place in her rather feminine bedroom. The ambulance people and one of the policemen left. The policeman who remained was quiet and respectful in the presence of the still, third person in the room. He seemed embarrassed and explained to me that he was required to stay there until there was an authorization for my mother to be released to a funeral parlor. But I knew she was already released from the prison of her life, her struggles for "my two boys," her swimming against the tide of an indifferent and callous world so that my brother would have a life of dignity. She was now on the other side and won the race.

The policeman expressed his condolences—odd that the first person to convey condolences was a policeman whom I had never before met. He told me he had lost his mother, and it seemed he wanted to talk, but this was not the place to talk.

I called my brother and told him. I cannot remember what I said or how I said it. He was silent.

His relationship with my mother was different and of a kind more profound than any other I could ever imagine. Beyond the arguments and shouting at her, he existed through her, and there was I suppose, a kind of pact—silent, unspoken—between them that they lived within each other and that all the anger and rage they shared, and often directed at each other, was meaningless and more than just that. Their anger was at the hand fate dealt them, and their rage against it was one that the powerless could only vent against the one closest, the one most loved. It was an expression of their love and was intimate and a bond that was part of their mutual protection against the world.

She, I believe, saw in him still a nine-year-old boy in braces and crutches that would survive and excel. The decades did not erase their silent bond.

I hoped these things of the past were not in my brother's thoughts as things like these often are when someone dies. He had already had his allotment of lifetime pain.

Thoughts jumbled and spilled over each other as I waited. One image played itself over and over again.

Several years earlier, my mother visited me in East Hampton. One evening, there was a rock 'n' roll concert in town at Guild Hall. I took my mother, and as it turned out, many of the songs performed were written by my brother.

The audience was very responsive, clapping to the music, standing at their chairs, singing along. I looked over and saw my mother standing, clapping, swaying to the songs, *his* songs, and I knew that she knew they had won. I turned away since I did not want her to see the tears running down my cheeks.

I had to make the funeral arrangements. This was my first experience in dealing with these people who traffic in other's grief and vulnerability.

A thirtyish young man with soft plump hands furtively swept the remnants of his sandwich lunch away as I entered his small, appropriately dimly lit office. His face was appropriately somber as he, in a low voice, expressed appropriate condolences. Did they teach this in a school?

He told me in an unguent murmur that he knew how I felt, and I asked him, "How? Did you know my mother?" He stammered and mumbled an unintelligible answer undoubtedly wishing he never should have abandoned his tuna-fish sandwich to meet with me.

"Then how could you know how I feel?" At this point, he probably wished that I had chosen a different funeral parlor.

He ignored my question and gave me a set of forms to sign. He then told me of the different types of funerals available and their respective costs.

He took me down a flight of stairs to a large room rather like an automobile showroom; only here, there were models of the various types of coffins available, each having a card with a sanctimonious name for the particular model, together with its price. Of course, grief-stricken people are not of a mind to bargain in much the same way that people who need a heart operation do not bargain with the surgeon. Only here, you are told the bill just before you are about to be wheeled into the operating room. It is worse. Here people overpay to expiate real or perceived wrongs they have done to the dead or even just to impress the neighbors in an ultimate display of conspicuous consumption.

I suppose the funeral director plays some role in the cycle of life. But so do maggots.

The funeral was a large one, and my brother managed to come, sitting in the back in his wheelchair. He came to the graveside burial service, but of course, could not get out of the car. He sat in the car with the door open while the service was conducted. Both our lives, from that moment on, forever changed.

* * *

My brother's death, a year later, the worst of all.

The Babylonian Talmud said that each life is a universe. The end of part of his universe began in the middle of the night with a call from my niece, Sharyn. She said my brother had telephoned her saying he was having trouble breathing. I told her to call an ambulance and dressed quickly. I cannot recall whether she came that night or not—there were many such nights to follow—but I arrived just as the ambulance attendants were leaving. They had given him oxygen, and he seemed to be all right. I waited a while with him and then went home.

A few nights later, there was a similar occurrence. My brother had not been to a doctor for many years. They brought back too many awful memories of doctors and hospitals. I insisted that he see an internist and through a doctor friend, obtained a recommendation of a competent one that had a hospital practice at NYU and whose office was wheelchair accessible. There were inherent difficulties in examining my brother. His weight and physical condition made access to modern diagnostic devices unrealistic even if my brother was so inclined. He was not prepared to get involved with the MRI and all the other devices of discomfort that are part of a modern doctor's armamentarium and was satisfied with the diagnosis of asthma.

He duly took the medicine prescribed. At one point, the doctor recommended someone expert in the art of "cupping." This involved striking my brother's back over his rib cage with rubber cups and also with cupped hands. This was supposed to clear the lung's passageways and alleviate that asthma. None of this helped. The calls continued to be made in the middle of the night. The ambulance drivers seemed to come and go like pizza-delivery people. Sometimes, they would see my brother's awards on the walls, and he would give them records or tapes.

Because I could never tell if there would be a call from him during the night, before I would go to bed, I would lay out my clothes for the next day, putting all the proper things in my pockets and pack my briefcase. This is a practice I follow to this day.

He continued to suffer the attacks at night. I finally told my brother that we should either go to another doctor or check into a hospital to get to the root of the problem. He was resistant and as was his way, would bluster and put me off, but the matter was soon taken out of our hands.

After one particularly bad attack, the ambulance attendant, as well as his doctor who we reached on the phone, insisted he go to the hospital.

The admittance facility was overflowing—this was during the AIDS epidemic—the beds were placed in the crowded corridors, and it looked like there would be no bed available for a long, indeterminable time. I called Bob Tisch, a major contributor to the institution and for whose family the main building of NYU hospital was named. He said he would see what he could do. Within a few hours, my brother was admitted to a large and comfortable room. For the first time in weeks, my brother, his children and I had a night secure from the chaos and fears of the prior weeks. But the real troubles had yet to begin.

The tests began. The blood tests, x-rays and physical examinations were fine, but what he needed was an MRI. However, these machines were not designed to accommodate someone as large as my brother. The doctors decided to examine his esophagus and lungs as far as might be possible by means of passing a scope down his throat.

His son, daughter and I waited in a small area down the hall from the room where the procedure was performed. As we waited, we made the kind of small talk people make to avoid dealing with a subject that hangs over them like an immense and threatening thundercloud.

After about forty-five minutes, the physician came out. I left my nephew and niece and walked down the hall to talk to him. He said, in a matter-of-fact voice, "He has cancer."

I had a brief conversation with him that had the reality of a conversation in a dream. It was as if I were someone else talking about a different person.

"Are you sure?"

"Yes, but I took some tissue to biopsy. That will take a few days to come back."

"Don't say anything to him."

"I had to. He asked me."

"How serious is it?"

"Very serious."

"Will he die?"

"Yes."

"How long? I mean, what can we expect?"

"I dunno. Three months, maybe. Your doctor will bring in an oncologist."

"How much does my brother know?"

"Nothing, other than he has cancer and he will be seeing another doctor. He asked to see you."

My nephew and niece were walking down the hallway toward me and the doctor. I told them what the doctor said, at least the cancer part, although he was standing beside me as I spoke to them. It was better I tell them than he.

This kind of news is like an anesthetic that has to seep into your tissues before it hits you. I tried to avoid looking at them because I knew I would have to try to hold things together, and I was hardly able to do it for myself and had to go in to see my brother.

While they continued to ask the doctor questions, I walked into the room. My brother was sitting in a wheelchair waiting to be taken back to his room. He was quiet and even seemed relieved and at peace like a person who has fretted over a long-expected visitor who has finally arrived. He motioned me close to him. I told him Sharyn and Geoffrey were in the hall outside the room. He waived off the thought and beckoned me closer so that the nurse could not hear him. He told me he wanted a will and gave me instructions of how he wanted to dispose of things. I said that we should concentrate on treatment and getting better and not rush into thinking about wills. He wanted to hear none of this and insisted on the will.

I left the room to give him an opportunity to be alone with his children.

His hospital room was large and as pleasant as a hospital room could be in a sterile and antiseptic way. He would change that.

He did not seem to be suffering or even in pain. Perhaps this was all some mistake, but we knew that he was dying, and there was no turning away from it. All the instruments agreed that he was dying, but his life ebbed away in increments so small that we could not perceive it on a daily basis. Some days, he said he felt weak, and then on other days with more and more frequency, he received oxygen through small tubes in his nose.

After my mother died, I used to make fried chicken in large batches and bring it to his apartment and later to the hospital. I learned how to do this from watching my mother: Put flour and spices in a brown paper bag, add the chicken pieces and shake the bag. The oil should be boiling, and not too many pieces should be fried at one time.

He soon regained his usual gruff persona, at least when he was talking to other people. I heard him say to people on the phone, "I'm going to beat this." Several times to friends, "Can you believe this shit?"

At home, the telephone was his instrument, sometimes far into the night and the next day. The breadth and depth of his telephone relationships were deep and wide and continued in the hospital.

The letters, cards and phone calls, to the annoyance of the hospital staff, kept coming, and there were records, and Ray Charles sent him a message on tape.

Well-known musicians visited him, creating excitement in the hospital staff. There was a complaint when we brought a phonograph into his room, but we somehow got around the problem.

There was some talk of his going home and that the cancer might be in remission. His apartment, although dreadful and dreadfully small, was the place of large parties and visits by famous people. He seemed to be indifferent to its squalor.

A fine new condominium building was just completed on Broadway, on the corner of the block on which he lived. I urged him that he needed to own a first-class apartment built around his needs to which he could come home. He was convinced he could not afford it, although his songs would earn enough money to support his children and children's children and perhaps beyond that. Although, on some level, he understood this because whenever I would bring up the subject of life insurance with him, he always said that his songs were his life insurance. At any rate, I lent him the money to buy the apartment, and we made the alterations necessary to construct it to his needs. This seemed to make him happy, and I heard him tell people he looked forward to his new home.

He never got to see this apartment although all the construction and customization had been made. The only time it was used was after he died and the family sat *shiva*—the proscribed days of mourning for the family when people visited to pay their condolences.

The doctors held out no hope, but at various times, they said the tumor was not getting bigger and at one point was actually smaller. Because of his size, they could not give him external radiation and administered it by putting a long polished thick tube down his throat and esophagus. It seemed barbaric.

The internist told me that he would be there "until the end." No mention was made of the fact that he misdiagnosed my brother's condition for months.

One day, I hailed a cab to take me to the hospital to visit my brother. The cab driver was black and from the sound of his voice, came from one of the Caribbean islands. I glanced at his hack license card casually. The name on the card was Jerome Felder, my brother's real name. I thought for a moment that I was under the spell of a hallucination and tried to engage the driver in conversation and to explain this extraordinary coincidence. He turned out to be the only New York cabbie who did not want to talk to his customers. Most of the time, the problem is the other way around. You cannot stop them from giving you a lecture on anything from the state of the economy to the state of their digestion.

I did not know what to make of all this. Doctor Freud said there was no such thing as a pure coincidence, but merely two independent things occurring at the same time. If this random event had a meaning, it eluded me.

There was another event that involved my brother's stay at the hospital that left me shaken.

A year or so earlier, a lawyer asked me to try to get his girlfriend out of jail. It turned out to be more complicated than that. I sent a young lawyer to court to obtain her release.

Mary Smith (that is not her real name, but the events related were reported in the media, and anyone of such a mind to do so can, I am sure, learn more of the bizarre facts that surrounded them) had been expelled from several European countries, the last being Switzerland. The Swiss authorities took her into custody and sent her back to the United States accompanied by two Swiss policewomen who (she said) shoved her head into a toilet and then handcuffed her. The plane's captain radioed ahead, and there were Port Authority police waiting to meet the plane upon its arrival at Kennedy. At the airport, a scuffle ensued that, I was told, resulted in Mary breaking a policewoman's arm. She was arrested for the assault.

After she was released, she came back to my office with the lawyer I sent to help her. We met for about ten minutes, and I had an idea. If a claim was made to the airlines for what happened to Mary, it might be willing to settle to avoid a lawsuit. She had never thought of this and instructed me to go forward. I sent a letter to the airline, made a few calls and received an offer of fifty thousand dollars. I telephoned her and relayed the offer.

The only thing I remember about our one meeting was that, although she was dressed in a conventional manner, she wore tooled white cowboy boots.

The next day, I heard shouting in the office and a female voice screaming, "You spread your legs for the insurance company."

After that she began multiple lawsuits representing herself in the federal court, all of them being thrown out virtually immediately. Finally, she was declared an "abusive litigant" and could only begin a new lawsuit with the permission of the chief judge, Charles Brieant.

She would periodically show up at the office in her cowboy boots and fling rolled-up sheaves of legal papers through the door.

The next I heard of the matter was a call I received from an FBI agent advising me that my name was on a sort of death list that Mary had prepared. The list also included Judge Brieant, therefore explaining the FBI's involvement. The judge was particularly sensitive since he was the object of an assassination attempt using poisoned chocolates. His wife had eaten them and was hospitalized.

In a telephone conversation with him, I told him that I believed there was no substance to Mary's threats and she was harmless. He said, "Those are just the ones who will get you." He once told a CBS interview "[People who represent themselves] very readily become paranoid [and can become] dangerous cases … every one of them."

The FBI, the NYPD and the federal marshals were unsuccessful in apprehending Mary. I told an FBI agent that I could make their work easy. She used to call my office making threats, obscene remarks, ethnic slurs and demanding money. I never would speak to her, and the receptionist was used to the calls and simply hung up on her. The next time she calls, I said, I would set up a meeting, and then they could arrest her.

She called about a week later, and I spoke to her.

"Mary, this must all really come to an end. How much money do you want?"

There was a pause. "Twelve million dollars."

"That's a lot of money. Can't we negotiate?"

"No, no negotiation. Twelve million dollars."

I thought, why quibble? She said she would meet me on the second floor of a bank on Park Avenue and Fifty-fifth Street. The bank was staked out by the FBI. I had a female FBI agent as my companion. We waited on the second floor, and when Mary arrived, she was arrested.

Before her arrest, during the period of her multiple lawsuits, my brother was in the hospital. After visiting him, I found that taking a path through the emergency-room area was a shortcut to First Avenue, the street where I could hail a cab.

One evening, after leaving my brother and feeling particularly low, I walked through the emergency area, my eyes downcast. I found myself staring at a pair of tooled white cowboy boots. They resonated with me in that brief second. I raised my gaze and found myself looking at Mary. Having only seen her for a few minutes months earlier, I did not immediately recognize her. But she recognized me. She began to shriek. "You gave me diabetes. You gave me diabetes." People came out from various rooms to ascertain the source of the screaming.

She was, of course, quite mad, and I suppose any emergency room has its share of loonies. So most of the staff shrugged it off. However, she followed me into the street while I tried to hail a cab, shouting, "You gave me diabetes. You gave me diabetes." Just my luck that there were few cabs available that night on First Avenue.

My brother became incrementally weaker, pauses between sentences became longer, and he seemed disinterested in the conversations around him. He was unduly harsh to his daughter, Sharyn, in a way a person can only be to someone he loves when anger is the only thing left to give. He worried about her, but felt her life was on track. I promised to watch over his son, and then I changed the topic.

Some days later, I received a call to come quickly to the hospital. His son and daughter and a few close friends were there. He seemed to be in and out of sleep the way my father was on warm

Sunday afternoons. His daughter played his old Joe Turner records as he drifted away to a place of no battles and nothing to prove. I remembered hearing the same music in our bedroom on Manhattan Avenue. It came from a battered phonograph beside his bed, but now, there were no neighbors to complain, and my mother was not down the hall in the kitchen and would not come down the hall when he called. It was over. Gone. I kissed him.

I doubt if New York has ever seen a funeral such as his. Perhaps, there are similar ones in New Orleans, but not here. A thousand people came, filled the main hall of the funeral parlor, and more stood out in the street to hear it over loudspeakers. Some were in the street because they could not get seats, and some for religious reasons, were not permitted to enter a building in which there is a dead body.

Little Jimmy Scott, whom my brother helped, sang—it was almost a lonely wail—Gershwin's *Someone to Watch Over Me*. I still cannot bear to hear the song. Among the writers with whom he wrote his last songs that many people said were his best, although they did not achieve first place on the charts (as many of his others did) nor were they recorded by Elvis Presley, was Doctor John. He performed and described how my brother put his life back on track for him and in quoting my brother's shouting at him, probably uttered the only curse words ever heard at a funeral. I looked at the people seated in the funeral parlor, and I saw a sea of black and white faces, musicians, at least one movie star and the kind of people I would never have expected to see at a funeral and even some, this side of the jailhouse walls.

They carried my brother out to a recording of him singing so many, many years ago.

The obituary writers were kind and generous, and he received some important awards posthumously. Eventually, a biography was written that was well received and praised in a full-page *New York Times* book review. A respected novelist dedicated his next book to him, and a tribute album was released.

After my brother died, B. B. King recorded an album of some of the last songs my brother had written, some during his illness. The title of the album is *There Is Always One More Time*. It won a Grammy, and I was told that King broke down after he recorded the title song.

> *If your whole life somehow*
> *Wasn't much till now*
> *And you've almost lost*
> *Your will to live*
> *No matter what you've been through*
> *Long as there's breath in you*
> *There is always one more time*

Down the road from where my parents are buried, a long plot with only one grave, my brother is buried. There is space next to him for his children and my family. Engraved on his headstone is another verse from that song, my brother wrote:

> *Oh turnin' corners*
> *Is only a state of mind*
> *Keeping your eyes closed*
> *Is worse than being blind*

I visit the cemetery often and try to make sure my children do, also. I think of him every day.

* * *

My children turned out well and are unusual people. My daughter is a freelance journalist. My son is a scriptwriter and teaches writing at the graduate school of a university.

I have also never had an argument with either one of them except for my son, James. He was accepted to Brown University—at the time the nation's most difficult college to obtain admission—but wanted to turn it down and go to a local commuter college. I gave up almost immediately.

Neither of my children drink, take drugs, smoke or can drive a car. And then, there is my eleven-year-old granddaughter, Millie, the love of my life or the life of my love. She also does not drink, take drugs, smoke or can drive a car. I wish I could preserve my moments with her in amber, but I know they will be blown away by the winds of time like the colored dust on butterfly wings.

If anybody were foolish enough to ask my advice about how to raise children, I would tell them that the first step is to have a good wife. And, oh yes, I would look out for kids who know exactly, precisely, absolutely, to a mathematical certainty what they want to do in life from the moment they climb out of diapers. For the others, the good ones, the best of them, it will be a crapshoot.

* * *

The other night, I dreamed that I was sitting in the small foyer just outside the kitchen in the apartment in Williamsburg. I sat next to the old Bakelite phone that was on a small table. I waited for something; perhaps a telephone call, perhaps a guest. Everything looked the same as it did when I was a boy: a faded, tan loveseat, the wall behind it marked by the back of the heads of the people who sat on it, the tired prints of old sailing ships hanging on the opposite wall, the linoleum floor that was worn down its center by the people, usually my mother, going back and forth from the kitchen to my brother's and my bedroom.

After a time, the front door opened, and my mother came in carrying a cardboard suitcase. She looked the way she did when I was a boy. Her face was smooth and pale, without wrinkles or the lines of time—the face of a young woman. Her hair was jet black and pulled into a bun.

She kissed me on my cheek and then removed her coat, and I saw that she wore a housedress, something she always wore when going about the house, tending to me, my brother or her other chores. She put the suitcase down on a chair, opened it and began to unpack.

My brother called her from our bedroom. "Ma, Ma, come, I need you." His voice sounded the same as it always did, as it did a thousand years ago when it all began, here in this apartment.

My mother stopped unpacking and turned to me and told me to wait and then went quickly down the hall to the bedroom.

After a while, I began to feel frightened and called, "Ma, can I come?"

She answered, faintly, from down the hall, "No, not yet."

"When?"

There was a long pause. "Soon . . . soon," she said. "Soon."

INDEX